AMBEDKAR LIFE AND VIEWS

AMBEDKAR LIFE AND VIEWS

D.C.VYAS

CYBER TECH PUBLICATIONS
4264/3, Ansari Road, Daryaganj, New Delhi-110002 (India)
Ph.: 011-23244078, 011-43559448 Fax: 011-23280028
E-Mail: cyberpublicationsdelhi@yahoo.com
Website: www.cybertechpublications.com

AMBEDKAR LIFE AND VIEWS

D.C.VYAS

First Edition 2011

Published by :

G.S. Rawat for Cyber Tech Publications
4264/3, Ansari Road, Daryaganj, New Delhi-110002 (India)
Ph.: 011-23244078, 011-43559448 Fax: 011-23280028
E-Mail: cyberpublicationsdelhi@yahoo.com
Website: www.cybertechpublications.com

CONTENTS

PREFACE

Dr. Ambedkar's constant fight for social justice, equality, constitutional and political safeguards for the millions of ex-untouchables. It also contains his correspondence with the top administrators, leaders besides some of his speeches as a rebel national leader. For years, Ambedkar waged a singular and lonely battle against India's Brahminical and higher-caste political establishment, which included Mahatma Gandhi, who resisted Ambedkar's effort to formalize the codify a separate identity for lower-caste Hindus.

Nonetheless, Ambedkar became Law Minister in the first government of independent India, and chairman of the committee which drafted the Indian constitution, and was able to modify Gandhian attempts to influence India's polity. In the final stage of his life Ambedkar distanced himself from politics and sought solace in Buddhism, to which he converted a short while before his death. The theme of the book is the main subject which runs throughout this work, an envisaged by Babasaheb Dr. B.R. Ambedkar.

The entire discussion is based mainly upon his original writings. Besides the main theme, this work also carries the detailed discussions on the related themes, which include: 'Buddha's Dhamma', 'Dalits and the conversion', Untouchability etc.. I intentionally have allowed Dr. Ambedkar to speak for himself, therefore the readers will find many quotations throughout this work.

The themes discussed are most relevant today, therefore it is being offered to the readers with this belief that Dr. B.R. Ambedkar's thoughts can became the basis of dealing with the current problems related to the Dalits, tribals, women, minorities and other weaker sections of the Indian society." This work, being a piece of research, has discovered certain parameters as to know how far one may be an Ambedkarite, both in spirit and action. "In this book I have endeavoured my best to place before the reader, thoughts, views Dr. Babasaheb Ambedkar in their own words quoted verbatim. My only passion has been to be dispassionate about several controversies on their relationship.

—*Author*

1

HISTORY OF THE AMBEDKAR LIFE

INTRODUCTION

On April 14th, 1891 a son was born to Bhimabai and Ramji Ambedkar. His father Ramji was an army officer stationed at Mhow in Madhya Pradesh-he had risen to the highest rank an Indian was allowed to hold at that time under British rule. His mother decided to call her son Bhim. Before the birth, Ramji's uncle, who was a man living the religious life of a sanyasi, foretold that this son would achieve worldwide fame. His parents already had many children. Despite that, they resolved to make every effort to give him a good education. Two years later, Ramji retired from the army, and the family moved to Dapoli in the Ratnagiri district of Maharashtra, from where they came originally. Bhim was enrolled at school when he was five years old. The whole family had to struggle to live on the small army pension Ramji received. Even from his boyhood Ambedkar had a mind of steel. Once it was raining very heavily. The boy Ambedkar said the would go to school. His friends said, "These are empty words, how can you go in this heavy rain?" In the downpour, the boy did go to school and that, too, without an umbrella! When some friends found Ramji a job at Satara, things seemed to be looking up for the family, and they moved again. Soon after, however, tragedy struck. Bhimabhai, who had been ill, died. Bhim's aunt Mira, though she herself was not in good health, took over the care of the children. Ramji read stories from the epics Mahabharata and Ramayana to his children, and sang devotional songs to them. In this way, home life was still happy for Bhim, his brothers and sisters. He never forgot the influence of his father. It taught him about the rich cultural tradition shared by all Indians.

Bhim began to notice that he and his family were treated differently. At high school he had to sit in the corner of the room on a rough mat, away from the desks of the other pupils. At break-time, he was not allowed to drink water using the cups his fellow school children used. He had to hold his cupped hands out to have water poured into them by the school caretaker. Bhim did not know why he should be treated differently-what was wrong with him? Once, he and his elder brother had to travel to Goregaon, where their father worked as a cashier, to spend their summer holidays. They got off the train and waited for a long time at the station, but Ramji did not arrive to meet them. The station master seemed kind, and asked them who they were and where they were going. The boys were very well-dressed, clean, and polite. Bhim, without thinking, told him they were Mahars (a group classed as 'untouchables'). The station master was stunned-his face changed its kindly expression and he went away.

Bhim decided to hire a bullock-cart to take them to their father-this was before motor cars were used as taxis-but the cart-men had heard that the boys were 'untouchables', and wanted nothing to do with them. Finally, they had to agree to pay double the usual cost of the journey, plus they had to drive the cart themselves, while the driver walked beside it. He was afraid of being polluted by the boys, because they were 'untouchables'. However, the extra money persuaded him that he could have his cart 'purified' later! Throughout the journey, Bhim thought constantly about what had happened-yet he could not understand the reason for it. He and his brother were clean and neatly dressed. Yet they were supposed to pollute and make unclean everything they touched and all that touched them. How could that be possible? Ambedkar ranks easily amongst the most highly educated and erudite leaders of India. He spent many years studying a host of subjects ranging from economics and anthropology to politics, law and religion, in colleges and universities such as Elphinstone College, Bombay where he earned a B. A., Columbia University, USA, from where he earned an M. A. and a Ph. D., London University where he earned a D. Sc. and entrance to the Bar from Grey's

Inn, London. Much of Ambedkar's education was made possible by financial support from the Gaikwad of Baroda who was known for his financial contributions to reformers and educators in what was the Bombay Presidency during colonial times.

Yet, Ambedkar's education did not grant him the status of a fellow human being when he returned to India. Untouchability, practiced by an overwhelming majority of caste Hindus as well as other religious communities, stigmatized him in the most pernicious ways. His own analysis refuted an understanding of untouchability as a racial oppression. He argued instead that it arose as a social, political, religious, and economic separation and denigration of practitioners of Buddhism in the historical period of renascent Hinduism (see his book The Untouchables, 1948). For Ambedkar, Buddhism represented the historical revolutionary experience in India, while Hinduism represented the counter-revolutionary experience seeking to bring back an orthodoxy founded upon the caste system.

Such an understanding of Hinduism was one of the main causes of Ambedkar's strong differences with Gandhi's approach to the struggle against oppressive practices such as untouchability. Throughout his active political life spanning more than three decades, Ambedkar spearheaded an alternative movement against the evils of the caste system—an alternative that was much more radical in content and modern in vision than the one that Mahatma Gandhi nurtured and led by example. The difference in their approaches is brought out by Dr. Eleanor Zelliot, a pioneer historian of Untouchables/Dalits in Maharashtra:

Ambedkar's programs were intended to integrate the Untouchable into Indian society in modern, not traditional ways, and on as high a level as possible. This goal stood in marked contrast to Gandhi's "Ideal Bhangi" (Harijan, 23 November 1936) who would continue to do sanitation work even though his status would equal that of a Brahmin. Ambedkar's ideal for the depressed (classes) was to "raise their educational standard so that they may know their own conditions, have asportation to rise to the level of the highest Hindu and be in a position to use political power as a means to that end." Both reformers had a vision of equality, but for Ambedkar equality meant not only equal status of the Varnas, but equal social, political, and economic opportunity for all. Ambedkar planned his programmes to bring the Untouchable from a state of "dehumanization" and "slavery" into one of equality through the use of modern methods based on education and the exercise of legal and political rights.

Ambedkar's adaptation of western concepts to the Indian scene is also reflected in the terms he used to justify Untouchable political rights: democracy, fraternity, and liberty. In his Marathi speeches, Ambedkar conveyed the implication of these concepts in a single word, manuski, that was readily understood by the most illiterate Mahar villager. Although manuski's literal meaning is "humanness", it serves to evoke feelings of self-respect and human attitudes towards one's fellow humans.

Ambedkar himself delineated his differences through minute study of Gandhi's vision of an ideal society and the specific practices which Gandhi upheld throughout his life. It is worth quoting a couple of paragraphs from his essay titled Gandhism: The Doom of the Untouchables, which forms part of his larger book titled What the Congress and Gandhi have done to the Untouchables.

Bhim never forgot this incident. As he grew up, such senseless insults made him realise that what Hindu society called 'untouchability' was stupid, cruel, and unreasonable. His sister had to cut his hair at home because the village barbers were afraid of being polluted by an 'untouchable'. If he asked her why they were 'untouchables', she could only answer-that is the way it has always been." Bhim could not be satisfied with this answer. He knew that-it has always been that way" does not mean that there is a just reason for it-or that it had to stay that way forever. It could be changed.

While in school, Bhim's teacher Ambedkar, entered his last name into the school records as Ambedkar. Teacher Ambedkar and Pendse, were the only ones in the entire school who were kind and affectionate to young him. They made the few fond memories Dr. B.R. Ambedkar had of his school days. At this time in his young life, with his mother dead, and father working away from the village where Bhim went to school, he had some good fortune. His teacher, though from a 'high' caste, liked him a lot. He praised Bhim's good work and encouraged him, seeing what a bright pupil he was. He even invited Bhim to eat lunch with him-something that would have horrified most high caste Hindus. The teacher also changed Bhim's last name to Ambedkar-his own name.

When his father decided to remarry, Bhim was very upset-he still missed his mother so much. Wanting to run away to Bombay, he tried to steal his aunt's purse. When at last he managed to get hold of it, he found only one very small coin. Bhim felt so ashamed. He put the coin back and made a vow to himself to study very hard and to become independent.

Soon he was winning the highest praise and admiration from all his teachers. They urged Ramji to get the best education for his son Bhim. So Ramji moved with his family to Bombay. They all had to live in just one room, in an area where the poorest of the poor lived, but Bhim was able to go to Elphinstone High School-one of the best schools in all of India. In their one room everyone and everything was crowed together and the streets outside were very noisy. Bhim went to sleep when he got home from school. Then his father would wake him up at two o'clock in the morning! Everything was quiet then-so he could do his homework and study in peace. In the big city, where life was more modern than in the villages, Bhim found that he was still called an 'untouchable' and treated as if something made him different and bad-even at his famous school.

One day, the teacher called him up to the blackboard to do a sum. All the other boys jumped up and made a big fuss. Their lunch boxes were stacked behind the blackboard-they believed that Bhim would pollute the food! When he wanted to learn Sanskrit, the language of the Hindu holy scriptures, he was told that it was forbidden for 'untouchables' to do so. He had to study Persian instead-but he taught himself Sanskrit later in life.

MATRICULATION AND MARRIAGE

In due course, Bhim passed his Matriculation Exam. He had already come to the attention of some people interested in improving society. So when he passed the exam, a meeting was arranged to congratulate him-he was the first 'untouchable' from his community to pass it.

Bhim was then 17 years old. Early marriage was common in those days, so he was married to Ramabai the same year. He continued to study hard and passed the next Intermediate examination with distinction. However, Ramji found himself unable to keep paying the school fees. Through someone interested in his progress, Bhim was recommended to the Maharaja Gaikwad of Baroda. The Maharaja granted him a monthly scholarship. With the help of this, Bhimrao ('rao' is added to names in Maharashtra as a sign of respect) passed his B.A. in 1912. Then he was given a job in the civil service-but only two weeks after starting, he had to rush home to Bombay. Ramji was very ill, and died soon afterwards. He had done all he could for his son, laying the foundations for Bhimrao's later achievements.

STUDIES IN THE USA AND THE UK

The Maharaja of Baroda had a scheme to send a few outstanding scholars abroad for further studies. Of course, Bhimrao was selected-but he had to sign an agreement to serve Baroda state for ten years on finishing his studies. In 1913, he went to the USA where he studied at the world-famous Columbia University, New York.

The freedom and equality he experienced in America made a very strong impression on Bhimrao. It was so refreshing for him to be able to live a normal life, free from the caste prejudice of India. He could do anything he pleased-but devoted his time to studying. He studied eighteen hours a day. Visits to bookshops were his favourite entertainment!

His main subjects were Economics and Sociology. In just two years he had been awarded an M.A.-the following year he completed his Ph.D. thesis. Then he left Columbia and went to England, where he joined the London School of Economics. However, he had to leave London before completing his course because the scholarship granted by the State of Baroda expired. Bhimrao had to wait three years before he could return to London to complete his studies.

The British Museum in London has a very good library. It used to open at eight in the morning, and every day Ambedkar would be there by eight. He read till five o'clock. In London he came to know a student called Asnodkar. He belonged to a rich family. He was not interested in study. Ambedkar said to him, "Your people may have made plenty of money. But think, you have born a man, what are you going to achieve? The Goddess of Learning will not come to you whenever you want. We must get her blessings when she comes." In 1922 Ambedkar became a barrister and the nest year he came back to India.

Return to India-Nightmare in Baroda: So he was called back to India to take up a post in Baroda as agreed. He was given an excellent job in the Baroda Civil Service. Bhimrao now held a doctorate, and was being trained for a top job. Yet, he again ran into the worst features of the Hindu caste system. This was all the more painful, because for the past four years he had been abroad, living free from the label of 'untouchable.'

No one at the office where he worked would hand over files and papers to him-the servant threw them onto his desk. Nor would they give him water to drink. No respect was given to him, merely because of his caste. He had to go from hotel to hotel looking for a room, but none of them would take him in. At last he had found a place to live in a Parsi guest house, but only because he had finally decided to keep his caste secret. He lived there in very uncomfortable conditions, in a small bedroom with a tiny cold-water bathroom attached.

He was totally alone there with no one to talk to. There were no electric lights or even oil lamps-so the place was completely dark at night. Bhimrao was hoping to find somewhere else to live through his civil service job, but before he could, one morning as he was leaving for work a gang of angry men carrying sticks arrived outside his room. They accused him of polluting the hotel and told him to get out by evening-or else! What could he do? He could not stay with either of the two acquaintances he had in Baroda for the same reason-his low caste. Bhimrao felt totally miserable and rejected.

Bombay-Beginning Social Activity: He had no choice. After only eleven days in his new job, he had to return to Bombay. He tried to start a small business there, advising people about investments-but it too failed once customers learned of his caste. In 1918, he became a lecturer at Sydenham College in Bombay. There, his students recognised him as a brilliant teacher and scholar. At this time he also helped to found a Marathi newspaper 'Mook Nayak' (Leader of the Dumb) to champion the cause of the 'untouchables'. He also began to organise and attend conferences, knowing that he had to begin to proclaim and publicise the humiliations suffered by the Dalits-'the oppressed'-and fight for equal rights. His own life had taught him the necessity of the struggle for emancipation.

Completion of Education-Leader of India's Untouchables: In 1920, with the help of friends, he was able to return to London to complete his studies in Economics at LSE. He also enrolled to study as a Barrister at Gray's Inn. In 1923, Bhimrao returned to India with a Doctorate in Economics from the LSE-he was perhaps the first Indian to have a Doctorate from this world-famous institution. He had also qualified as a Barrister-at-Law.

Back in India, he knew that nothing had changed. His qualifications meant nothing as far as the practice of Untouchability was concerned-it was still an obstacle to his career. However, he had received the best education anyone in the world could get, and was well equipped to be a leader of the Dalit community. He could argue with and persuade the best minds of his time on equal terms. He was an expert on the law, and could give convincing evidence before British commissions as an eloquent and gifted speaker. Bhimrao dedicated the rest of his life to his task.

He became known by his increasing number of followers-those 'untouchables' he urged to awake-as Baba Saheb. Knowing the great value and importance of education, in 1924 he founded an association called Bahiskrit Hitakarini Sabha. This set up hostels, schools, and free libraries. To improve the lives of Dalits, education had to reach everyone. Opportunities had to be provided at grass roots level-because knowledge is power.

Leading Peaceful Agitation: In 1927 Baba Saheb presided over a conference at Mahad in Kolaba District. There he said:-It is time we rooted out of our minds the ideas of high and low. We can attain self-elevation only if we learn self-help and regain our self-respect." Because of his experience of the humiliation and injustice of untouchability, he knew that justice would not be granted by others. Those who suffer injustice must secure justice for themselves. The Bombay Legislature had already passed a Bill allowing everyone to use public water tanks and wells. (We have seen how Bhim was denied water at school, in his office, and at other places. Public water facilities were always denied to 'untouchables' because of the superstitious fear of 'pollution.')

Mahad Municipality had thrown open the local water tank four years earlier, but so far not one 'untouchable' had dared to drink or draw water from it. Baba Saheb led a procession from the Conference on a peaceful demonstration to the Chowdar Tank. He knelt and drank water from it. After he set this example, thousands of others felt courageous enough to follow him. They drank water from the tank and made history. For many hundreds of years, 'untouchables' had been forbidden to drink public water.

When some caste Hindus saw them drinking water, they believed the tank had been polluted and violently attacked the Conference, but Baba Saheb insisted violence would not help-he had given his word that they would agitate peacefully. Baba Saheb started a Marathi journal Bahishkrit Bharat ('The Excluded of India'). In it, he urged his people to hold a satyagraha (nonviolent agitation) to secure the right of entry to the Kala Ram Temple at Nasik, 'untouchables' had always been forbidden to enter Hindu temples. The demonstration lasted for a month. Then they were told they would be able to take part in the annual temple festival. However, at the festival they had stones thrown at them-and were not allowed to take part. Courageously, they resumed their peaceful agitation. The temple had to remain closed for about a year, as they blocked its entrance.

Round Table Conferences-Gandhi: Meanwhile, the Indian Freedom Movement had gained momentum under the leadership of Mahatma Gandhi. In 1930, a Round Table Conference was held by the British Government in London to decide the future of India. Baba Saheb represented the 'untouchables'. He said there:-The Depressed Classes of India also join in the demand for replacing the British Government by a Government of the people and by the people... Our wrongs have remained as open sores and have not been righted although 150 years of British rule have rolled away. Of what good is such a Government to anybody?"

The British had done nothing to alleviate the status of the depressed classes. He declared that India must have a minimum of Dominion Status. He pressed for a separate electorate for the depressed classes.

Soon a second conference was held, which Mahatma Gandhi attended representing the Congress Party. Baba Saheb met Gandhi in Bombay before they went to London. Gandhi told him that he had read what Baba Saheb said at the first conference. Gandhi told Baba Saheb he knew him to be a real Indian patriot.

At the Second Conference, Baba Saheb asked for a separate electorate for the Depressed Classes-Hinduism, "he said-has given us only insults, misery, and humiliation." A separate electorate would mean that the 'untouchables' would vote for their own candidates and be allotted their votes separate from the Hindu majority.

Baba Saheb was made a hero by thousands of his followers on his return from Bombay-even though he always said that people should not idolise him. News came that separate electorates had been granted. Gandhi felt that separate electorates would separate the Harijans from the Hindus. The thought that the Hindus would be divided pained him grievously. He started a fast, saying that he would fast unto death.

The Mahatma's Fast: Gandhiji felt that separate electrorates would only separate the Harijans from the Hindus. The very thought that the Hindu would be divided pained him much. He started a fast against separate electorates. He said he would fast unto death in necessary. There was anxiety in the country because of Gandhiji's fast.

Many Congress leaders went to Ambedkar to save Gandhiji. "Muslims, Christians and Sikhs have obtained the right of separate electorates. Gandhiji did not fast to oppose them. Why should Gandhiji fast to oppose Harijans getting separate electorates?" questioned Ambedkar. "If you are unwilling to give the 'untouchables' separate electorates, what other solution is there? It is essential to save Gandhiji. But just to save him I am not prepared to give up the interests of the backward classes," he declared. He said, reserve a larger number of seats for the untouchables' than the British have given; then I will give up the claim for separate electorates."

Only Baba Saheb could save Gandhi's life-by withdrawing the demand for separate electorates. At first he refused, saying it was his duty to do the best he could for his people-no matter what. Later he visited Gandhi, who was at that time in Yeravda jail. Gandhi persuaded Baba Saheb that Hinduism would change and leave its bad practices behind. Finally Baba Saheb agreed to sign the Poona Pact with Gandhi in 1932. Instead of separate electorates, more representation was to be given to the Depressed Classes. However, it later became obvious that this did not amount to anything concrete.

In the Prime of His Life: Baba Saheb had by this time collected a library of over 50,000 books, and had a house named Rajgriha built at Dadar in north Bombay to hold it. In 1935 his beloved wife Ramabai died. The same year he was made Principal of the Government Law College, Bombay.

Also in 1935 a conference of Dalits was held at Yeola. Baba Saheb told the conference:-We have not been able to secure the barest of human rights... I am born a Hindu. I couldn't help it, but I solemnly assure you that I will not die a Hindu." This was the first time that Baba Saheb stressed the importance of conversion from Hinduism for his people-for they were only known as 'untouchables' within the fold of Hinduism.

During the Second World War, Baba Saheb was appointed Labour Minister by the Viceroy. Yet he never lost contact with his roots-he never became corrupt or crooked. He said that he had been born of the poor and had lived the life of the poor, he would remain absolutely unchanged in his attitudes to his friends and to the rest of the world.

The All-India Scheduled Castes Federation was formed in 1942 to gather all 'untouchables' into a united political party.

Architect of the Constitution: After the war Baba Saheb was elected to the Constituent Assembly to decide the way that India-a country of millions of people-should be ruled. How should elections take place? What are the rights of the people? How are laws to be made? Such important matters had to be decided and laws had to be made. The Constitution answers all such questions and lays down rules.

When India became independent in August 1947, Baba Saheb Ambedkar became First Law Minister of Independent India. The Constituent Assembly made him chairman of the committee appointed to draft the constitution for the world's largest democracy.

All his study of law, economics, and politics made him the best qualified person for this task. A study of the Constitutions of many ccuntries, a deep knowledge of law, a knowledge of the history of India and of Indian Society-all these were essential. In fact, he carried the whole burden alone. He alone could complete this huge task.

On July 15, 1947, the British Parliament passed the act of Indian Independence and on August 15, 1947, India became free. The Constituent Assemble of Independent India appointed a Drafting Committee with Dr. Ambedkar as its Chairman to draft the Constitution of India. Dr. Ambedkar was also invited to join the Cabinet as the Minister of Law. Ambedkar toiled over the Constitution while he took care of his ministry. In February 1948, Dr. Ambedkar presented the Draft Constitution before the people of India.

After completing the Draft Constitution, Baba Saheb fell ill. At a nursing home in Bombay he met Dr. Sharda Kabir and married her in April 1948. On November 4, 1948 he presented the Draft Constitution to the Constituent Assembly, and on November 26, 1949 it was adopted in the name of the people of India. On that date he said: I appeal to all Indians to be a nation by discarding castes, which have brought separation in social life and created jealousy and hatred."

Later Life-Buddhist Conversion: In 1950, he went to a Buddhist conference in Sri Lanka. On his return he spoke in Bombay at the Buddhist Temple. In order to end their hardships, people should embrace Buddhism. I am going to devote the rest of my life to the revival and spread of Buddhism in India." Why did he choose Buddhism?: Ambedkar told his friend Dattopant Thengadi:

"I am in the evening of my life. There is an onslaught of ideas on our people from different countries from the four corners of the world. In this flood our people may be confused. There are strong attempts to separate the people struggling hard, from the main life-stream of this country and to attract them towards other countries. This tendency is fast growing. Even some of my colleagues who are disgusted with 'untouchability', poverty and inequality are ready to be washed away by this flood. What about the others?

They should not move away from the main stream of the nation's life; and I must show them the way. At the same time, we have to make some changes in the economic and political life. That is way I have decided to follow Buddhism." There is a way of life which has come down as a steady stream in India for thousand of years. Buddhism is not opposed to it. The backward people must rebel against the injustice done to them; they must wipe it out. But 'untouchability' is a problem of the Hindu Society. To solve this, a path which does not harm the culture and the history of Bharat must be followed. This is the basis of his resolution.

He did not believe in the theory that Aryans came from a different land and that they defeated the Dasyus' (the Dravidians) of this country. There is no foundation for this in the Vedas. The word 'Arya' appears some 33 or 34 times in the Vedas. The word has been used as an adjective meaning 'the noble' or 'the elder'. It is said in the Mahabharata that 'Dasyus' can be found in all 'varnas' (castes) and 'ashramas' (stage of life). In this way Ambedkar used to support this view.

On 14th October 1956 at a big function in Nagpur, Ambedkar, with his wife, embraced Buddhism. In May 1956, on Buddha's Anniversary, Dr. Ambedkar announced that on October 14 he would embrace Buddhism. With him his wife and some three lakh followers also converted to the faith. When asked why, Dr. Ambedkar replied, "Why can't you ask this question to yourself and... your forefathers...?" For the next five years Baba Saheb carried on a relentless fight against social evils and superstitions. On October 14, 1956 at Nagpur he embraced Buddhism. He led a huge gathering in a ceremony converting over half a million people to Buddhism. He knew that Buddhism was a true part of Indian history and that to revive it was to continue India's best tradition. 'Untouchability' is a product only of Hinduism.

Bhim was an average student. He became fond of gardening and, whenever he could, he bought saplings and with great devotion nurtured them to full growth. While studying in Satara, many of his classmates left for good jobs in Bombay. He too wanted to go to Bombay and get a job and become independent. He realized that if he ever were to be successful, he would have to concentrate more on his studies. He became interested in reading. He read not just the prescribed books in school but any book in general. His father was too pleased when he digressed from school books but he never said "no" when Bhim wanted a book.

Fight against Untouchability: As a leading Dalit scholar, Ambedkar had been invited to testify before the Southborough Committee, which was preparing the Government of India Act 1919. At this hearing, Ambedkar argued for creating separate electorates and reservations for Dalits and different religious communities. In 1920, he began the publication of the weekly Mooknayak (Leader of the Dumb) in Mumbai. Attaining popularity, Ambedkar used this journal to criticize orthodox Hindu politicians and a perceived reticence in the Indian political community to fight caste discrimination. His speech at a Depressed Classes Conference in Kolhapur impressed the local state ruler Shahu IV, who shocked orthodox society by dining with Ambedkar and his untouchable colleagues. Ambedkar exhorted his Mahar community to abandon the idea of sub-castes, and held a joint communal dinner in which the principle of segregation was abandoned. Upon his return from Europe, Ambedkar established a successful legal practise, and also organised the Bahishkrit Hitakarini Sabha (Group for the Wellbeing of the Excluded) to promote education and socioeconomic upliftment of the depressed classes.

In the same vein, he was highly critical of the practice of untouchability in Indian Muslim Society, lending credence to the view that he was not exclusively against Hindus or Hinduism, but was speaking of reforming social evils. In his illustrious publication "Pakistan and the Partition of India", he writes that, while Islam speaks of "brotherhood", the practice of slavery and caste discrimination were rampant in Muslim society in South Asia, such as the Ashraf/Ajlaf caste divide and the severe discrimination against the Arzal castes or Dalit Muslim untouchables. With the help of Shahu Maharaj of Kolhapur, a sympathizer of the cause for the upliftment of the depressed classes, Bhimrao started a fortnightly newspaper, the Mooknayak (Leader of the Dumb) on January 31, 1920. The Maharaj also convened many meeting and conferences of the "untouchables" which Bhimrao addressed. Impressed by Ambedkar, the Maharaj declared at a meeting, "You have found your saviour in Ambedkar. I am confident he will break your shackles."

In July 1924, Ambedkar founded the Bahishkrut Hitkarini Sabha. The aim of the Sabha was to uplift the downtrodden socially and politically and bring them to the level of the others in the Indian society. The Sabha aimed at scrapping the caste system from the Hindu religion. The Sabha started free school for the young and the old and ran reading rooms and libraries. Dr. Ambedkar took the grievances of the "untouchables" to court and gave them justice. Soon he became a father-figure to the poor and downtrodden and was respectfully called "Baba Saheb."

On March 19-20, 1927 a conference of the depressed classes was held at Mahad. Ten thousand delegates attended, workers and leaders attended. Baba Saheb condemned the British for banning the recruitment of "untouchables" into the military. He declared:

> "No lasting progress can achieved unless we put ourselves through a threefold process of purification. We must improve the general tone of our demeanour, retone our pronunciation and revitalize our thoughts. I, therefore, ask you now to take a vow to renounce eating carrion, the... flesh of... animals, from this moment....Make an unflinching resolve not to eat the thrown away crumbs. We will attain self-elevation

only if we learn self-help, regain our self respect and gain self-knowledge."

On December 25 of the same year, thousands responded to Ambedkar's call. Speaker after speaker spoke, passions rose and the vast gathering waited for the satyagraha to begin with intense anticipation. The satyagraha was deferred when the matter was referred to the court. At the end of conference, a copy of the Manusmruti, the age-old code of the Hindus that gave rise to the caste system, was ceremoniously burnt. In a thundering voice, Ambedkar demanded in its place a new smruti, devoid of all social stratification. This act sent shockwaves through the nation. On October 13, 1935, at a conference at Nasik, Dr. Ambedkar reviewed the progress made on the condition of the "untouchables" in the decade since Ambedkar started his agitation. Ambedkar declared that their efforts had not borne the kind of results he had expected. He then made a fantastic appeal to the "untouchables." He encouraged them to forsake the Hindu religion and convert to a religion where they would be treated with equality. The nation was shocked.

The British Government agreed to hold elections on the provincial level in 1937. The Congress, Muslim League and Hindu Mahasabha started gearing up for the elections. Dr. Ambedkar set up the Independent Labour Party in August 1936 to contest the elections in the Bombay province. On February 17, 1937, Ambedkar and many of his candidates won this a thumping majority. Around the same time, the Chavdar Taley water dispute which was referred to the Bombay High Court in 1927 finally handed down its verdict in favour of the depressed classes. The Constituent Assemble adopted the Draft Constitution as the Constitution of India on November 26, 1949 with all its 356 Articles and eight Schedules and Article 11 which abolished untouchability in all forms.

A Legacy Marking Indian Sociopolitical History: Ambedkar's legacy, as a sociopolitical reformer, has been long-lasting on modern India. In post independence India his sociopolitical thought has acquired respect across political spectrum and influenced various spheres of life like socioeconomic, education and Government policies of affirmative action by socioeconomic and legal incentives.

Ambedkar organized untouchable political parties and social organizations, and served in the legislative councils of British India. He would intensify his criticism of orthodox Hindu society, as well as his criticism of slavery and exclusivism in Islam. Despite this, his reputation as a scholar led to his appointment as free India's first law minister, and chairman of the committee responsible to draft a constitution. Ambedkar's work would guarantee political, economic and social freedoms for untouchables and other ethnic, social and religious communities of India.

His polemical condemnation of Hinduism and attacks on Islam would make him unpopular and controversial, although his conversion to Buddhism sparked a revival in interest of Buddhist philosophy in India. In 1926, he became a nominated member of the Bombay Legislative Council. By 1927 Dr. Ambedkar decided to launch active movements against untouchability. He did begin with public movements and marches to open up & share public drinking water resources to which until then untouchable communities had no access; also he put up a struggle for entry in Hindu Temples which was not allowed by upper caste communities.

Poona Pact: Ambedkar had become one of the most prominent untouchable political figures of the time. He had grown increasingly critical of mainstream Indian political parties for their perceived lack of emphasis for the elimination of the caste system. Ambedkar criticized the Indian National Congress and its leader Mahatma Gandhi, whom he accused of reducing the untouchable community to a figure of pathos. Ambedkar was also dissatisfied with the failures of British rule, and advocated a political identity for untouchables separate from both the Congress and the British. At a Depressed Classes Conference on August 8, 1930 Ambedkar outlined his political vision:

> "...Safety of the Depressed Classes hinged on their being independent of the Government and the Congress" both: "We must shape our course ourselves and by ourselves... Political power cannot be a panacea for the ills of the Depressed Classes. Their salvation lies in their social elevation. They must cleanse their

evil habits. They must improve their bad ways of living.... They must be educated.... There is a great necessity to disturb their pathetic contentment and to instill into them that divine discontent which is the spring of all elevation."

Born in a class considered low and outcast. Dr. Ambedkar fought untiringly for the downtrodden. The boy who suffered bitter humiliation became the first Minister for Law in free India, and shaped the country's Constitution. A determined fighter, a deep scholar, human to the tips of his fingers.

We Need Dharma-But Casteism Should Go: 'Undouchablity' is a branch of casteism; until casteism is wiped out 'untouchability' will not go - this was Ambedkar's firm belief. He argued that to wipe out casteism, political power was very necessary. He believed that Dharma was essential for men. But he revolted against those who, in the name of Dharma, treated some of their fellowmen like animals. Many people criticised him.

Some newspapers also wrote against him. There were many occasions when his life was in danger. Also, Ambedkar knew from his own experience that even a bright man could not come up in life vacuse of casteism. People give his cast importance and make him powerless. Ambedkar fought casteism. He was disgusted to find how difficult it was to secure justice and to find how many men were still narrow-minded. He even said that it would be better to give up the Hindu Dharma itself.

Muslim and Christian priest and missionaries learnt about this declaration; they tried very hard to attract Ambedkar. They met and assured him that the 'untouchables' who changed their religion would be given equal status in their society.

Dr. B.R. Ambedkar is viewed as messiah of dalits and downtrodden in India. He was the chairman of the drafting committee that was constituted by the Constituent Assembly in 1947 to draft a constitution for the independent India. He played a seminal role in the framing of the constitution. Bhimrao Ambedkar was also the first Law Minister of India. For his yeoman service to the nation, B.R. Ambedkar was bestowed with Bharat Ratna in 1990.

Dr. Bhimrao Ambedkar was born on April 14, 1891 in Mhow (presently in Madhya Pradesh). He was the fourteenth child of Ramji and Bhimabai Sakpal Ambedkar. B.R. Ambedkar belonged to the "untouchable" Mahar Caste. His father and grandfather served in the British Army. In those days, the government ensured that all the army personnel and their children were educated and ran special schools for this purpose. This ensured good education for Bhimrao Ambedkar, which would have otherwise been denied to him by the virtue of his caste.

Bhimrao Ambedkar experienced caste discrimination right from the childhood. After his retirement, Bhimrao's father settled in Satara Maharashtra. Bhimrao was enrolled in the local school. Here, he had to sit on the floor in one corner in the classroom and teachers would not touch his notebooks. In spite of these hardships, Bhimrao continued his studies and passed his Matriculation examination from Bombay University with flying colours in 1908. Bhimrao Ambedkar joined the Elphinstone College for further education. In 1912, he graduated in Political Science and Economics from Bombay University and got a job in Baroda.

In 1913, Bhimrao Ambedkar lost his father. In the same year Maharaja of Baroda awarded scholarship to Bhimrao Ambedkar and sent him to America for further studies. Bhimrao reached New York in July 1913. For the first time in his life, Bhimrao was not demeaned for being a Mahar. He immersed himself in the studies and attained a degree in Master of Arts and a Doctorate in Philosophy from Columbia University in 1916 for his thesis "National Dividend for India: A Historical and Analytical Study." From America, Dr. Ambedkar proceeded to London to study economics and political science. But the Baroda government terminated his scholarship and recalled him back.

The Maharaja of Baroda appointed Dr. Ambedkar as his political secretary. But no one would take orders from him because he was a Mahar. Bhimrao Ambedkar returned to Bombay in November 1917. With the help of Shahu Maharaj of Kolhapur, a sympathiser of the cause for the upliftment of the depressed classes, he started a fortnightly newspaper, the

"Mooknayak" (Dumb Hero) on January 31, 1920. The Maharaja also convened many meetings and conferences of the "untouchables" which Bhimrao addressed. In September 1920, after accumulating sufficient funds, Ambedkar went back to London to complete his studies. He became a barrister and got a Doctorate in science.

After completing his studies in London, Ambedkar returned to India. In July 1924, he founded the Bahishkrit Hitkarini Sabha (Outcastes Welfare Association). The aim of the Sabha was to uplift the downtrodden socially and politically and bring them to the level of the others in the Indian society. In 1927, he led the Mahad March at the Chowdar Tank at Colaba, near Bombay, to give the untouchables the right to draw water from the public tank where he burnt copies of the 'Manusmriti' publicly.

In 1929, Ambedkar made the controversial decision to cooperate with the all-British Simon Commission which was to look into setting up a responsible Indian Government in India. The Congress decided to boycott the Commission and drafted its own version of a constitution for free India. The Congress version had no provisions for the depressed classes. Ambedkar became more skeptical of the Congress's commitment to safeguard the rights of the depressed classes.

When a separate electorate was announced for the depressed classes under Ramsay McDonald 'Communal Award', Gandhiji went on a fast unto death against this decision. Leaders rushed to Dr. Ambedkar to drop his demand. On September 24, 1932,

Dr. Ambedkar and Gandhiji reached an understanding, which became the famous Poona Pact. According to the pact the separate electorate demand was replaced with special concessions like reserved seats in the regional legislative assemblies and Central Council of States.

Dr. Ambedkar attended all the three Round Table Conferences in London and forcefully argued for the welfare of the "untouchables". Meanwhile, British Government decided to hold provincial elections in 1937. Dr. B.R. Ambedkar set up the "Independent Labour Party" in August 1936 to contest the elections in the Bombay province. He and many candidates of his party were elected to the Bombay Legislative Assembly.

In 1937, Dr. Ambedkar introduced a Bill to abolish the "khoti" system of land tenure in the Konkan region, the serfdom of agricultural tenants and the Mahar "watan" system of working for the Government as slaves. A clause of an agrarian bill referred to the depressed classes as "Harijans," or people of God. Bhimrao was strongly opposed to this title for the untouchables. He argued that if the "untouchables" were people of God then all others would be people of monsters. He was against any such reference. But the Indian National Congress succeeded in introducing the term Harijan. Ambedkar felt bitter that they could not have any say in what they were called. In 1947, when India became independent, the first Prime Minister Pt. Jawaharlal Nehru, invited Dr. Bhimrao Ambedkar, who had been elected as a Member of the Constituent Assembly from Bengal, to join his Cabinet as a Law Minister. The Constituent Assembly entrusted the job of drafting the Constitution to a committee and Dr. Ambedkar was elected as Chairman of this Drafting Committee. In February 1948, Dr. Ambedkar presented the Draft Constitution before the people of India; it was adopted on November 26, 1949.

In October 1948, Dr. Ambedkar submitted the Hindu Code Bill to the Constituent Assembly in an attempt to codify the Hindu law. The Bill caused great divisions even in the Congress party. Consideration for the bill was postponed to September 1951. When the Bill was taken up it was truncated. A dejected Ambedkar relinquished his position as Law Minister. On May 24, 1956, on the occasion of Buddha Jayanti, he declared in Bombay, that he would adopt Buddhism in October. On October 14, 1956 he embraced Buddhism along with many of his followers. On December 6, 1956, Baba Saheb Dr. B.R. Ambedkar died peacefully in his sleep.

Overcoming numerous social and financial obstacles, Ambedkar became one of the first untouchables to obtain college education in India. He went on to pursue higher studies in the United States and England, where he earned law degrees and multiple doctorates for his studies and works in law, economics and political science. A famous scholar, Ambedkar practised law for a few years before he began publishing journals advocating political rights and social freedom for India's untouchables. Leading numerous public agitations, he would become a fierce critic of Mahatma Gandhi and the Indian National Congress.

Ambedkar organised untouchable political parties and social organisations, and served in the legislative councils of British India. He would intensify his criticism of orthodox Hindu society and would oppose nationalist rebellions. Despite this, his reputation as a scholar led to his appointment as free India's first law minister, and chairman of the committee responsible to draft a constitution. Ambedkar's work would guarantee political, economic and social freedoms for untouchables and other ethnic, social and religious communities of India. His polemical condemnation of Hinduism and attacks on Islam would make him unpopular and controversial, although his conversion to Buddhism sparked a revival in interest of Buddhist philosophy in India.

Bhimrao Ramji Ambedkar was born in the British-founded town and military cantonment of Mhow in the Central Provinces (now in Madhya Pradesh). He was the 14th and last child of Ramji Maloji Sakpal and Bhimabai Murbadkar. His family was of Marathi background from the town of Ambavade in the Ratnagiri district of modern-day Maharashtra. They belonged to the Hindu Mahar caste, who were treated as untouchables and subjected to intense socioeconomic discrimination. Ambedkar's ancestors had for long been in the employ of the army of the British East India Company, and his father served in the Indian Army at the Mhow cantonment, rising to the rank of Subedar. He had received a degree of formal education in Marathi and English, and encouraged his children to learn and work hard at school.

Belonging to Kabir Panth, Ramji Sakpal encouraged his children to read the Hindu classics, especially the Mahabharata and the Ramayana. He used his position in the army to lobby for his children to study at the government school, as they faced resistance owing to their caste. Although able to attend school, Ambedkar and other Untouchable children were segregated and given no attention or assistance from the teachers. Ramji Sakpal retired in 1894 and the family moved to Satara two years later. Shortly after their move, Ambedkar's mother died. The children were cared for by their paternal aunt, and lived in difficult circumstances. Only three sons-Balaram, Anandrao and Bhimrao-and two daughters-Manjula and Tulasa-of the Ambedkars would go on to survive them. Of his brothers and sisters, only Ambedkar succeeded in passing his examinations and graduate to a bigger school. His native village name was "Ambavade" in Ratnagiri District so he changed his name from "Sakpal" to "Ambedkar" with the recommendation and faith of a Brahmin teacher that believed in Bhimrao.

Ramji Sakpal remarried in 1898, and the family moved to Mumbai (then Bombay), where Ambedkar became the first untouchable student at the Government High School near Elphinstone Road. Although excelling in his studies, Ambedkar was increasingly disturbed by his segregation and discrimination. In 1907, he passed his matriculation examination and entered the University of Mumbai, becoming one of the first persons of untouchable origin to enter college in India. This success provoked celebrations amongst his community, and after a public ceremony, he was given a biography of the Buddha by his teacher Krishnaji Arjun Keluskar also known as Dada Keluskar a Maratha caste scholar. Ambedkar's marriage had been arranged the previous year as per Hindu custom, to Ramabai, a nine-year old girl from Dapoli. In 1908, he entered the Elphinstone College and obtained a scholarship of Rs. 25 a month from the Gaikwad ruler of Baroda, Sahyaji Rao III for higher studies in USA. By 1912, he obtained his degree in economics and political science, and prepared to take up employment with the Baroda state government. His wife gave birth to his first son, Yashwant in the same year. Ambedkar had just moved his young family and started work, when he dashed back to Mumbai to see his ailing father, who died on February 2, 1913.

A few months later, Ambedkar was selected by the Gaikwad ruler to travel to the United States and enrol at Columbia University, with a scholarship of $11.5 pounds per month. Arriving in New York City, Ambedkar was admitted for graduate studies at the political science department. After a brief stay at the dormitory, he moved to a housing club run by Indian students and took up rooms with a Parsi friend, Naval Bhathena. In 1916, he was awarded a Ph.D. for a thesis which he eventually published in book form as The Evolution of Provincial Finance in British India. His first published work, however, was a paper on Castes in India: Their Mechanism, Genesis and Development. Winning his degree and doctorate, he travelled to London and enrolled at Gray's Inn and the London School of Economics, studying law and preparing a doctoral thesis in economics. The expiration of his scholarship the following year forced him to temporarily abandon his studies and return to India amidst World War I.

Ambedkar wrote very learned and theories obtained his M.A and Ph.D. degrees. He returned to India on the 21st of August 1917. There is one thing to note in the years of Ambedkar's education. He studied English and Persian languages in India. In America he studied Political Science, Ethics, Anthropology, Social Science and Economics. In this way he studied many subjects. He obtained his doctorate. Even at that time Ambedkar had a revolutionary mind. He had made an unshakable resolution to wipe out the injustice done to the people of the low cast; in this way he wanted to bring about a revolution in the Hindu Society. But-and this is important before becoming a revolutionary he increased his knowledge. Because of this his thoughts were not mere froth. They had a solid foundation of information. This enabled him to pay a very effective part in framing the Constitution of India. Returning to work as military secretary for Baroda state, Ambedkar was distressed by the sudden reappearance of discrimination in his life, and left his job to work as a private tutor and accountant, even starting his own consultancy business that failed owing to his social status. With the help of an English acquaintance, the former Bombay Governor Lord Syndenham, he won a post as professor of political economy at the Syndenham College of Commerce and Economics in Mumbai. He was able to return to England in 1920 with the support of the Maharaja of Kolhapur, his Parsi friend and his own savings. By 1923 he completed a thesis on The Problem of the Rupee. He was awarded a D.Sc. by the University of London, and finishing his law studies, he was simultaneously admitted to British Bar as a barrister. On his way back to India, Ambedkar spent three months in Germany, where he conducted further studies in economics at the University of Bonn. He would be formally awarded a Ph.D. by the Columbia University on June 8, 1927.

In 1926, he became a nominated member of the Bombay Legislative Council, and led a satyagraha - nonviolent protest and civil disobedience as pioneered by Mahatma Gandhi - Mahad to fight for the right of the untouchable community to draw water from the main water tank of the town. On January 1, 1927 Ambedkar organised a ceremony at the Koregaon Victory Memorial near Pune, which commemorated the Indian soldiers who died during World War I. Here he inscripted the names of the soldiers from his Mahar community on a marble tablet. In a Depressed Classes Conference on December 24, he condemned the ancient Hindu classical text, the Manusmriti (Laws of Manu).

Condemning it for justifying the system of caste discrimination and untouchability, Ambedkar and his supporters burned copies of the texts. In 1927, he would begin his second journal, the Bahiskrit Bharat (Excluded India), later rechristened as Janata (The People). He would be appointed to the Bombay Presidency Committee to work with the all-European Simon Commission in 1928. This commission had sparked great protests across India, and while its report was ignored by most Indians, Ambedkar himself wrote a separate set of recommendations for future constitutional reforms. He was injured in an accident that occurred during a visit to Chalisgaon on October 23, 1929. Hoping to help the untouchable community, which was facing a social boycott from orthodox Hindus, he was confined in bed there till the end of the year.

In this speech, Ambedkar criticized the Salt Satyagraha launched by Gandhi and the Congress. Ambedkar's criticisms and political work had made him very unpopular with orthodox Hindus, as well as many Congress politicians who had condemned untouchability and worked against discrimination across India. His prominence and popular support amongst the untouchable community had increased, and he was invited to attend the Second Round Table Conference in London in 1931. Here he sparred verbally with Gandhi on the question of awarding separate electorates to untouchables. A fierce opponent of separate electorates on religious and sectarian lines, Gandhi feared that separate electorates for untouchables would divide Hindu society for future generations.

When the British agreed with Ambedkar and announced the awarding of separate electorates, Gandhi began a fast-unto-death while imprisoned in the Yeravada Central Jail of Pune in 1932. Exhorting orthodox Hindu society to eliminate discrimination and untouchability, Gandhi asked for the political and social unity of Hindus. Gandhi's fast provoked great public support across India, and orthodox Hindu leaders, Congress politicians and activists such as Madan Mohan Malaviya and Pawlankar Baloo organized joint meetings with Ambedkar and his supporters at Yeravada. Fearing a communal reprisal and killings of untouchables, had Gandhi died, Ambedkar agreed to drop the demand for separate electorates, under massive coercion from the supporters of Gandhi, and settled for a reservation of seats. Ambedkar was to criticise the fast of Gandhi as a gimmick to deny political rights to the untouchables and the coercion he faced to give up the demand of separate electorates, in all his writings later.

THE MODERN MANU

Today Ambedkar's name is remembered in the history of India also because of the role he played in framing the Constitution of India. Ambedkar became the first Minister of Law in independent India. With one voice all India welcomed his appointment. He took oath as a minister.

The country, no doubt, got freedom. It was to be decided how a country with crores of people should be rules. How should elections take place? What are the rights of the people? How are laws to be made? How should the government works? How should courts of law function?-Such important matters had to be decided, and laws had to be made. The Constitution answers all such questions and lays down rules.

It was a very difficult task to prepare the Constitution. A study of the Constitutions of many countries, a deep knowledge of law, knowledge of the history of India and of the Indian society, the patience and wisdom to weigh different opinion-all these were essential. On 29th August 1947, a committee was constituted to frame the Constitution of India. Ambedkar was chosen as its Chairman. Shri T. T. Krishnamachari, a member of the committee, himself has said:

> "Though a committee of seven members was formed, one of then resigned. Another was nominated in his place. Another member died. No one took his place. One of the members was very busy with government work. Owing to ill health two other members were far away from Delhi. As a result, Dr. Ambedkar alone had to carry the entire burden of preparing the draft of the Constitution. The work he has done is admirable".

As the Minister for Law, Dr. Ambedkar placed the draft Constitution before the Constituent Assembly on 4th November 1948. He gave satisfactory answers to many questions about the Constitution.

The part of the Constitution wiping out 'untouchanblity' was approved on 29th November 1948. Ambedkar's struggle bore fruit in his own life time. A new chapter began in social life. We should remember the words of Ambedkar in answer to the debate on the Indian Constitution:

> "India has lost her freedom only owing to treason of her own people. Raja Dahir of Sindh was defeated by Muhammad Bin Qasim. The only reason for this defeat was that the generals of the Sindh army took bribes from Jasim's men and did not fight for the king. It was Raja Jaichand of India who invited Muhammad Ghori to fight against Prithviraj. When Shivaji was fighting for the freedom of the Hindus, other Maratha leaders and Rajputs were fighting for the Mughals. When the Sikhs were fighting against the British, their leader did nothing.... Such things should not happen again; therefore, everyone must resolve to fight to the last drop of his blood, to defend the freedom of India"

The Constituent Assembly accepted the draft India Constitution on 26th November 1949.

A Life of Fulfilment: Ambedkar's entire life was dedicated to one purpose - securing justice and equality to those people who are called 'untouchalbes'. He had said many times "God will spare me till I complete my work for the 'untouchables'. "He lived to see 'untouchability' declared a crime. The 'untouchables' had secured political equality. They should enjoy social equality also - this feeling was beginning to grow in the country.

As early as in 1951, Ambedkar's health had begun to fail. Yet he continued to work saying that he would not succumb to ill health when there was work to be done. On 6th December 1956 he breathed his last. Thousand and thousands of people watched the funeral procession and expressed their sorrow and admiration. Five hundred thousand people witnessed the last rites.

Ambedkar was very fond of books. He had set apart a part of his house "Rajagriha' for them. When he suffered from an eye trouble, he was particularly unhappy that he could not read. Whenever he went abroad, he used to buy books. Once he bought more than two thousand books in New York, "untoucalbes', 'Buddha and His Gospel', 'Revolution and Counter - Revolution in India', 'Buddha and Karl Marx' and 'The Riddle of Hinduism'- these are some of the books he wrote. His books show how widely he had read, how he had gathered information, and how he could think for himself.

It appears that anger and perseverance are the two most important qualities that stand out in Ambedkar's life. This is true from one point of view. The Hindus had called some people 'untouchables' and treated them very unjustly. This went on for hundreds of years. Ambedkar struggled hard to strengthen his people; he knew that those who are weak are bound to suffer. Once he said," Goats are sacrificed, not lions.' He attacked like lightening those who practised injustice. He opposed the British, he opposed the Hindu that were victims of the past, he opposed even Gandhiji, he opposed the Government of free India; he brought justice to the 'untouchables'. At times his own life was in danger; but he gave no thought to it. It is important to notice another aspect of his Himalayan personality. He was very learned. At school he was not allowed to study Sanskrit, but later in life he did learn Sanskrit.

As the president of the people's Education Society he opened a number of schools and colleges; as a result people of backward classes could get education. He spent some days in Aurangabad. He saw that there were no plants or trees in the bit compound of the college. He said that any one who wanted to meet him should plant a sapling; otherwise he (Ambedkar) would not see him. In a few days more than a hundred saplings appeared inside the compound. Once in front of a hostel he saw shrubs. He himself began to clean the ground with a pickaxe and shovel.

The root of his anger was kindness. It is no wonder that at the end he turned to Buddha, 'the ocean of compassion'. His heart melted in pity when he saw those who, born as men, lived worse than animals, without the respect and the justice every man should receive. That is why he opposed 'untouchability'. He felt that men need Dharma. "Food alone is not enough. Man has a mind, which also requires food. Dharma gives man hope and makes him active" he said. Once he went to Ambedkar. He said he had made avow to God and he begged for Ambedkar's permission to carry out the vow. Ambedkar asked with a smile, "Who told you that I have no faith in God? Go, do as you wish." Once an old lady knocked at his door at early in the morning. Weeping, she said, "My husband is very sick. I tried for 12 hours to admit him to the hospital. They said that there was no room in the hospital." Ambedkar himself went with her and admitted her husband to the hospital. Once, when Dr. Ambedkar resigned as Principal, a boy came to him crying. He was a Brahmin boy. He was very poor. He had a scholarship for two years. He was doubtful whether he would get it during the last year of his stay.

Ambedkar was grieved at his story. He comforted him. He made him sit with him for food. Then he gave him fifty rupees. He patted him on his back and said "if you are in trouble again, come and tell me." When Ambedkar himself was in poor health, he heard that his gardener was not well. He took another man with him and, using a stick for support, went to see the gardener. "Who will look after my wife, if I should die?" - this thought troubled the gardener. Ambedkar comforted him. He said "Do not cry, everyone has to die one day or the other. I too have to die one day. Be brave. I will send you medicine. You will be all right." He sent the medicine. The very next day Ambedkar died in his sleep.

A Lion Among Men: Ambedkar was born in a cast which was considered as the lowest of the low. People said that it was a sin if they offered him water to drink, and that if he sat in a cart it would become unclean. But this very man framed the Constitution for the country. His entire life was one of struggles. And his personal life was too misirable; he had lost his first wife and sons. But even though he did not lost hid dareness. It is no wonder that everyone called him 'Baba Saheb', out of love and admiration. Bhimrao Ambedkar was the lion-hearted man who fought for equality, justice and humanity.

"Inequality is the soul of Hinduism," wrote Ambedkar. He characterized the oppressive caste system as the tyranny of Hinduism. After spending a lifetime in a crusade against the oppressive Hinduism, Ambedkar finally renounced Hinduism, and converted to Buddhism and exhorted his followers to do the same. It is an irony that BJP and other Sangh Parivar outfits are trying to appropriate such a historic personality as Dr. B.R. Ambedkar.

They have started unveiling Ambedkar photos and statues. Some Sangh ideologies have torn some quotations of B.R. Ambedkar on Islamic invasions out of context and misinterpreted them to fit Ambedkar in their own anti-Islamic framework. Vinay Katiyar took out an Ambedkar Yatra in UP. Mayawati unveiled a statue of Ambedkar's wife even though her party, the BSP, shamelessly betrayed the Ambedkar tradition by aligning with his arch ideological-political foes, the Hindutva brigade, in a coalition for the sake of power.

To attract dalits to its fold, the BJP made Bangaru Laxman its ornamental chief but he had to ignominiously bow down from office for accepting Tehelka cash bundles. But before his resignation he made a speech in the Nagpur session of the BJP National Council almost equating Ambedkar with Hedgewar. In fact, the actual history convincingly refutes the dirty tricks of the Sangh Parivar.

During the freedom movement, because of the failures and neglect of the Congress a few political streams arose independent of it. Because of the Congress neglect of Muslims and the influence of Hindu conservatism and Hindu dominance in Congress leadership, Muslims rallied independently under the

Muslim League. For similar reasons, Sikhs also rallied under the Akali Dal. Brahminical upper caste forces dominated the Congress leadership and the party turned a blind eye to the aspirations of nationalities. In Tamil Nadu, Periyar E.V. Ramasamy fought against this, first through the anti-Brahmin movement and then went on to represent the nationality aspirations of Tamils.

It was Ambedkar who squarely put social reform on the agenda during the freedom struggle and launched a simultaneous movement against untouchability and the caste order that were the hallmarks of Hinduism, and championed the interests of dalits. In this he was far to the left of Gandhi. On the other hand, far to the right of Gandhian leadership there was first Hindu Mahasabha and later RSS streams, which often collaborated with the British and considered, with open hostility, even Gandhi too liberal. This hostility finally culminated in the assassination of Gandhi by an RSS man Nathuram Godse. Ambedkar was lifelong at loggerheads with the Hindu fundamentalists. Even in his Thoughts on Pakistan, (on which Katiyar's portrayal of him as an anti-Muslim Hindutva figure rests), he ruthlessly critiques the Hindu Mahasabha and Savarkar. He writes: "The Hindu nationalist who hopes that Britain will coerce the Muslims into abandoning Pakistan, forgets that the right of nationalism to freedom from an aggressive foreign imperialism and the right of a minority to freedom from an aggressive majority's nationalism are not two different things, nor does the former stand on a more sacred footing than the latter."

This clearly illustrates his criticism of aggressive majorotarian nationalism. He further criticizes Savarkar, commenting that "strange as it may seem, Mr. Savarkar and Mr. Jinnah instead of being opposed to each other on the two nations issue, are in complete agreement about it". But Ambedkar exposes Savarkar's authoritarian intent: "Mr. Savarkar wants the Hindu nation to be the dominant nation and the Muslim nation to be the subservient nation under it."

Such being the historical evolution of different political streams in India, it is clear that the legacy of Ambedkar and Hindu fundamentalism are irreconcilably hostile to each other.

Hindutva forces today are trying to delink Ambedkar from his entire legacy, cover up their hostility towards him and try to appropriate him for electoral use.

The fundamental hostility of the Sangh Parivar against Ambedkar was clearly brought to the fore by the vile campaign unleashed against him by RSS ideologue and a BJP minister in Vajpayee's cabinet Arun Shourie through his book Worshipping False Gods. Shiv Sainiks, the soul mates of Hindutva forces, also launched a struggle against Ambedkar's book The Riddles of Hinduism. This is the actual record of Hindutava forces vis-a-vis the heritage of Ambedkar, which they are trying to hide now in order to appropriate his glorious image for their own vested interests.

Ambedkar was the architect of the constitution of India. Sangh Parivar is even opposed to the marginal secular and liberal features of this Constitution and that is why they have formed a committee to tinker with it. While Ambedkar had total enmity towards Hindu Mahasabha and RSS and other Hindu fundamentalists, he was generally pro-left and, befitting a true democrat in a semi-feudal society, he had a positive attitude towards Marxism though it was unfortunate that the communists in those days failed in their united front tactics and failed to develop a proper relationship with Ambedkar. This was part of their general weakness and shortcomings in India.

The Contrast between Ambedkar and Savarkar: Savarkar's strategy of dissolving more than 3,000 castes into one pan-Hindu identity involves pan-Hindu temples, pan-Hindu dinners, inter-caste marriages, anti-untouchability programmes and the removal of injunctions on caste-ridden vocations and sea-voyage. Thus, Savarkar seems to have admonished Hindus to break off the seven shackles that according to him hindered the progress of the Hindu society. Did this programme really denounce Hinduism? The answer to this question has to be in the negative because the anti-caste programme particularly relating to injunctions against inter-caste marriage and advocating vedic rights for the sudras and ati-sudras given by Savarkar did not have vigour and genuine thrust to attack the Hindu shastras and caste system.

Savarkar's contention regarding inter-caste marriages looked to be so casual that he offered only a qualified support to such marriages, thus replacing the need for creating any conscious motivation necessary for the radical mobilisation of the people towards reaching the desired end. Similarly, Savarkar's attempt to grant the study of vedas and vedic rituals to non-Brahmins though apparently liberal may effectively lead to the Brahminisation of the non-Brahmin castes thus according legitimacy to Hindu shastras.

On the contrary, Ambedkar considers inter-caste marriages as the effective means for abolishing caste system. But Ambedkar is also aware that inter-caste dining or even inter-caste marriages are not enough to eliminate casteism. He was of the opinion that for realising the desired goal of casteless society through inter-caste marriages it is necessary to destroy the belief in the sanctity of Hindu shastras.

And for destroying this belief, Ambedkar suggests that people should not only discard the shastras, but they should deny their authority as Buddha and Nanak did. Thus; it can be argued here that socially radical Ambedkar was very unlikely to be attracted by Savarkar whose proposal, according to one of the sincere Savarkarites, contained reformative zeal aimed at revival of Hinduism rather than its denunciation.

Ambedkar was never a Marxist. He could not carry forward his struggle for thorough going abolition of semi-feudalism and against imperialism through a democratic revolution like Mao did in China. He focused mainly on the petty bourgeois and bourgeois intelligentsia from the oppressed communities and worked largely within the system representing their interests in the form of reservation etc. Nevertheless, despite this limitation, he remained an outstanding bourgeois revolutionary democrat who was head and shoulders above many in the Congress leadership and was clearly far more radical than Gandhi.

In the course of his differences against the Congress, he never made any concession to the Hindu Right and always remained hostile to them.

Against Brahminical Hinduism During his boyhood Ambedkar had to suffer lots of personal humiliation due to untouchability. In Chowder Tank satyagraha led by Ambedkar in 1927, the upper caste Hindus attacked him and physically injured him. During the freedom movement Ambedkar emerged as the tallest leader of social reform in India.

Ambedkar asserted: "I was born a Hindu, but never will die a Hindu. What is required is to get rid of the doctrine of 'Chatuvarna'. That is the root cause of all inequality and is also the parent of the case system and untouchability, which are merely other forms of inequality". It is relevant to note here that while both Hedgewar and Golwalkar upheld Manu and thus rationalised the caste system inherent to the Hindu religion, Ambedkar even burnt copies of Manusmruti through a campaign. On December 25, 1927 Ambedkar observed a "Manu Smruti Dahan Din", and publicly burnt Manusmruti. The struggle was known as the "Maha-Sangharsha" of Mahad Satyagraha, and it is an important milestone in Dalit struggle against Brahmanism and Brahminical Hinduism.

Manuvadis had conspired so that Ambedkar did not get a ground for the meeting, but a Muslim gentleman, Mr. Fattekhan, gave his private land to observe this protest. There was a strong reaction in the Brahmanical press, Baba Saheb was called "Bheemaasura" by one paper. Dr. Ambedkar justified the burning of Manusmruti in various articles.

Ambedkar made a scathing attack on Hinduism: "I tell you, religion is for man and not man for religion. If you want to organise, consolidate and be successful in this world, change this religion. The religion that does not recognise you as a human being, or give you water to drink, or allow you to enter temples is not worthy to be called a religion. The religion that forbids you to receive education and comes in the way of your material advancement is not worthy of the appellation 'religion'. The religion that does not teach its followers to show humanity in dealing with its co-religionists is nothing but a display of a force. The religion that teaches its followers to suffer the touch of animals but not the touch of human beings is not a religion but a mockery. The religion that compels the ignorant to be ignorant and the poor to be poor is not a religion but a visitation!"

He added this on the upper castes: "It is your claim to equality which hurts them. They want to maintain the status quo. If you continue to accept your lowly status ungrudgingly, continue to remain dirty, filthy, backward, ignorant, poor and disunited, they will allow you to live in peace. The moment you start to raise your level, the conflict starts. Untouchability is not a transitory or temporary feature; it is eternal, it is lasting. Frankly it can be said that the struggle between the Hindus and the Untouchables is a never-ending conflict. It is eternal because the religion which assigns you the lowest status in society is itself divine and eternal according to the belief of the so-called high caste Hindus. No change warranted by change of time and circumstances is possible." Such being the views of Ambedkar, those who offer political patronage to outfits like Ranvir Sena can have no claim over Ambedkar. The ideologies of Hindutva are trying to rationalise caste system saying that it is a division of labour. Ambedkar refuted this saying, "Caste System is not merely a division of labour.

It is also a division of labourers. It is an hierarchy in which the divisions of labourers are graded one above the other." While the Hindutva brigade is known for defending Manu and the caste system, Ambedkar made a trenchant criticism of the caste system associated with Hinduism: "There cannot be a more degrading system of social organisation than the Chaturvarna.

It is the system which deadens, paralyses and cripples the people from helpful activity." He further added, "Caste in the hands of the orthodox has been a powerful weapon for persecuting the reforms and for killing all reform." Relating the inseparable relation between caste system and Hinduism, Ambedkar wrote, "Hinduism is a veritable chamber of horrors. The sanctity and infallibility of the Vedas, Smritis and Shastras, the iron law of caste, the heartless law of karma and the senseless law of status by birth are to the untouchables veritable instruments of torture which Hinduism has forged against untouchables."

In Buddha and His Dhamma, Ambedkar has enumerated the evils of Hinduism in the following manner:

1. It has deprived moral life of freedom;
2. It has only emphasized conformity to commands; and

3. The laws are unjust because they are not the same for one class as of another.

Besides, the code is treated as final. According to Ambedkar, "what is called religion by Hindus is nothing but a multitude of commands and prohibitions." The Sangh Parivar is out to make this code the official code in India under their scheme of authoritarian Hindu rashtra.

Sensing the alienation of dalits, many people, from Savarkar to Gandhi, made token gestures against casteism. The RSS was also forced to come out with some tokenist pronouncements. But Ambedkar put things in the right perspective by saying, "Caste cannot be abolished by inter-caste dinners or stray instances of inter caste marriages. Caste is a state of mind. It is a disease of mind. The teachings of the Hindu religion are the root cause of this disease. We practice casteism and we observe untouchability because we are enjoined to do so by the Hindu religion. A bitter thing cannot be made sweet. The taste of anything can be changed. But poison cannot be changed into nectar."

Ambedkar even made a sarcastic comment against Gandhi: "There have been many mahatmas in India whose sole object was to remove untouchability and to elevate and absorb the depressed classes, but everyone has failed in their mission. Mahatmas have come, mahatmas have gone but the untouchables have remained as untouchables." Ambedkar told dalits that, "You must abolish your slavery yourselves. Do not depend for its abolition upon god or a superman. Remember that it is not enough that a people are numerically in the majority.

They must be always watchful, strong and self-respecting to attain and maintain success. We must shape our course ourselves and by ourselves." He further stressed that, "What you have lost others have gained. Your humiliations are a matter of pride with others. You are made to suffer wants, privations and humiliations not because it was preordained by the sins committed in your previous birth, but because of the overpowering tyranny and treachery of those who are above you. You have no lands because others have usurped them; you have no posts because others have monopolised them. Do not believe in fate; believe in your strength." It may be recalled that Advani recently raised a controversy over a Buddhist symbol like Ashoka chakra figuring in the national flag and a Buddhist symbol being the national emblem. Regarding their origin Ambedkar explained, "Even though Buddhism is almost extinct in India, yet it has given birth to a culture, which is far better and richer than the Brahminic culture. When the question of the national flag and the national emblem was being considered by the Constituent Assembly we could not find any suitable symbol from the Brahminic culture. Ultimately, the Buddhist culture came to our rescue and we accepted the Wheel of Law (Dhamma-Chakra) as the national symbol." No wonder, a Brahminical high-priest of Hindutva like Advani wanted to do away with these symbols introduced by Ambedkar and his colleagues.

In his slanderous campaign against Ambedkar, the RSS ideologue Arun Shourie questioned the patriotism of Ambedkar. Ambedkar, however, defined patriotism thus, "I do not want that our loyalty as Indians should be in the slightest way affected by any competitive loyalty whether that loyalty arises out of our religion, out of our culture or out of our language. I want all people to be Indians first, Indian last and nothing else but Indians." And despite all his differences with the Congress, Ambedkar remained a staunch nationalist.

For Ambedkar, the conception of a secular state is derived from the liberal democratic tradition of the West. In contrast to the Gandhian misinterpretation of secularism as 'sarva dharma samabhava', Ambedkar said, "No institution, which is maintained wholly out of state funds, shall be used for the purpose of religious instruction irrespective of the question whether the religious instruction is given by the state or by any other body". He further explained the corruption of the concept of secularism in India, "This country has seen the conflict between ecclesiastical law and secular law long before Europeans sought to challenge the authority of the Pope. Kautilya's Arthshastra lays down the foundation of secular law. In India unfortunately ecclesiastical law triumphed over secular law. In my opinion this was the one of the greatest disasters in the country."

Ambedkar effectively punctured the false supremacy of the narrow Brahminical elite: "In every country the intellectual class is the most influential class. This is the class which can foresee, advise and lead. In no country does the mass of the people live the life for intelligent thought and action. It is largely imitative and follows the intellectual class. There is no exaggeration in saying that the entire destination of the country depends upon its intellectual class. If the intellectual class is honest and independent, it can be trusted to take the initiative and give a proper lead when a crisis arises. It is true that the intellect by itself is no virtue. It is only a means and the use of a means depends upon the ends which an intellectual person pursues. An intellectual man can be a good man but he may easily be a rogue. Similarly an intellectual class may be a band of high-souled persons, ready to help, ready to emancipate erring humanity or it may easily be a gang of crooks or a body of advocates of narrow clique from which it draws its support."

Though changing one's religion through conversion is not going to abolish the semi-feudal inequalities, Ambedkar's decision to convert to Buddhism in the evening of his life-just a couple of months before his demise on 6 December 1956-only underlined his disgust and bitterness with the highly iniquitous Hinduism. About 2 lakh dalits converted to Buddhism along with him in October 1956. Since then neo-Buddhism has remained a trend. This clearly rattled the Hindutva bosses who are clamouring for anti-conversion legislation in every state.

A THOROUGH DEMOCRAT

Though Ambedkar headed the committee that drafted the Constitution of the democratic republic of India, he was never fully satisfied with the democracy which came to be established in India. In his opinion, "A democratic form of government presupposes a democratic form of a society. The formal framework of democracy is of no value and would indeed be a misfit if there was no social democracy. It may not be necessary for a democratic society to be marked by unity, by community of purpose, by loyalty to public ends and by mutuality of sympathy. But it does unmistakably involve two things. The first is an attitude of mind, and attitude of respect and equality towards their fellows. The second is a social organisation free from rigid social barriers. Democracy is incompatible and inconsistent with isolation and exclusiveness resulting in the distinction between the privileged and the unprivileged." "Democracy is not a form of government, but a form of social organisation", he asserted.

He further elaborated, "What we must do is not to content ourselves with mere political democracy. We must make our political democracy a social democracy as well. Political democracy cannot last unless there is at the base of it, a social democracy."

Ambedkar underlined the limitations of formal law and Constitution: "The prevalent view is that once the rights are enacted in law then they are safeguarded. This again is an unwarranted assumption. As experience proves, rights are protected not by law but by social and moral conscience of the society. If social conscience is such that it is prepared to recognise the rights which law proposes to enact, rights will be safe and secure. But if the fundamental rights are opposed by the community, no law, no parliament, no judiciary can guarantee them in the real sense of the world. What is the use of fundamental rights to the untouchables in India?" "If I find the constitution being misused, I shall be the first to burn it," he declared.

Ambedkar also had certain premonitions about the rise of authoritarian forces in India which is coming true before our eyes: "On the 26th January 1950, we are going to enter into a life of contradictions. In politics we will have equality and in social and economic life we will have inequality. In politics we will be recognising the principle of one-man-one-vote and one-vote-one-value. In our social and economic life, we shall by reason of our social and economic structure, continue to deny the principle of one-man-one-value. How long shall we continue to live this life of contradictions? How long shall we continue to deny equality in our social and economic life? If we continue to deny it for long, we will do so only by putting our political democracy in peril". The Sangh Parivar outfits rally tribals and dalits only to use them to attack Christian missionaries as witnessed in Orissa or to launch pogroms against Muslims as seen in Gujarat, and thereby endanger democracy. To frustrate the designs of the Sangh Parivar it is necessary that today communists and genuine Ambedkarites should come together to defend democracy from communal fascists, a democracy to establish which Ambedkar fought so hard.

In his last days, Ambedkar raised a note of warning: "The point is that India once lost the independence she had. Will she lose it a second time? It is this thought which makes me most anxious for the future. What perturbs me greatly is the fact that not only India has once before lost her independence, but she lost it by treachery of some of her own people...Will history repeat itself? It is this thought which fills me with anxiety.. Will Indians place the country above their creed or creed above their country? I do not know, But this much is certain that if the parties place creed above country, our independence will be put in jeopardy a second time and probably be lost forever. This eventuality we all must resolutely guard against. We must be determined to defend our independence with the last drop of our blood!" The rise of Hindutva forces who totally cringe before the US imperialism but at the same time are bent upon establishing a fascistic Hindu rashtra has proved how correct this warning was. As Ambedkar called upon us, we must defend this freedom and democracy with the last drop of our blood.

Baba Saheb Ambedkar has undoubtedly been the central figure in the epistemology of the Dalit universe. It is difficult to imagine anything serious or important in their collective life that is totally untouched by Ambedkar. For the Dalit masses he is everything together; a scholar par excellence in the realm of scholarship, a Moses or messiah who led his people out of bondage and ignominy on to the path of pride, and a Bodhisatva in the pantheon of Buddhism. He is always bedecked with superlatives, quite like God, whatever may be the context in Dalit circles.

It is not difficult to see the reason behind the obeisance and reverence that dalits have for Ambedkar. They see him as one who devoted every moment of his life thinking about and struggling for their emancipation, who took the might of the establishment head on in defence of their cause; who sacrificed all the comforts and conveniences of life that were quite within his reach to be on their side; who conclusively disproved the theory of caste based superiority by rising to be the tallest amongst the tall despite enormous odds, and finally as one who held forth the torch to illuminate the path of their future. Few in the history of millenniums of their suffering had so much as looked at them as humans and empathised with them as fellow beings. He was their own among these few. It was he, who forsook his high pedestal, climbed down to their level, gave them a helping hand and raised them to human stature. It is a commonplace occurrence to see dalits right from the humble landless labourer in villages to the highly placed bureaucrat in corridors of power, emotionally attributing their all to him. They all believe that but for him, they would still be living like their forefathers, with spittoons around their necks and broom sticks to their behind.

It is thus natural for dalits to place him at the centre as their beacon and conduct their collective affairs as directed by its beam. This beam however is not monochromatic like a laser beam, to use an analogy from physics, but is composed of many light frequencies, the filters for which are controlled not by the masses but by some others. They manipulate this beam as per their desire, sometimes letting some frequencies pass and some times some other. They could selectively amplify some part and de-amplify the other and present an entirely different spectrum. What reaches the masses, thus, is not the holistic and true picture of 'Ambedkar' but its part, sometimes a distorted part, carefully filtered out and amplified by the 'technicians'.

This fragmented and false Ambedkar is what reaches the masses. For them, Ambedkar is no more a historical personality named Bhimrao Ramji Ambedkar. He is already metamorphosed into a symbol-a symbol for their collective aspiration, an icon for the thesis of their emancipation. Because for the masses icons come handy. They are sans complexity of the main body, practical useable artefacts. Iconisation of the great heroes and their ideas at the hands of masses is thus inevitable. Human history is replete with such icons; rather it is largely made of them. The Dalit politicians who never let the masses see the material aspects of their problems and kept them entangled in the cobweb of emotional issues have moreover promoted iconisation of Baba Saheb Ambedkar.

The history of post-Ambedkar Dalit movement is largely influenced by the icons of Ambedkar that were produced by the sociopolitical dynamics of post-independence India The process of iconisation, whatever be the motivations, has to have the basis, howsoever tenuous, in the material reality, in the facts about the subject. Being essentially a simplification of a complex reality, it involves the playing up of facts as per one's proclivities and propensities. The icons in Ambedkar himself and simultaneously highlights the motive force behind the underlying distortions that they embody. While it largely holds these icons responsible for the current sorry State of the Dalit movement based on the near-monotheistic devotion of dalits towards Baba Saheb Ambedkar, it still considers that the conceptual framework that he reflects could be used, not only to further the emancipatory struggles of dalits to its logical end but also to promote a true democratic revolution in India, provided it is seen in a radical light.

The first part reviews the post-Ambedkar Dalit movement, essentially in relation to certain significant milestones or trends and attempts to trace the specific icon of Ambedkar that underscores each. The second part discusses the general limitations of transpositioning the ideologies, characterising specific episodes in the history across the historical periods and in specific reviews the predominant profiles of the Ambedkar-icons.

It outlines the need to redefine Ambedkar, if he is to be the ideological icon to guide the Dalit movement to its logical end. The third part discusses certain predominant issues that will have to be essentially resolved in the redefinition project and gives clues for profiling 'Ambedkar' for the future Dalit movement. The fourth and final part sums it up, emphasising the relevance and validity of the basic framework implied in Ambedkar's work-to view the contradictions in the society from the standpoint of the worst victim and work for their resolution, to bring about a democratic revolution in India.

NEED FOR A REVIEW

Various icons that the post-Ambedkar movement of dalits appear to have built up, characterise Ambedkar as the maker of the Indian Constitution, provider of the present order, a Bodhisatva, a constitutionalist, a messiah, a saviour, an SC leader, a liberal democrat, a staunch anti-Communist, a social engineer who believed in the reform process and disliked revolutions. It is heavily sculpted by the petty-bourgeoisie outlook that has completely hegemonised the Dalit movement. It rarely reflects the dreamer in him who was perpetually in search of ways and means to see the human society sans exploitation, injustice and humbug.

Many students of the Dalit movement are influenced by these post-Ambedkar reflections in characterising Ambedkar as the bourgeoisie liberal democrat. Does it really project what Ambedkar stood for? Does it capture the full essence of his movement? More importantly, is that the Ambedkar whom we are going to use as the weapon in the emancipatory struggle of dalits?

Dalits as a social group, are still the poorest of poor. A negligible minority has managed to escape poverty limits and to locate itself on to a continuum ranging up to a reasonable level of prosperity with the help of certain State policies like reservation and political patronage. In social terms however, all dalits, irrespective of their economic standing, still suffer oppression. This social oppression varies from the crudest variety of untouchability, still being practised in rural areas, to the sophisticated forms of discrimination encountered even in the modern sectors of urban life. Although, the statistics indicate that dalits have made significant progress on almost all parameters during the last five decades, the relative distance between them and non-dalits seems to have remained the same or has increased.

More than 75 per cent of the Dalit workers are still connected with land; 25 per cent being the marginal and small farmers and the balance 50 per cent being landless labourers. The proportion of dalits landless labourers to the total labourers has shown a steady rising trend.

In urban areas, they work mainly in the unorganised sector where the exploitation compares well with that of a feudal rural setting. Out of the total Dalit population of 138 million, the number of dalits in services falling in the domain of reservations does not exceed 1.3 million including sweepers; less than even a percent. And this too would be grossly misleading, as out of this 1.3 million the relatively well-off group A and B officers (in which most of the clerical staff of the PSUs also come), count only 72,212 as against 131,841 sweepers.

With the new politico-economic order emerging in the world, the grammar of the Dalit liberation struggle is going to be totally different from that familiar to dalits. The onslaught of the adversarial forces is being felt world over by all the oppressed people and it would be folly for dalits not to feel a part of the latter. Their objective situation as a social block is not represented by the minuscule minority that managed to find themselves in the organised sectors of economy, but by the vast majority who are left behind in the villages or the numbers who toil in the unorganised sectors in towns and cities. They need the weaponry for battling out their salvation. This battle is to be waged simultaneously on two fronts, marked by the caste and class. These terms under segmented and sectarian usage came to bear an erroneous exclusivity.

Since, Ambedkar still provides a better framework for their problems than any other, and since he commands an unchangeable place in their hearts, the weapons in his armoury needs dusting and sharpening. They will need a review for their effective application in the changing context and possibly, substantial supplementation and replenishment. Ambedkar, quite similar to Buddha in his own hands, needs redefinition. The folklore 'Ambedkar' needs to be replaced by the radical 'Ambedkar', who would inspire people to claim the whole world as theirs and not to beg for petty favours from the robbers.

It is the responsibility of all those who are capable of seeing the reality, to contribute to this task. For, without such a redefinition, Ambedkar could be fossilised as god but would fail in the emancipation project; he might be raised to the highest pedestal by the vested interests but then he would be unable to reach out to where he is most needed; he would lose out to the parody of history.

2

VISIONS AND ICONS OF GREAT PERSON

INTRODUCTION

Every great person has a vision that impels all her/his works. Its discernibility may vary from case to case, generally being the function of the degree of turbulence around her/him, her/his relative position within the power structure in the given environment, her/his own equipment and conception of self-role. Marx, for instance, offers an articulate vision in clearest terms as he assumed the primary role of a philosopher to bring about revolutionary change, whereas Ambedkar had donned the mantle of mass-leadership in his primary role to spearhead the change; the degree of turbulence in the work domain of Marx had been minimal as he basically struggled in the realm of thought spanning complete human history whereas Ambedkar situated himself in the political turbulence that obtained in India as his strategy; Ambedkar's position in the power structure that bounded his work domain was certainly weak relative to Marx's. This is neither to undermine the role of Marx as the activist constantly trying out his philosophy in the realm of practice nor to belittle the problems he suffered in life. With regard to personal equipment, both Ambedkar as well as Marx, could be taken to be equally equipped to undertake their respective tasks that they had undertaken. Marx had started off with philosophy and adopted the class-consciousness of the proletariat quite unlike Ambedkar, in whose case it was his own consciousness-the consciousness of an untouchable built up through concrete experience that had propelled his philosophical search.

Marx was well aware of his role in the revolutionary project, that he had to provide requisite tools and tackles for the working class for bringing about a change in the overall interest of humanity. But, Ambedkar was always loaded with anxiety as he had to strategize his way through the political maze around him, winning for dalits the maximum he could in a short span of time. In process, his role also underwent transformation with the expanse of the battleground. Inevitably, his thoughts and action always remained context-laden, polemical and pragmatically purposeful. It is therefore a relatively difficult task to discern a coherent vision underscoring the life work of Baba Saheb Ambedkar.

It is a moot point as to what extent a great person, who is essentially anchored in her/his space and time, could transcend these barriers and be equally effective in a different situation. A great person basically is the product of prevailing social relations. It is a particular moment in history that reflects an acute demand for such a person. Depending upon her/his location in the social setting, she/he imparts her/his individual feature to the historical moments and movements in terms of working out specific means for resolving contradictions that engender them and releasing the forces of history in a specific direction. The masses whose cause she / he espouses throng around her/ him in this process, depending upon the level of their collective consciousness. The longevity of the ideas a great person propounds in a historical setting depends upon the nature of contradictions, the size and expanse of problems and the time domain in which they are situated.

Generally, the classes that share the vision and ideology of such persons tend to iconise them with specific attributes of their class choice, in an attempt to institutionalise the latter. In this process, they would de-contextise some of the ideas and proffer them as universal theorems, if they perceive a pay-off for themselves in the sphere hegemonised by them.

This phenomenon becomes clear only over a long time horizon. For instance, the religious principles that were sprouted in the soil of certain specific social relations have basically blossomed in an alien soil with the help of the nutrients of class interests. Very broadly speaking, the trend of iconisation of great persons and the attempt of institutionalising their ideas is a gauge to assess the forces of status quo in the society.

COMMITMENT AND CONSTRAINT

In the case of Baba Saheb Ambedkar, iconisation was inevitable. The combination of factors like his high stature, his devotion to the cause of his people; the historical setting in which he lived, the low level of literacy and political consciousness in masses; and the vested interests of internal as well as external people have been its cause. The problem is not with iconisation as it is with its multiplicity. A question may be pertinently asked can Ambedkar be uniquely represented by a single icon? As Prof. Upendra Bakshi had outlined in one of his articles during the centenary year of his birth anniversary that there were many Ambedkars and had questioned as to which Ambedkar do we commemorate? When he said so, Prof. Bakshi was referring to different facets of Ambedkar's personality that could be virtually segregated.

One can even periodise some of them. For example, the pre-1942 Ambedkar as a young, untouchable man endowed with highest scholastic distinctions, struggling within and without for the emancipation of his people is a grossly different personality than the Ambedkar as a member of the viceroy's Executive Council or the Ambedkar as the law minister in the Nehru cabinet in the post-independence India or the Ambedkar as the chairman of the drafting committee for the Indian Constitution or even the Ambedkar of still later years who had completely identified himself with Buddhism and in a way completely spiritualised himself.

What comes clearly however, is that the changes in his outlook and role were essentially driven by his unstilted commitment to the cause of emancipation of oppressed humanity in general and dalits in particular. He might not have had appropriate methodological tools to deal with the problem at hand. With the equipment that basically belonged to a school of social engineers, he tried to dissect history. Paradoxically, he attempted to demolish the establishment with the very tools that were forged to serve the ruling classes. By training he did not have the facility to look at history as the continuum of human struggle with a certain inherent logic. He did use history as a repertoire of human episodes and attributed even logic to it but its source was externalised.

NON-DIALECTICAL SOLUTION: STATE AND RELIGION

It appears that Baba Saheb Ambedkar had really internalised the doctrine of momentariness (Anityatawad and later Kshanikwad) of Buddha and therefore even refused to care for consistency in his views and opinions. This doctrine states that every thing changes every moment, that things are constantly becoming. It follows that in this situation of flux not even mental processes could be static, they had essentially to match the dynamicity of the material world. He thus never hesitated in changing his thoughts or strategy as per the unfolding situation. Viewed another way, these changes can be understood in relation to foci of control.

The degree of consistency in thought and action is generally inversely proportional to the distance of the subject from the foci of control of its surrounding. Ambedkar had nil or little control over his situation. He had to consistently create space for himself and strategize to influence the situation to his advantage. (The dynamics of the situation was propelled by the forces that were variously placed in the adversary camps.) The framework within which he conceived his struggle had exposed him to his lot to respond to this dynamics.

The hallmark of Ambedkar's thoughts is the dynamic rationale, which he has consistently employed to comprehend situations and to strategize his response thereto. 'Ambedkar' therefore cannot be captured in static terms. His icon will have to represent the dynamism that he lived. Since, this is an infeasible proposition; we will have to discern the underscoring vision behind his works, the intransient essence of his entire mission to create a suitable icon. This icon, even if it does not resemble the familiar Ambedkar, alone could be the beacon of the Dalit movement. The concept of Anityawad in Buddhism essentially belongs to dialectics that has made Buddha an early dialectician philosopher. The dichotomy that creeps in can only be resolved by dialectical method. It may be questioned whether Ambedkar's method was dialectical. It appears that while he accepts constant becoming of things as the principle underscoring the universe, he faces a dilemma with respect to the conception of order in this State. It could be resolved dialectically in terms of systemic attribute of self-regulation-a characteristic of internal control. But the conventional conception of order, essentially a non-dialectical conception, leads to externalisation of control. Ambedkar, having experienced the brutal aspects of history and unbridled exploitation of man by man, appears in need of a control mechanism operating at two levels, viz., internal and external, so as to maintain the societal order in the desired State. His internal control mechanism is the moral code provided by the religion and the one for external control is the State.

If this moral code is internalised by all individuals and in turn by society as the summation of the latter (as the liberal tradition held), society is expected to have an internal order. If however the baser instincts of some people or group of people defy this order, either as a result of conflicting codes they follow or for any other reason, then in such case the State will step in and restore the order. The will of the collective is supposed to be embodied in the State by the Constitution. It is therefore that Ambedkar has reservation in agreeing with Marx that 'religion was the opium of masses' or the 'State shall eventually wither away'. Ambedkar certainly did not know that the order could be the attribute of the system itself. It is only in the sixties that Cybernetics principles came to lime light that the complex probabilistic systems, which the social systems certainly are, do have the inherent capability of self-regulating and self-organising control.

AGAINST EXPLOITATION

The underscoring vision in Ambedkar's thought and action is to be found in his yearning for the end of all kinds of exploitation. Whenever and wherever he smelt exploitation, he raised his voice against it. The caste system that subjugated more than one fifth of the population to levels worse than animals' for more than two millennia and which represented institutionalisation of the most heinous inequality by the Hindu religion as ordained by its gods, became the prime target of his life. He attacked it from the standpoint of its victims-the untouchables. He waged many battles; initially targeting the citadels of Brahminism-the custodian of the Hindu religious code, and later politicised the battle, realising the ineffectiveness of the former. He did not let this objective out of sight even for a moment and worked incessantly for its achievement. This Herculean task almost completely overshadows the fact that his struggles extend well beyond the caste struggles and rather encompass all other forms of exploitation.

Even the credit for struggling against untouchability was reluctantly granted to him by the establishment which had belittled him initially as merely a leader of his own caste-Mahar. This prejudicial treatment of Ambedkar could itself be taken as a measure of the severity of the problematic of caste. The facts are clear today that not only was his struggle directed towards the emancipation of all the untouchables but also towards annihilation of the entire caste system. It was basically against the systemic exploitation that ran unabated for centuries.

The protest against this inhuman system could be articulated only in a concrete situation, not in a vacuum. He did not theorise the struggle on a hypothetical plane. He built it on the basis of real problems in a concrete situation. Unlike many cases, the motive force for his life mission was provided by his experience itself. Although he pitched his tents against Brahminism, he never bore any enmity against the Brahmins or identified any one for his friend or foe by caste. The Bahishkrit Hitkarini Sabha that was the launch vehicle of his movement had majority from the forward caste people in its executive body. Even later, this intention of having a non-caste base for the organisation could be consistently seen in his movement, be it the Mahad struggle or the Indian Labour Party. He was perceptive enough to say that the Brahminism could exist in all the castes including the untouchables, for that was the essence of the casteism. It is tragic to find his legacy being monopolised today by only the scheduled castes.

Although, he considered the magnitude of the problem of emancipation of dalits is such as to warrant his sole attention, he did take cudgels for other oppressed entities like workers, peasants and women. At one occasion in response to the accusation that he did not care for the tribals, he had to squarely admit the fact that he considered the problem at hand big enough to outlast his life and provokedly put that he never claimed to fight for whole humanity. Such instances though disturbing enough could be understood within their specific context. While dealing with the socioeconomic depravation of dalits, he comprehensively exposed certain systemic dimensions that help perpetuate exploitation. For instance, he was well aware of the capitalist and imperialist oppression besides the decadent feudalism within which domain his problem lay.

CAPITALISM

During the colonial British regime, capitalism started taking root in India with the collaboration of Indian mercantile capital and British capital. Unlike Europe, it did not have to battle against feudalism; rather it was implanted on the trunk of the latter in India. As a result, even in the capitalist institutions in the cities, caste discrimination simultaneously existed. Ambedkar was quite aware of the exploitative potential of capital and hence he had declared capitalism and Brahminism as the twin enemy of his movement. Capitalism was in an infantile stage then but Brahminism encompassed the phases of slavery, feudalism and extended its tentacles as we see to the phase of imperialism. Moreover, he noted the reactionary compradore character of rising capitalism in the contemporary sectors of the economy and the inhuman exploitation of workers that it unleashed.

His, Indian Labour Party (ILP) was an attempt to take up the question of capitalist exploitation, as well as to combine the struggle on both caste and class basis. Various workers' problems were taken up by the ILP, the leadership of combined strike of the mill workers, parliamentary fight for the workers' interest in relation to the Industrial Disputes Act, and various legal reforms that were brought about while he was in the Executive Council of the Viceroy, can be the examples of his concern for workers' exploitation. It cannot be denied that his approach to these contemporary problems was closer to that of the Fabian socialists with whom he was more familiar. But, it was a model adopted out of familiarity and pragmatism, a matter of strategy, never thought out on an ideological plane to be a theoretical plank. Although, there cannot be any doubt that he stood against capitalism, he could not articulate a sound theoretical basis for doing so. Resultantly, his efforts remained constricted with a short view of workers' welfare but could not provide them a vision of their liberation.

IMPERIALISM

Ambedkar's attitude towards imperialism has been projected in a distorted manner right from the beginning, mainly because he refused to take part in the freedom struggle or opposed Gandhi who for certain category of ignoramuses was the anti-imperialism personified. He strategically sought to maintain neutrality vis-a-vis the colonial State. As per him, it would not be possible for the resourceless dalits to fight its mighty foes all together. He did not want to dissipate and squander his extremely limited resources on several fronts. He however knew the basic exploitative character of the colonial regime. At several occasions, he burst out saying that British imperialism and Indian feudalism were the two leaches that clung to Indian people. However, there was a fundamental difference between his and others' viewpoint. For instance, he did not approve equating opposition to imperialism with opposing the British. He noted that the opposition to imperialism couldn't be effective until its supporters within the country are left untouched.

The then leader of the Communist Party of India-Manabendranath Roy once met him at his residence and during discussions insisted that destruction of imperialism had to be the first and foremost objective of Indian politics. Ambedkar's response to him summarised his outlook towards this problem. He replied to Roy in explicit terms that without struggling against the landlords, mill owners, moneylenders-the friends of imperialism within the country, it was not possible to wage an effective fight against imperialism. It may be a matter of research but a priori his anti-imperialist attitude pervades even his writings as a student.

The validation of his stand comes from an entirely unrelated corner and nearly half a century later. Suniti Kumar Ghosh, (1985 and 1995) in his books has shown in great detail how the Congress representing landlords and capitalists had played a compradore role to serve the interest of imperialism during the so-called freedom struggle and how even after the transfer of power in 1947 the grip of imperialism instead of weakening became stronger. Does it not indicate that he was more correct than any of his contemporary politicians? The ones who biasedly wish to pronounce their half baked verdict that Ambedkar was a stooge of British merely on the basis of his acceptance of membership of Viceroy's Executive Council or talking to the Simon Commission, not only display their ignorance of history but also their casteist fangs. They ought to rethink the comparison between Ambedkar who, even being apparently a part of the imperialist apparatus was perhaps striking at its roots by empowering the people and many others, so called nationalists, who after wearing the mask of anti-imperialism were indirectly strengthening its pillars.

In relation to British rule, Ambedkar basically makes two points. The first is that he questions the so-called freedom struggle launched under the leadership of Congress as an anti-imperialist struggle. He contended that the Congress basically represented the class of feudal lords and the urban capitalists-the two some exploiters of Indian masses. Although, it succeeded through the charismatic leadership of Gandhi in galvanising masses in its support, it essentially relied on bargaining with the colonial rulers for securing itself more share of power.

It always throttled the mass spontaneity as in the case of 1942-uprisings and actively opposed the genuine anti-imperialist struggles of the revolutionaries like Bhagat Singh. Ambedkar reflects the understanding of true character of the Congress in his own way, when he says that if Congress was fighting a real anti-imperialist war, he would whole heartedly support it. The rhetoric of such statement apart, for he never appears to even take a note of other truly anti-imperialist struggles like the one referred to above, it is enough to reveal his attitude towards imperialism and understanding of the class character of the Congress. He knew that the class character of the Congress would not permit it to don this role in reality. Ambedkar could see through the anti-imperialist masks the real fangs of an exploiter of masses.

He thus not only saw no point in siding with this more real exploiter of people than perhaps the colonial rulers, but also did not hesitate to openly oppose it when it came in the way of Dalit liberation. He smelt rot in all such struggles that refused to notice existence of inhuman exploitation of some of their own people within their precincts and tended to over-externalise their woes. Here lay his second point when he raised a question of Hindu imperialism perpetrated through its caste system that was certainly seen as more vicious by its victims than the British rule. It may be pertinent to ask of those who raise the issue of Ambedkar's attitude and conduct towards imperialism, to answer as to why the problem of untouchability or caste system that reduced its one-fifth of the population to subhuman levels did not find a mere mention in the lofty discussions of freedom struggle that predated Ambedkar's raising it. The anti-imperialist aspiration also could be seen in the context of the class/caste division in the society.

The battle for the lost kingdom waged by the vanquished lords also could be camouflaged as an anti-imperialist struggle and at the same time the genuine peoples' anti-imperialist aspiration manifested in the form of say anti-feudal struggle could be condemned as the pro-imperialism, merely because it directed its gun towards the props of the imperialism. The real anti-imperialist aspirations belong to the masses of people the manifestation of which is possible only through the peoples' war. Whatever anti-imperialist struggle people waged were soon hijacked by the phoney war whose real intent was to extract political power to native ruling classes. While the scenes of anti-British struggles were being enacted for the 'mother' India of exploiters, Ambedkar busied himself to liberate the other India- the India of the exploited and oppressed.

OPPRESSION OF WOMEN

Besides these mainstream forms of exploitation even the subaltern forms like women's exploitation, could not escape his agenda. He viewed them as the most oppressed of all. His approach to the problems was typically that of a liberal democrat constitutionalist. This certainly constrained his articulation of this problem as in many others. This issue will have to be seriously rethought by dalits under the redefinition project. But suffice here to say that at any opportunity, he raised his voice against women's discriminatory situation in the society.

His basic law of social engineering was that the social revolutions must always begin from the standpoint of the most oppressed or the ones on the lowest rung of the society. Right from the days of Mook Nayak and Bahiskrit Bharat, he appears to take cudgels for women. He always involved women in his struggles and tended to give them vanguard positions. For example, about 500 women had marched at the head of the historical procession at Mahad to assert the untouchables' right to drink water from the public tank. He was immensely pained to see the permanent denial of education and religious rights to women ordained in the Shastras of the Hinduism (e.g. Manusmriti). His democratic consciousness never reconciled with any thing lesser than the equality of men and women though its expression was acutely constrained perhaps by his anxieties about the possibilities, so much so that it might even be mistaken as the male centric tactic.

While he asked women to be good mothers so as to shape up their son or to be good wives to their husbands or be a carrier of community's cultural baggage, he did struggle for their equal rights as in the case of Hindu Code Bill. He described sacramental marriages (Mathew, 1991) as polygamy for men and perpetual slavery for women because under no circumstances within that system the latter would get liberty from their husbands, however bad or undesirable they may be. He insisted that women should have the freedom to break this contract.

ON REVOLUTION

Revolution, on the face of it, appears to be an anathema to Ambedkar who seems to dread it and instead advocates reforms. But it would be disaster to take it at face value. For, like many other terms, his usage of the term 'revolution' does not bear the same meaning as is in vogue, particularly in

Marxist circles. What Ambedkar seems to detest in revolution is the violence. At many places he tends to equate rebellion, revolution and revolt with violence. He also seems to disagree with the method of insurrection. He thought that without mass consciousness being ripe enough for revolutionary change, insurrectionary methods would not succeed.

Moreover, he appears to be sceptical of the justness of revolutions as they invariably represent the triumph of the collective over the individual. It may be attributed to the influence of liberal democracy in which he got his indoctrination in his formative days. Liberal democracy always put an individual on a high pedestal and considered it precious.

His concern for the individual is not again doctrinaire but emanates from the value that any and every human being is precious and the belief that alone can act as the best guarantee against the collective tyranny and totalitarian excesses any time. In the context of the collapse of erstwhile Soviet block, where the totalitarian states that came into being in the name of dictatorship of proletariat and played havoc with people, this human-centric value assumes importance. One needs to be however reminded that even the values do need to have some material bases.

They do not fall from sky. The contradiction between collective and individual has thus to be resolved in the concrete situation. As for Ambedkar, apart from this scepticism, he does not seem to have any dispute with the general aim and object of revolution.

Revolution, inasmuch as it seeks to bring about a fundamental change in the social relations in the society, will always be opposed by the forces of status quo, whose material interests are directly threatened by this change. In corollary, it becomes imperative for the forces of revolution to overcome this resistance whatever be the means. Whereas, the antagonist camp will always project codes of ethics and morality for their tactical defence in face of the onslaught of revolution, the revolutionaries discard them as decadent; for them revolution itself represents the highest value. Being the upsurge of the suppressed ones, revolutions do have a tendency to be bloody, but it is always in response to the resistance of its opponents.

Therefore it is a representation only by the vested interest to associate violence or moral turpitude with revolutions. On the contrary, it would be more logical to say about the revolutionaries that being propelled by an external motivation to deliver mankind from the existing traps at the risk of their own lives; they cannot be bloodthirsty people. The revolutionary violence is almost an inevitability that arises at the instance of the oppressors.

In that sense Marx called "violence as the midwife of history", emphasising its inevitability. It is the inevitability that marks the compulsion of the vast majority of people to resist the antirevolutionary violence of the minority. The prerequisite here is that the revolution truly represents the majority consciousness. If it does not, then the violence of the few exercised with howsoever a lofty objective could transform into its antithesis, fortifying itself against the majority will. In this sense and insofar as the recent history showed the scepticism that revolutions trample upon individual's rights therefore cannot be dismissed as baseless.

Historically, revolution is the process of identifying and destroying the obstacles in the existing order to take productive forces to the qualitatively next higher level, for the overall progress of human race. The progress achieved by mankind so far is basically due to the qualitative transformation from quantitative continuum that characterises revolutions. The qualitative transformations always need concentrated inputs, akin to latent heat in the case of phase transformation of water. In social transformation it takes the form of revolutionary energy that in turn may manifest into violence. Ambedkar does not neglect the necessity of violence. As he himself said that if dalits wanted to be effective they would need the canons.

It is erroneous to construe that his opposition to violence was idealistic or doctrinaire. Violence was not a taboo for him; it could be practised when it was absolutely necessary. Even his mentor Buddha, who is respected as the greatest apostle of non-violence had the same pragmatic approach towards violence. Ambedkar was not obsessed either with the idea of non-violence or the value of individualism professed by the classical school of liberal democracy. His reservations were against the possibility of the cunning of a few overriding the will of majority as had happened in the case of caste institution. He would hate to see any thing like caste getting institutionalised again. In his scheme of things he therefore was not ready to compromise the value of democracy, the will of majority of people, whatever may be the end.

Ambedkar did not juxtapose reform against revolution, as many people tend to do. He does not reflect comprehension of technicality of dialectical materialism in his usage of these terms. Often his revolution is the violent overthrow of the existing rule and establishment of the new rule. Likewise, he does not seem to mean that reforms will not entail a qualitative transformation. What he certainly means by revolution is the change brought about in a 'big bang' manner. Notwithstanding what Ambedkar said about his own work, revolution does not always entail a 'big bang'; it is not a point concept as mistakenly regarded in common parlance, but a line concept. Mao's Great Proletarian Cultural Revolution may be a good example of this.

There could be many bits of work, which contributes to taking society to a qualitatively higher rung in the ladder of progress that qualify to be the revolutionary work. The qualitative change itself occurs over a discrete time horizon and not a moment. The moment that marks out transformation of power and looks like a 'big bang', alone is not the revolution. The particular phase of history puts constraints on the kind of changes that can be conceived in its womb. Some one dreaming of a socialist revolution in the slave society would only at best be a daydreamer; a romanticist but he cannot be a revolutionary. Likewise, certain phase of history demands a lot of quantitative preparation before a revolutionary change can be planned for. Ambedkar largely reflects these kinds of concerns while dealing with the issue of revolution. He did not see Indian situation ripe enough for any revolutionary change. Any change without resolution of the caste question, according to him, would not only be detrimental to dalits but also be an extremely short-lived.

The importance of Ambedkar's work can be gauged in relation to contemporary social situation and its transitional social context. Indian society was ridden with a peculiar brand of feudalism, the most prominent feature of which was caste. Caste had incapacitated over 15 per cent of its population and maintained them at the subhuman level. The large part of the balance population also suffered the degradation in a varying degree. This decadent institution had far outlived its minimal utility and as a result for centuries kept Indian society in a fossilised form. It served the material needs of a handful of people but all perceived varying stakes in the system on account of its hierarchical structure and faithfully practised it because they internalised it as their Dharma ordained by none other than God.

The possible exception in generic terms were dalits who were placed at the lowest rung of the caste ladder and had hardly anything to their share. However, in particular terms only a few castes from the Dalit castes, who did not have any specific caste profession and hence little stake in the system and consequently who as the general workmen of villages had better exposure to the changing urban life than any one else came out of the hegemony of Brahmins to articulate the challenge to the system. The hierarchy among dalits however prevented them to come together and consequently this challenge had to be articulated caste by caste. Capitalism that took root in India in big cities also had struck compromise with the caste institution like its harbingers, the British imperialism. It was an arduous task, as it still is, to conceive a model for this struggle and still more difficult to build.

During the colonial times for various reasons these struggles had germinated largely in Maharashtra and Southern states where the social structure reflected sharper polarisation between dalits and balance society. Ambedkar's advent in the Indian sociopolitical scene marked their zenith. It articulated its attack on Brahminism and capitalism that accepted its alliance, focused its organisation on dalits and gave a clarion call for annihilation of castes for achieving the ultimate aim of society based on Liberty, Equality and Fraternity to provide wider umbrella for all progressive forces to work. It reflects the distinct historical need to democratise Indian society without which it was bound to suffer constriction of its productive forces. This work had to have large content in the sociocultural realm; it is a credit to Ambedkar's acumen that he gave it a political dimension.

It had to be approached as reform. Ambedkar clearly found the talks of communist revolution as out of phase with the history although he never fully accepted the tenets of historical materialism as he thought it negatived human ingenuity and carried it through a predetermined channel. He insisted that India did not provide congenial soil for germination of class-consciousness because of castes. Their annihilation therefore constituted the first task in the revolutionary agenda. It is unfortunate that many communist revolutionaries still parrot the same characterisation of his work as in years back their predecessors proclaimed using the spoon fed theories from the West.

One day it is hoped that the contributions of all the caste struggles to democratisation of Indian society would be restored as a native revolutionary heritage by these well meaning people. Till then it will always sound puerile to pigeonhole the historical work as reform or revolution merely on the basis of syntax and not the content. However, it is much more unfortunate for Ambedkarite dalits to deny themselves the credit for this historical contributions by dissociating from the revolutionary agenda, mistakenly thinking that it something alien to them. Effectively, not only they are denying themselves a historical opportunity to contribute to revolution but also delaying their own emancipation.

Dalits have to rethink their position vis a vis revolution. Ambedkar's dream of a society based on liberty, equality and fraternity cannot be realised except through revolution. They will have to understand Ambedkar's life and mission only from this perspective. His contribution to Indian revolution lies in the fact that he tried to comprehend Indian reality independently and tried to contribute to the resolution of its contradictions in his own way. Indian history held out the gauntlet of fossilised Indian feudalism for so long to the Indian revolutionaries but every one conveniently wished it away, initially as a superstructural matter that would disappear automatically when the material base is revolutionised and now after seven decades as a problem belonging to both structure and superstructure, that could be solved through revolutionary practice. It still lacks the clarity and courage to hold the bull by horn.

Ambedkar did not confuse issues, he saw clearly that the annihilation of caste will have to be consciously worked for before taking up any revolutionary project. He went beyond and found out the institutional base of castes in the Indian village whose economic support lay in the land-relations and caste division of labour. But, unlike many communists who still use the stereotype of land reform-a slogan of land to the tiller as the only revolutionary programme, he did not hamper on it because he knew that firstly it was economically impossible to satisfy the land hunger of the landless in the country, secondly the likely transformation of landless to a marginal farmer through land reforms was unlikely to solve the problems of dalits and thirdly, as the later empirical data showed, contrary to expectations the land reforms could aggravate the problem of caste. Instead, he proposed nationalisation of land and co-operativisation of farming.

He realised the necessity of detaching substantial village population from land and absorbing it into the industrial sector that was to be mainly under State sector. Even in retrospect, these points could have constituted a viable agenda for democratic revolution. As one naxalite scholar-(Ashok Kumar, 1995) perceptively puts it, for having independently seen the question of annihilation of castes linked with the question of land one could unhesitatingly call Ambedkar as the torchbearer of the people's democratic revolution.

'AMBEDKAR' AS THINKER

Dalits are never tired of projecting Ambedkar as the greatest of all the leaders. That unfortunately smacks of sectarian attitude and of their blind devotion to him. They need to understand that the measure of greatness of any person could only be her / his contribution to better the human situation, in terms of correct understanding of its ailment and contribution to cure it. What Ambedkar did could be seen in relation to the broad five currents in Indian politics of his times:

- The Reformists current that wanted to bring about development on the western pattern, possibly with the support of British imperialism,

- o Congress, that represented Indian capital and which demanded self-rule under the domination of British imperialism,
- o The Terrorist Nationalists who had taken up arms in their fight for freedom against British imperialism,
- o The Communists who were trying to implant Bolshevik revolution in India, and
- o The Muslim League which opened up a separatist front of Muslims.

All of them scarcely reflected an understanding of the Indian situation. For instance, none showed even a cursory concern about the problems of one fourth of their countrymen who were forced to live worse than animals as ordained by their decadent religion. It was indeed surprising that although all craved for self-rule from the British, none concerned with the caste-system which basically was responsible in pushing the country repeatedly into slavery. None seemed to attempt an objective analysis of either the history or the present of this country. It could circumstantially be said that their motivations came from their narrow class-caste interests. These movements were motivated by the desire of an abstract freedom for country and a refusal to see the concrete slavery of their own people. Granted that the problems before the country were really intricate, still no one would dare say that the need for democratisation was in anyway subordinate.

The real people's movement in the country was required to wage simultaneous war against imperialism, internal compradore bourgeoisie, landlords and Brahminism. It was only Ambedkar who clearly indicated this requirement. In this light, he was certainly ahead of all others. His own bitter experiences with untouchability had stood him in good stead in seeing this more clearly than any other. He strove to build his movement along this understanding but unfortunately it was neither in his power to deal comprehensively with all the issues, nor was there an ideological and programmatic clarity required therefore. He inevitably had to focus his attention on dalits who were the worst victims of this multifaceted oppression. It was the misfortune of Indian history that this struggle progressed in a constricted manner and eventually got dissolved into regressive statist politics. It reflected both the limitation of Ambedkar as well the situational compulsion on him.

The anti-caste movements before Ambedkar were mainly welfare oriented. Some wanted a higher rank for their own caste in the caste hierarchy and some taking the inferior culture of their caste to be the reason for their suffering, aimed at improving the same. Mahatma Phuley's movement was an exception to this trend insofar as it attempted to unite the Sudra and Ati-Sudra castes against the exploitation by the parasitic castes of Shetjis (capitalists) and Bhatjis (priests). While Ambedkar accepted the lineage/inheritance of this movement and held Phuley in greatest esteem as his one of the three Gurus, he went beyond to declare annihilation of caste to be the object of his movement in the direction of the goal of 'liberty, equality and fraternity'. In the historical context it certainly was a radical step. He rightly diagnosed that the caste system is basically sustained by the peculiar economic constitution of the Indian village of which the land relations were the main features. Towards breaking this link he toyed with an idea of separate settlement for dalits at one time and at another exhorted them to leave villages for cities.

He had clearly understood that castes stood on multiple props, viz., the religio-cultural relations, feudal relations in village setting of which land relations constituted the crux and the sociopolitical nexus with the State. Annihilation of castes thus needed destruction of all of them. He soon realised the necessity of political power for this multi-fronged attack. Even to bring about the residual change in the belief system either through the cultural or religious route, he stressed the necessity of political power. In this way, for the first time he brought the problem of untouchability and caste out of the confines of culture to the political agenda. Unfortunately, this political agenda got lost into the maze of parliamentary politics that soon became be-all-end-all with Dalit leaders. Even during Ambedkar's times the economic aspects of the problem remained largely untouched giving the impression to his followers as though they did not count. In the overall context it can be seen that they could not be as easily dealt with as the religio-cultural and political aspects of the problem. Moreover, it meant direct confrontation with the State for which Ambedkar was certainly not prepared. Alternately, the feudal relations in villages could be destroyed only if the private ownership of land is abolished and co-operativisation of farming is introduced. He thought, this structural change could be effected through the Constitution. It was a folly that he would soon realise when even as the 'chief architect' of the Constitution he failed so much as to bring this point on the agenda of the Constituent Assembly.

A VISIONARY'S PLAN

B. R. Ambedkar is well known as the principal architect of the Indian Constitution, a social reformer and an emancipator of the poor and the deprived. Having studied bar at the Gray's Inn in UK, he had established himself as a legal luminary. He was a great scholar and a prolific writer in diverse areas like sociology, anthropology, history, economics, politics, law and religion.

However, what is not so well known is the fact that he was also an eminent economist. His academic achievements in economics include a Ph.D. degree from Columbia University, Master of Science in Economics from the London School of Economics and Doctor of Science in Economics from the University of London. He contributed a great deal to the formulation of India's postwar economic development plan in general and planning and development of water resources and electric power in particular.

In his book, Abraham elaborates on Ambedkar's economic philosophy and seeks to trace the relevance of his ideas on economic planning and development to the present day problems of the economy. Evidently, Ambedkar's views on Centre-State financial relations, fiscal deficit, necessity to reduce non-plan expenditure, Government's responsibility towards the weaker sections of society, necessity of land reforms, transfer of surplus labour from agriculture to industry etc. are of contemporary relevance.

Ambedkar enunciated the principles of Centre-State financial relations in the Constitution of India keeping in view the need for a strong Centre and proximity of state governments to the people based on his analysis of 'The evolution of Provincial Finances in British India'. No less important is his contribution to incorporate in the Constitution the provision for the appointment of a Finance Commission every five years to decide on the sharing of the tax kitty between the Centre and States. The crucial importance of this provision can be seen from the fact that even after five decades, and 10 Finance Commissions, the financial relations between the Centre and States remain somewhat strained.

During the discussion on the functions of the Comptroller and Auditor General at the time of framing the Constitution in 1949, Ambedkar enunciated that the Governments should spend the resources mobilised from the public not only as per rules and regulations but should also ensure that 'faithfulness, wisdom and economy' have gone into the acts of expenditure by public authorities. Ambedkar's initiative to ensure that electricity is listed in the 'Concurrent List' in the VII Schedule of the Constitution enabled the Centre to take positive steps for intensified growth of the power sector in subsequent years. The subsequent creation of the Central Electricity Authority (CEA) has been singularly instrumental in planning, developing and nurturing the mammoth system of generation, transmission and distribution facilities that span the length and breadth of the country today.

Thanks to Ambedkar's initiatives during pre-independence years, the need to generate more power at a faster pace for accelerating the country's all round development was recognised since the inception of planning process in 1950. In successive Five Year Plans, power development was accorded a very high priority.

Ambedkar had clearly visualised that India should exploit not only the hydropower resources but also all natural resources such as coal and petroleum. The book clearly brings out Ambedkar's significant contribution to economic planning and development and his emphasis on the need for land reforms, infrastructure development and industrialisation in order to eradicate poverty and improving the standard of living of the people. The author also highlights his vision and agenda for the social and economic emancipation of the Dalits and other weaker sections of the Indian society.

While fighting relentlessly against inequalities, Ambedkar felt that even in a democracy, leaving economic and social matters to be determined exclusively by a political majority could lead to the dictatorship of the 'haves' and perpetuation of age-long tyranny. He, therefore, saw to it that the economic and social objectives were enshrined in the Constitution itself as Directive Principles of State Policy.

Ambedkar also influenced the country's labour policy. His tenure as Labour Member in the Viceroy's Council during 1942-46 was a watershed in the history of labour legislation and labour welfare in India. According to Ambedkar, unemployment and underemployment were the greatest enemies of labour. Hence he tried to formulate a full employment policy for labour and a state supported labour welfare system.

He adopted a multi-pronged approach in the formulation of labour policy with provisions for: providing safeguard and social security measures for workers; giving equal opportunity to workers and employers to participate in the formulation of labour policy; and establishing a machinery for enforcing labour laws and settling disputes.

Abraham has made a commendable effort in piecing together the scatter information from Ambedkar's speeches and writings as also from articles and contributions of eminent political personalities, legal experts and social scientists. His book will be a source of inspiration to the younger generation.

AMBEDKAR'S REPLY TO GANDHI

A village was on fire, and the wind that swirled the flames high above the ancient banyan tree carried with it an unmistakable sound: a lone woman crying over a corpse. It was grief at its most elemental, purer than the wind and fire devouring this village in the dark night of southern India.

The woman wailed and shuddered while cradling her dead husband. She is an untouchable, and so was her young husband, Perumal Radhakrishnan. An invisible line divides this village, called Karisakulam, and thousands of others like it across

India, separating the untouchables-those beneath Hinduism's rigid caste hierarchy-from the upper-castes. Radhakrishnan had crossed that line. As a leader of the village's untouchables, he had dared to defy the higher-caste community of Thevars.

That evening, Radhakrishnan, a thin and bare-chested man, had ambled over to the upper-caste side to watch the evening news on the village's only TV, rigged up under the stars. While he sat there, four men from the Thevar caste pinned him to the dirt while a fifth man pulled out a sword and butchered him. Enraged by the killing, the untouchables burned down the houses of all the Thevars in the village and slaughtered their animals. They even smashed the TV; its fragments lay scattered next to Radhakrishnan's corpse. Then the untouchables took fright-they were afraid the Thevars would rouse the upper-castes from nearby villages and seek revenge-and so they fled into a wasteland of thorn bushes, leaving Radhakrishnan's widow alone, silhouetted against the flames as she rocked her husband's corpse.

A few years ago, these untouchables would have dragged away Radhakrishnan's body and cowered in their mud-huts, resigned to their subhuman status. But now, scenes of defiance like the rampage at Karisakulam are taking place throughout India. The country's more than 150 million untouchables (who prefer to call themselves Dalits, Hindi for "the oppressed") are striking back. They are instigating a social revolution that is long overdue, one whose aim is to topple the 2,500-year-old juggernaut of the Hindu caste system. Increasingly, Dalits are challenging Hinduism's tenets that a person is condemned to his caste-determining whether he becomes a doctor or a scavenger, whom he marries, which village well he drinks from, and his social standing in a complex, ordered hierarchy-all by his actions in a past life. In this rebellion, the Dalit's main weapons are education and the vote. But in some rural areas, where resistance to their demands for equality is entrenched, they are taking up the gun. "Power was gradual

By slipping through the hands of the dominant castes for several decades," says Ashis Nandy, director of the Centre for the Study of Developing Societies in New Delhi. "It had already slipped down to the lower castes and is now reaching the Dalits.

This will help democracy." Or will it? Consider the caste warfare and chaos now engulfing the northern states of Bihar and Uttar Pradesh, where Dalits are trying to grab what they believe is theirs after so many centuries.

Dalits make up one-sixth of India's population, yet only a few have managed to occupy top places in society as politicians, lawyers and scientists. A poor Dalit from Kerala, Kocheril Raman Narayanan, encountered discrimination in school and work.

And yet this year he rose to become India's President, the first untouchable to hold that post. Before, Dalits had to support their landlords' candidates or they were beaten away from the polling booths when they tried to vote; now they are asserting themselves with the ballot, and their newfound power has jolted all of the national political parties, especially the long-ruling Congress. Ram Vilas Paswan, a Dalit member of the Janata Dal Party, is now serving in the United Front cabinet. Twice now, a Dalit woman, Mayawati, has been elected Chief Minister of populous Uttar Pradesh state, though her last six months in office were squandered in a vendetta against high-caste rivals. Says Mayawati: "Earlier I had thought it would take longer, but change is now so rapid that in a few years we will have a Dalit Prime Minister in New Delhi."

Politicians and their promises offer little, however, to the most radical Dalits. They would prefer an armed insurrection, and they are willing to settle scores with higher-caste landlords using guns and home-made bombs. Says Ram Prit, a 75-year-old Dalit labourer in Bihar: "If you keep pouring water into a rat hole, the rats will come out fighting."

Religious sanction has allowed this apartheid to survive Muslim invasions, British colonialism and even 50 years of democracy. Defenders of the caste system usually cite a verse from the Upanishads, Hinduism's ancient sacred texts: "Those whose conduct on earth has given pleasure can hope to enter a pleasant womb, that is, the womb of a Brahman or a woman of the princely class. But those whose conduct on earth has been foul can expect to enter a foul and stinking womb, that is the womb of a bitch, or a pig, or an outcaste." A hymn from the sacred Rig Veda describes how this human stratification came about: a cosmic giant, Purusha, sacrificed parts of his body to create mankind. "His mouth became the Brahman, his arms were made into the Warrior (Kshatriya), his thighs the People (Vaishiya) and from his feet the Servants (Sudra) were born." Through the centuries, these four main divisions (called varnas), were silvered into more than 3,000 sub-castes, based on the purity of their professions.

A goldsmith is higher up the ladder than a blacksmith, and a priestly Brahman, whose rituals bring him in touch with the gods, is highest of all. The untouchables, however, are off the ladder completely. By origin, many were India's dark-skinned first inhabitants, conquered by Aryans and assigned such awful tasks as burning bodies, skinning carcasses and removing "night soil"-human excrement-from latrines. For thousands of years, outcastes were burdened with these denigrating chores.

In many villages, untouchables still live in poverty and subjugation. They are forbidden from entering temples or drinking from the same wells as upper-castes. It was customary for higher-caste landlords to deflower a Dalit bride on her wedding night, before her helpless groom. (To cleanse himself after such a dalliance, according to the more than 2,500-year-old Laws of Manu, an upper-caste man must give alms and make "daily mutterings" of prayers.)

These Hindu rules are far from evenhanded: even today in some parts of India, if an untouchable is caught sleeping with a high-caste woman, both he and the woman are executed. A Dalit also can be considered too uppity, and risks a beating, if he wears a wristwatch or trousers instead of a traditional dhoti or loincloth.

In some places in the south, Dalits aren't allowed to use an umbrella. Some roadside tea stalls refuse to serve them out of ordinary cups, and often Dalit children are warned not to try sharing classrooms with upper-caste kids. In some villages like Vembakkotai, in Tamil Nadu, the Dalits are forced to live on the leeward side to prevent the wind that touches their bodies from defiling the upper-castes.

Faced with such persecution, Dalits are finally running out of patience. What's surprising is that it took them so long, Their emancipation began only in this century, behind the efforts of India's two great social reformers, Mahatma Gandhi and Bhimrao Ramji Ambedkar, an angry, brilliant Dalit lawyer and politician. Through a scholarship from the Maharajah of Baroda, Ambedkar, an impoverished village boy, was able to study abroad and eventually earned several degrees. He worked as a financial adviser to the Maharajah but quit in disgust because the prince's upper-caste servants would fling documents onto his desk, rather than hand them to him, for fear of contamination.

Yet his genius was unstoppable, as was his grit. "Nothing can emancipate the outcaste except the destruction of the caste system," Ambedkar once declared. "Nothing can help to save the Hindus and ensure their survival in the coming struggle except the purging of the Hindu faith of this odious and vicious dogma." As an author of the Indian constitution, he secured guarantees for the advancement of outcastes. For decades, these promises were often blocked by upper-caste bureaucrats, but a new generation of Dalits inside the civil service is helping their downtrodden people.

In Uttar Pradesh, for example, 150 positions are held by Dalits in the elite 540-member Indian Administrative Service. The government gives Dalits a lift by reserving 15% of all government jobs and college places for them.

Many of these educated Dalit bureaucrats are infuriated when, on visits to their villages, they are mistreated by upper-caste neighbours poorer and less educated than they. Man Dahima, a Dalit who is one of the most senior civil servants in Bhopal, capital of Madhya Pradesh state, says he still encounters "feudal harassment" when he goes back to his village. "Even today, we're not allowed in some temples," he says. "There are no signs outside, but these things are well understood."

Other urbanized Dalits seethe when being served out of coconut shells instead of teacups or when forced to sit at a village Brahman's feet. Says Ezhilmalai, a Dalit politician in Tamil Nadu: "The Dalit would rather die than live without self-respect. And when he prefers to die for honour, what is there to care for?"

Ambedkar wanted to destroy the caste pyramid through democracy, but the rule of law has been slow in reaching many villages where upper-caste landlords, often in league with local police, are keeping the Dalits down. In such places, many Dalits are opting for armed resistance.

"The condition of the Dalits in the villages is so bad that the concern for most is how to gain minimum self-respect and security," says a senior state official in Uttar Pradesh. "What they want today is not jobs, but to be able to live without being humiliated and harassed." In Uttar Pradesh, Bihar, Tamil Nadu and Andhra Pradesh, caste conflict is rife, and it has spread to other states such as Madhya Pradesh and Maharashtra. Many Dalits, along with forest-dwelling tribals, have signed up with armed leftist groups like the Maoist Communist Centre, Liberation and People's War Group, which go around shooting or slitting the throats of feudal upper-caste landowners and policemen. This communist insurgency, which flared in the 1970s, still rages in the backward regions of central and eastern India.

Not surprisingly, the upper-castes are hitting back. In Bihar, high-caste landowners raised a private army called the Ranvir Sena, and hardly a day goes by without caste killings. Even Rabindra Chowdhary, a Ranvir Sena leader, concedes that the landlords had cruelly exploited the Dalits. "We were abusive and did not treat these people well," he says. "We do not believe in killing. But if we do not kill, they will think that we are weak."

Tension runs high, and even the most nonsensical incident can trigger a bloody outburst. In Tamil Nadu, a game of tag between Thevar and Dalit schoolboys led to the beheading of a Dalit and the revenge killing of 13 people, both Thevars and Dalits, many of them dragged off a bus and hacked to death. In Bihar's Belaur village, a tiff over a pack of cigarettes led to a mini-war between Dalits and the upper-caste Bhumihars that ultimately left 16 dead and dozens wounded. Even today, that feud festers: more than 350 Dalit families have deserted the village, and the Bhumihars-who patrol their village at night with guns and spears, ready for attack-cannot hire labourers for their fields. Some Dalits are even refusing to carry out their repugnant jobs. "My generation is fighting," says Sri Prakash, a Dalit whose house was set ablaze in a caste feud. "We've told the Thevars we're not going to cremate their dead any more. Let them do it themselves." Says Sociologist Nandy: "The Dalits are much more aggressive. Now that they have tasted power, they don't want to be denied it."

A mini-partition based on caste lines is taking shape in areas where Dalits are especially politicized. In some districts, police say, Dalits are probably better armed and organized than their upper-caste adversaries. It has become too dangerous for a Thevar family to live among the Dalits.

Thevars are migrating to villages where they are in control, while Dalits are moving to places where they are in the majority. A Thevar knows better than to wander into some villages in the Srivilliputhur district, where Dalits humiliate upper-caste strangers by making them walk through the village with their sandals on their heads, ridiculing Vedic order by putting the lowliest on top.

Dalits toiling in stone quarries and match factories have allegedly pilfered enough explosives to gain a lethal edge. Says Mahboob Batacha, a Tamil social worker in Madurai: "There's no village around here where the Dalits aren't armed. Now, more Thevars are getting killed than Dalits."

Envy is often the spark for caste warfare. It is not usually the top-rung Brahmans and Kshatriyas who clash with the Dalits but rather the castes lower down: those slightly above the untouchables, such as the Thevars in Tamil Nadu and the Yadavs in Bihar and Uttar Pradesh. As Dr. K. Krishnaswamy, a prominent Dalit politician in Tamil Nadu, explains, "Some Dalit youth are climbing fast through reserved government jobs.

Others have gone to the Gulf for employment, and they are all bringing back TVs, refrigerators and vcrs. This is causing a lot of heartburn among the other castes." Krishnaswamy's own life is an illustration of this jealousy. When he was granted a scholarship to a prestigious college, the upper-caste postman pocketed his admissions letter, and Krishnaswamy never found out that he was accepted until too late.

Eventually he made it to medical school and, after leaving, set up practice near his village. Many of his patients were Dalit women who wanted abortions after being raped by upper-caste landowners. "I went to the upper-caste men and told them this wasn't right. They should marry these girls," he says. It was not a popular idea; a mob of 1,000 upper-caste men besieged the doctor's house one night, attacking him and his family. After a month in the hospital, he returned, full of fight. "It made me angry, more determined than ever," he says. Today, Krishnaswamy is one of only a few Dalits elected to Tamil Nadu's assembly, even though Dalits comprise about 20% of the state's voters.

His life has been threatened so often that, while driving through upper-caste-dominated areas of the state, he is accompanied by two armed bodyguards. Says Krishnaswamy: "The political parties are the real culprits for keeping the caste conflict going." But caste politics is alive and well, and is contributing to a stirring-up of anti-Dalit sentiment in Bombay. In July, slum-dwellers awakened to find that their statue of the bespectacled Ambedkar had been garlanded not with the customary flowers but with a wreath of dirty sandals. That was all it took to start a riot.

Hundreds of angry Dalits poured onto the streets, hurling stones and setting up roadblocks with burning tires. Fearing the rioters would set fire to a parked gas tanker, police started shooting in the shanty lanes, killing about a dozen people. Once news of the deaths spread, Dalits began protesting in the neighbouring states of Gujarat, Karnataka and in the capital, New Delhi.

The police shootings also revived antagonism between the Dalits and Maharashtra's ruling Shiva Sena party. Its militant Hindu leader Bal Thackeray has often attacked job reservations and the renaming of a university after Ambedkar.

The Bombay incident also revealed the Dalits' disillusionment with their own leaders. When a former State Minister and Dalit leader visited the shantytown the day after the killings, he was attacked and had to run for his life. The funeral procession for those shot by police was attended by 150,000 Dalits, but not one Dalit politician dared to show up.

Says Savita Ambedkar, the 81-year-old widow of the Dalit leader: "If we can stay together, we have the power to make a party succeed. But it's a great disappointment that the movement has been captured by people who cannot really lead it properly."

A doctor and a Brahman who became Ambedkar's second wife, Savita now lives alone in a shabby house in central Bombay. She has written a biography of her late husband, but because of her high caste, she was never really accepted by Dalits. Ambedkar's grandson Prakash hasn't fared much better. Ambedkar died in late 1956, soon after founding the Republican Party of India, but grandson Prakash, who now leads one of its many factions, lacks his visionary fire.

Desperate, the Dalits in Bombay's slums are flailing for an alternative leadership-or at least a godfather. Shortly after the funeral of the slain Dalits, a lower caste Bombay underworld chieftain named Arun Gawli offered himself as their saviour. When the gangster called a Bombay rally, thousands of Dalits flocked to it. Says social worker Sushoba Barve: "After the killings, many Dalit youth felt that the only way to protect themselves was to ally with someone who could give them protection." Elsewhere in India, Dalits are feeling equally deceived by the national parties, which are top-heavy with high-caste politicians. Dalits have yet to unite. "All that keeps India from having a bloody revolution is that we Dalits are a divided lot," says civil servant Dahima. Even among the Dalits, strong caste rivalries exist; one study discovered 900 Dalit "sub-castes" in the country.

Basically, everyone is squirming not to fall to the bottom of India's massive pile of humanity. Predicts one Dalit official: "As benefits trickle down, the conflicts between sub-castes are bound to sharpen." Lately, a number of regional leaders have been trying to bring unity to lower-caste aspirations. Several could easily cripple their state capitals with 100,000-strong demonstrations. So far, the only Dalit politician to challenge the mainstream parties is Kanshi Ram, a former technician at a government defence laboratory. Armed with wiliness and an ability to survive in the venal world of Indian politics, Ram has no qualms about forming alliances with his high-caste adversaries if it brings his Bahujan Samaj Party to power. His abrasive protege Mayawati governed Uttar Pradesh for six months in alliance with the Hindu nationalist Bharatiya Janata Party, many of whose followers adhere stoutly to Manu's ancient law.

During her term, Mayawati ordered 13,000 statues of Ambedkar and began work on a $30 million park in Lucknow in honour of the Dalit leader. She also reshuffled 1,400 bureaucrats and police officers. Dalit civil servants, whose promotions had been mothballed by their high-caste superiors, were elevated to top posts. State funds and projects for roads, schools and electricity were channelled to neglected Dalit villages. Above all, Dalits were treated to the spectacle-unimaginable a few years back-of an acid-tongued Dalit like Mayawati ordering around upper-caste grandees in the administration who in the past had either bullied or, at best, ignored them.

3

CONCEPTION OF AN IDEAL

INTRODUCTION

Babasaheb Ambedkar envisioned his ideal in the famous three principles: liberty, equality and fraternity. They were the basis for the ideal society of his conception. He denied that he had adopted them from the French Revolution. He said he had derived them from the teachings of Buddha. These principles were the clarion call of the French Revolution but later became the ideological props of the liberal bourgeoisie in Europe. Since Marx had ridiculed these principles as the fantasy of the bourgeois society, many people tended to stereotype Ambedkar as the petty-bourgeois liberal democrat. As according to Ambedkar the source of these principles is different from the French Revolution, familiar to Marx, there is a prima facie scope to argue that Marx's ridicule does not apply to him. His conception of these principles is indeed substantially different from that associated with the liberal bourgeoisie. Actually, what Marx refers to are the slogans of liberty and equality of the bourgeois parliamentary democracy.

There, 'liberty' is the liberty to contract and 'equality' refers to equality in market. Ambedkar insists that the conception of the ideal society ought to have them all the three together. Absence of any would not be acceptable to him. The ideal society of his dream could only be seen within a kind of spiritual frame. It would be interesting to compare this society with the communist society of Marx's conception. Marx reached his inference following the dialectical track of historical materialism.

In Ambedkar' case it was just his vision. Inevitably, he had to attribute the origin of them to some spiritual source.

For Ambedkar they meant to denote the State of society sans exploitation and with an emotive ambience of fellow feeling. It was beyond him to describe this State further in concrete terms and much so to indicate the forms of struggle to reach it. Known for his obsession with pragmatism and belief that any definitive laws could not bind the flow of human history, he would avoid the speculative construction of this distant stage of human society.

Not even Marx could describe what his dream communist society would be like beyond that it would be freed of the familiar contradictions. It essentially reflected a contradiction between human desire and material reality. It would be disaster to derive the meaning of this ideal State of Ambedkar's conception from what he did. He left that to posterity to decide as per their circumstances. But, rationally there could be little doubt that the vision of Ambedkar can only be realised in the communist society of Marx's conception where most (not all) of the contradictions in human society would have been resolved.

Dalits ought to internalise this vision and strive for its realisation. Ambedkar had a radical enough interpretation of his principles of liberty, equality and fraternity so as to feel inadequacy even in Marxism. He said that Marxism supported only equality. He was in need of a body of thought that would give equal importance to all these three principles. He met it with a convenient conceptualisation of religion. It is paradoxical that a person who is rational enough not to bind the posterity with his vision volitionally binds himself with what is said more than 25 centuries before.

It is natural to find ideals better articulated in spiritual spheres but it is equally true that these dream worlds are incapable to provide any clue for their realisation on the earth except for their pet prescription to ignore the material reality and imagine it happened in the mind. They run away from the fact that the evil humans suffer from are the attributes of the divisions in human society, and their abolition essentially calls for struggles by the sufferers against those who perpetrate sufferings. Howsoever, inherently rational the religion may be or radical its interpretation may be it cannot fully escape these limitations.

It can be seen in relation to Buddhism handed down by Babasaheb Ambedkar with his radical interpretation. Notwithstanding the familiar quibbling around the Dhamma and Dhamma among dalits, what remained of Buddhism with them is what would happen to any religion. It is a different question whether Marxism embodied Ambedkar's ideals or not but it is certain that they are neither realisable neither through any kind of constitutional acrobatics nor through any religious practice.

STATE

Ambedkar's conception of State reflects some amount of autonomy from the hegemony of the ruling classes. It is why he expected it to act as per the constitutional structure and endeavoured to incorporate the pro-Dalit bias into the Constitution. He must have realised the true nature of it, the boundaries of the autonomy and basic class bias of the State, when he actually reached not only the Constituent Assembly but also became the chairman of its Drafting Committee.

In his anxiety to secure some provisions in favour of dalits, he accepted to be the 'hack' to write what was acceptable to the ruling caste-class representatives. He must have thought that within the given constraints he had done a good job of making the Constitution responsive to the needs of the downtrodden people. Indeed, many of the provisions in the directive principles and elsewhere apparently bear clear imprint of his zeal and owe their existence to him. But, even they had to be within the strategic space provided by the rulers. His realisation of the folly was near complete when he had to burst out in utter dejection at its ineffectual implementation, that he would be the first man to burn the Constitution as it was of no good to any one. He was inaccurate, as the Constitution had proved good enough to the upper caste-class combine who had hegemonised complete political space in post-1947 India. He attributed it to the 'devils' in the Congressmen who had occupied the constitutional 'temple' he and others had built.

Ambedkar could not reach the point of understanding that the State is a mere instrument in the hands of the ruling classes to coerce the ruled ones into submission to their interests. Until the downtrodden themselves become the ruling class, they cannot expect the State to do good to them. Whatever good that appears to come to their share, in ultimate balance accrues to the other side in multiple measure.

The post-1947 State, which has never tired of propagandising its concern for dalits and poor, has in fact been singularly instrumental in aggravating the caste problem with its policies. Even the apparently progressive policies in the form of Land Ceiling Act, Green Revolution, Programme of Removal of Poverty, Reservations to Dalits in Services and Mandal Commission etc. have resulted against their professed objectives. The effect of the Land Ceiling Act, has been in creating a layer of the middle castes farmers which could be consolidated in caste terms to constitute a formidable constituency. In its new incarnation, this group that has traditionally been the immediate upper caste layer to dalits, assumed virtual custody of Brahminism in order to coerce Dalit landless labourers to serve their socioeconomic interests and suppress their assertive expression in the bud. The Green Revolution was the main instrument to introduce capitalisation in agrarian sector.

It reinforced the innate hunger of the landlords and big farmers for land as this State sponsored revolution produced huge surplus for them. It resulted in creating geographical imbalance and promoting unequal terms of trade in favour of urban areas. Its resultant impact on dalits has been far more excruciating than that of the Land Ceiling Act. The much publicised programme for Removal of Poverty has aggravated the gap between the heightened hopes and aspirations of dalits on one hand and the feelings of depravation among the poorer sections of non-dalits in the context of the special programmes especially launched for upliftment of dalits. The tension that ensued culminated in increasingly strengthening the caste-based demands and further aggravating the caste-divide. The reservations in services for dalits, notwithstanding its benefits, have caused incalculable damage in political terms. Reservations created hope, notional stake in the system and thus dampened the alienation; those who availed of its benefit got politically emasculated and in course consciously or unconsciously served as the props of the system. The context of scarcity of jobs provided ample opportunity to reactionary forces to divide the youth along caste lines. Mandal Commission, that enthused many progressive parties and people to upheld its extension of reservation to the backward castes, has greatly contributed to strengthen the caste identities of people. Inasmuch as it empowers the backward castes, actually their richer sections, it is bound to worsen the relative standing of dalits in villages.

Thus, the State, its welfare mask notwithstanding, has viciously and consistently acted against dalits and poor people. It is a complete contra-evidence to hopes of Ambedkar who strove to maximise and make use of the autonomous space of the State for the benefits of the have-nots, particularly dalits. It is one thing to assume autonomous space but quite another to equate it with caste-class neutrality. Unfortunately, the Dalit political behaviour always reflected this erroneous notion of caste-class neutrality of the State. It has already caused great damage to the Dalit interests. The radical Ambedkar might have strategy to use State for Dalit cause but would never see it as caste-class neutral.

SOCIALISM

Despite his ambivalence and reservations about the emphasis on the economic dimension in socialism, Ambedkar broadly remained a socialist. Some scholars do find little scope for suspecting his socialist credentials because of his disapproval of Russell's criticism of property, his non-acceptance of Marxian formulations and his placement of social issues higher than the economic and political issues. He called the complaint against love of money as 'philosophy of sour grapes' and ridiculed materialism as 'the ideology of pigs'. This impression is moreover strengthened by his reservations to accept the economic interpretation of history. But, in all fairness it may be said that what he appears to mean is the integrative consideration of all the factors that are needed for any society to be based on liberty, equality and fraternity. Notwithstanding his variant conception, there should not be any doubt about his socialistic antecedents.

His conception of socialism also underwent evolution. Once he had stated that there was hardly any difference between his socialism and communism. As such, his disagreement with the communists was about the means and not about the aim. He warns the communists that the classless society can emerge only after the emergence of a casteless society. It implies that his quarrel with the then communists was over the stages of revolution. In the 1920s and 30s, these people had borrowed the communist dogma and parroted class struggle in utter disregard of the reality.

Ambedkar, on the contrary, was firmly rooted in it. They believed that the soviet Russian model of revolution was importable for bringing about a socialist revolution into India whereas Ambedkar realistically postulated that unless the consciousness of the working class was congenial for revolution, there was no question of it materializing. And, unless the caste system is destroyed, creation of the pro-revolution consciousness was out of question. His annoyance with the Bombay communists was largely because of their dogmatic behaviour. It is unfortunate that the ideal of classlessness that was latent in his agenda never really surfaced during his lifetime.

Ambedkar relies on the concept of 'State' for materialisation of his conception of socialism. His conception of State is largely idealist. He wanted the State to intervene in the economic structure and its monitoring. He wanted to constitutionalise this State intervention so that it would not be subject to change any time with the whims of simple majority vote in the legislation. Ambedkar who taught, "The lost rights cannot be regained by making appeals or requests to the robbers; it needs struggles"; did not say anything on how the oppressed people will get such strength as to create the constitutional provisions, that would put the class structure upside down.

On behalf of his party-Scheduled Caste Federation, he had submitted a draft for the future constitution to the Constituent Assembly for the independent India. It was published later as "States and Minorities". This book has really aided students in understanding some aspects of his conception of socialism.

Nevertheless, one cannot afford to forget the constraints placed by the context in which it was written. The context was that he had failed to get into the Constituent Assembly and was therefore anxious to strike a feasible and still radical note that could find the support of the vast majority of the have-nots which might then create some pressure either for its inclusion in the Constitution or for his entry into the Constituent Assembly. For some years, during the preceding turbulence of negotiations for transfer of power, he found himself totally marginalised. Notwithstanding the probable limitations of this draft, its provisions in operational terms were still very radical. The main provisions are:

- o All important industries and services shall belong to the nation.
- o Insurance industry shall be in public sector and insurance will be compulsory for every citizen.
- o Private sector and entrepreneurs shall have a role in the economy but it shall not be dominating.
- o Nationalisation of land and promotion of cooperative farming on a collective principle.

These provisions, if implemented, would have gone a long way towards supporting democratic revolution in the country. It would have limited inequality and exploitation in the economic and political sphere. Politically, it would have had far-reaching impact. Ambedkar till the end could not completely remove the Fabian influence (which he might have gathered while in England) on him. In his times, particularly before World War II, few people in India were well versed in Marxist philosophy. The knowledge of Marxism seldom exceeded some broad principles and 'Stalin's dictatorship' painted by imperialists or the 'revolt of the workers, the insurgency of the poor. Ambedkar also does not seem to have gone very far from this point. Without indulging into the debate of ifs and buts, there should not be any iota of doubt that the ideal society of his conception could materialise only through socialism.

DEMOCRACY

Ambedkar had unshakeable faith in democracy. In his conception of an exploitation-less society, democracy has an extraordinary role. Democracy means 'one person, one vote';

and 'one vote, one value'. Democracy means empowerment of any person for participating in the process of decision-making relating to her/him, democracy means liberty, equality and fraternity-Ambedkar's definition of democracy had such a tone. Because he presided over making of the Constitution and is being projected as its chief architect, there is a misunderstanding that parliamentary democracy is what he wanted. But nothing could be farther from the truth than this. He himself spoke against parliamentary democracy. For instance, he defined parliamentary democracy as "voting by the people in favour of their owners and handing over the rights of ruling over themselves". This provides a glimpse of the expanse of his ideal, which certainly was much beyond the Indian Constitution or any common place understanding about him.

His conception of democracy appears to be purely people oriented. He showed that the bookish concepts of equality are detrimental to the disabled sections of society in the prevailing social setting and proposed a fundamental change in the concept of equality. It envisaged complete abolition of inequality. His principle of positive discrimination is based on this very concept of equality. But the operational aspects of this concept involved the need for some kind of autonomous institution, which was met by 'State' and 'religion'. It is necessary to stress that his greatness lies in the radicality of his conceptions, his vision of a human society sans any kind of exploitation; not in the remedies or apparatus he proposed in the circumstances prevailing in his time.

ASPECTS OF THE STRATEGY AND TACTICS

In the context of strategy, some of Ambedkar's contributions are really noteworthy. He brought the struggle against Brahminism into the political battlefield. He inferred that without political power the social and religious structures will collapse and motivated his followers to capture political power. But his conception of political power being acutely constrained by the parliamentary framework where bargaining is the predominant medium of securing political power, inevitably it made way for all kinds of aberrations and perversities to creep in. The prevailing politics being the game of possibilities, he was soon sucked into its vortex. Politics came to dominate the other aspects of his personality. Slowly, the impact of politics started becoming visible everywhere. This phase significantly contributed to multiplication of his inconsistencies out of tactical imperatives. Dalits have taken this legacy of parliamentary politics very seriously, almost as the be all and end all of their political being. It may be, interesting to probe how much damage this kind of political orientation inflicted on the Dalit movement.

It is altogether a different question whether Ambedkar had any other alternative to parliamentary politics for political practice. It may be argued that in the context of his resources, adversarial environment and to some extent his personal limitations, he had none. Even if it is taken as correct, it should not be forgotten that it was a matter of strategy and tactic that presuppose contextual variables: it cannot be taken as the lasting value.

The fundamental source of most of Ambedkar's political thoughts and action is his conception of State and religion, that he had adopted as the extraneous instruments to reconcile the state of flux of things and the necessity of order in them. It is necessary to understand that both, the State as well as religion, are the products of the evolutionary process of the human society. There is nothing inevitable about them. Marx took State as the instrument of coercion in the hands of ruling classes and religion as the opium of the masses. Dalits have a long experience of nearly five decades with the so-called welfare State of Ambedkar's design. What does it say? Does the State side with them in their conflict with the landlords? Does it come to their rescue when every day three or four of their daughters are raped?

Does it come to save the shame of their women when they are paraded naked in the streets? Does it take their side when they come in conflict with landlords, moneylenders in villages or with management in the modern settings? Does it really ensure they get their dues as provided in the Constitution or punish the defaulting management for noncompliance? To all of such questions the answer could only be in the negative. It is not a matter of 'devils occupying the temples' as Ambedkar lamented seeing the people occupying the Constitutional positions. The State possesses the characteristics of its master class. In India the upper caste capitalists, landlords, top bureaucrats, etc. being the ruling class, the State can never have saints who would favour dalits. It is a fact that even the government by a Dalit party like the BSP could not transform it into a Dalit State.

Religion, in Ambedkar's conception is necessary to maintain the moral order of the society. It may be interesting to examine to what extent it conforms to this idealistic expectation. Buddhism, which undoubtedly is the most rational of all the religions, does not have any evidence of having created over its near millennium long tenure in India such an order of the society which could claim liberty, equality and fraternity of Ambedkar's conception. Ambedkar's argument that the Bhikku Sangha in Buddhism was the prototype of this kind of society becomes invalid once we call into question the role of Sangha in the production process.

Before that, the order that envisaged nostalgically to recreate the value of the vanishing Gana Rajya in microcosm against the evil of rising monarchies, cannot just sublimate to the era of capitalism without being an alley of exploiters unless it transforms itself in some way as a catalyst for the revolution. The moral tenets of Buddhism likewise cannot submerge the lure of surplus extraction, that is its dominating ethos. If at all, it may help it become more pronounced by weakening the resistance of the exploited masses. As we empirically see, the Buddhism of his conception could not produce even a trace of morality in its adherents. On the contrary, for the masses it presents the distorted, if not inverted, worldview; it orients them to look inwards for their misery and be blind to the reality that some one exploits him. He could certainly derive mental peace and pleasure but it is a state of an intoxicated mind. Keeping in mind the causal links in Ambedkar's adoption of these instruments, the redefinition project needs to address these issues afresh.

The strategy of the ruling class always stresses on diversion of peoples' attention from their real problems and their disarmament-both in physical and ideological terms. They invariably have a multilayered strategy in place for this purpose. The vanguard parties of the ruling classes open up sentimental fronts and attempt to divert the attention of people as their real problems get aggravated. Secondly, their time-tested methods of adulterating radical ideas with the masses are always in operation. Towards this end, we see all the ruling parties vying with each other in co-opting Ambedkar. 'Ambedkar' represents a potentially dangerous ideological weapon in the hands of the Indian proletariat and so the ruling class will be hell bent on blunting its edge. They will do everything to eulogise him not only for wooing dalits for their immediate electoral gains but also to neutralise him as the radical ideological force by propagandising a distorted version of the latter. Dalits will have to exercise vigil over their ideological assets even after redefining Ambedkar.

CONCLUSION

For at least over last four decades Dalits have devotedly followed Ambedkar as their ideal, as a virtual God and zealously practised, as they claim, his teachings. Their social being could be seen to be totally imbued with what they call Ambedkarism-the veritable science of their emancipation. If it is true, and no one would deny it is not, it should be pertinent to ask why despite this flawless following of Ambedkar they continue to be in a pathetic state in every sense. Barring a handful dalits in the government and public sector services and of course politicians, they continue to occupy the lowest rung in the social as well as economic hierarchy of Indian society. Their politics, notwithstanding the media hype, gauged by the measure of general empowerment, continues to be in shambles. Over these decades, their relative situation either shows stagnation or decline. The insinuation to relate this State with their faith in Ambedkar itself would be distasteful for many dalits. But, it is vital for ones that are committed to their liberation to squarely face the facts and dispassionately find out where the rot lay.

Generally, beyond the first burst of anger in reaction to this question, one would face the defensive arguments to discount this relationship. Typically, they tend to attribute their miserable situation to the lack of competent leadership after Babasaheb Ambedkar, to the educated dalits who they think have become

Dalit Brahmins and have deserted the community; and sometimes to the people themselves for their extreme self-centredness. Sometimes, the finger is raised at the high caste hegemony that has neutralised the impact of the Constitution that Ambedkar created. Some, particularly the leadership, even would dismiss the basic premise itself that there is something wrong with the Dalit movement. They might even go so far as to claim net achievements indicating the prosperity of themselves or some others of their like. More sober may argue that what is seen is the transition state. Conceding them all some amount of validity even would not erase the stark fact that the general situation of the vast majority of Dalit masses remains still alarmingly pathetic. Externalisation of the reasons for this state has not helped dalits wee bit. The time has come for dalits to self-critically see whether anything was wrong with their ideology and / or with their practice thereof.

Reviewing the post-Ambedkar Dalit movement at some significant milestones, one finds a queer underscoring behaviour, believed to be in accordance with the teachings of Babasaheb Ambedkar, that is certainly incongruent with the essence of what he taught. This dichotomy between the essential Ambedkar and the 'Ambedkar' in the faith of Dalit masses-the icon of Ambedkar, comes out as the problematic in this review. In relation to almost every aspect of his teaching there emerged an icon that represented varying amount of distortion.

Insofar as they constituted the ideology that gripped the masses, these icons can be seen to be at the root of the Dalit pathos. Among the myriad sources for these icons, Ambedkar himself might come out as the major source. Because, even a myth can not sustain for long without some material base. The icons of Ambedkar thus could be linked to some such bases, howsoever tenuous, within his own life. The rationalist in Ambedkar never hesitated to change his opinions and behaviour if the facts so warranted. They appear to be inconsistencies to the ones who see it sans context.

His distance from the focus of control in his sociopolitical environment, the vastly varying target audience (ranging from the Englishmen to the illiterate dalits) to whom he had to communicate, the exigency to respond to the dynamics of communities set in motion by the pre-independence politics, his anxiety to accomplish as many gains for dalits as he could in his life time, the exigencies for 'short' actions at the expense of 'long' vision inevitably led to mark patterns that could support array of behaviours. The first to take advantage of it were his own lieutenants for serving their personal ambitions that set the trends of distortion of Ambedkar in the minds of gullible Dalit masses.

The ruling classes that always look for the grounds to divide masses had severally reinforced this distortion and accelerated fragmentation of dalits in every field. They, along with willing collaboration of Dalit politicians and emerging elite, promoted and sustained the particular icons of Ambedkar that would prevent political coalescence of dalits and suck them into the vortex of parliamentary politics in order to bring the establishment much needed legitimacy. Dalits failed to note this cunning and let themselves flow in the currents of confusion the ruling classes deliberately created. Today, with increasing political crises the ruling classes seem vying with each other in co-opting Ambedkar, as though that may be their last chance of survival. If dalits stood their grounds well, that might have proved to be their last act.

But, unfortunately dalits are giving them new leases of life by blinding themselves to the reality. Not only that they have not resisted these ruling class machinations but on the contrary they are curiously seen to swell the cadres of these castiest, communalist and anti-poor groups and parties. These parties who openly profess the ideology of Hindu revivalism and represent all that is decadent in Indian tradition show the temerity to project Ambedkar among their ideologies. Apart from the reasons of security that propel Dalit youth into their fold, the compradore behaviour of Dalit elite certainly has influenced the phenomenon. What is common in all the attempts by the ruling classes is to sap 'Ambedkar' of its rebellious content.

It is advantageous for them to show that he was the chief architect of the Indian Constitution, committed to parliamentary democracy and opposed to any ideology that propagates violence or revolution. He is projected to favour gradual change implying that dalits should patiently wait and strive persuasively to better their own lives. He is projected as the Bodhisatva that inspires nirvana-the State of total detachment from worldly matters. All these images have caused significant damage to the emancipatory struggles of dalits.

Some of these images might be the purposeful and blatant disfiguring of Ambedkar but some of them represent genuine dilemma arising from Ambedkar's own stands on various issues. From the viewpoint of the comprehensive pro-people change in the present historical phase a democratic revolution is an imperative. The motive force for this revolution ought to sprout from dalits. The history provides a strong testimony that any radical movement in the country could be sustained by dalits and tribals at its base. Ambedkar as a symbol for Dalit aspirations holds a key to the barrage that has so far bound the revolutionary upsurge in India below the alarming levels. If one concedes that Ambedkar's framework is going to haunt revolutionary commitment till the Indian Democratic Revolution actually happens and that Ambedkar represents the ideological weaponry in the hands of dalits who along with other oppressed people are going to be the axis of this revolution, then one would clearly see the need to redefine Ambedkar in radical terms commensurate with this purpose.

Many aspects of confusion with regard to the facts could be cleared with rational interpretation of his thoughts. But much might need the logical extrapolation of his basic thinking which for some reason appears to have settled in erroneous forms. As he himself showed the way in the case of his redefinition of Buddha's Dhamma, dalits will have to undertake this task, for giving themselves a powerful ideology. Their future as a social group almost hinges on this task. There are enough clues left behind by Ambedkar himself that point to this need.

There is no doubt that he was frustrated at the end of his life seeing the undesired aftermath of his lifelong struggle. He had to lament over the betrayal of the educated dalits in whom he had seen the crusaders of his mission. He had to weep with remorse that he could not do anything for his people in the villages. He had to disown the Constitution for working on which he had cut short his life at least by a few years. He had to swallow the frustration of not being able to pilot the Constitution of his conception (States and Minorities). He had to regret the anti-people State that emerged in republican India. He obviously lacked the analytical tools to see through the reasons for these happenings. His excessive religiosity and spirituality at the fag end of his life perhaps could be taken as the manifestation of this frustration.

The social engineer could only be busy with problems; he is unlikely to come to grip with the design defects in the system. Almost every thing that Ambedkar pinned his hopes on can be found today in antithetical shambles. His educational society, his vision of Buddhism, the political party of his conception, the social reforms could be some of the examples. These tragic aftermaths also would denote the necessity of a critical review of Ambedkar's thoughts if they were to be used as the ideology to further the Dalit movement towards its logical end. If this process is sincerely followed, there cannot be any doubt that this 'redefined Ambedkar' would be a revolutionary icon, organically linking the Dalit struggle to the revolutionary struggle in the world. It will truly globalize the Dalit struggle.

EFFORTS TO END INJUSTICE

There was no cast system during the Vedic age. There was no 'untouchability'. When and how did this system creep into the Hindu society? We do not know for certain.

Did no one try to wipe out this injustice? Buddha admitted may 'untouchables' to his religion. Ramanujacharya, Basaveshwara, Chakradhara, Ramananda, Kabir, Chaitanya, Ekanath, Tukaram, Raja Rammohan Roy and other great men preached that no one is high and no one is low among God's children. Mahatma Phooley and his wife dedicated their lives to the education of the 'untouchables.' Sayyaji Rao Gaikwad, the Maharaja of Baroda, established a school for the 'untouchables' as early as in 1883. In this way many thoughtful leaders of the Hindu Society have been trying for hundreds of years to wipe out 'Untouchability'. Both before and after India became free, many great man have sacrificed their lives for the truth and the principles they believed in. Ambedkar was one of them.

Ideas of high and low had crept into the Hindu Society; Ambedkar suffered because of this; he also fought hard against such differences; later he became the first Las Minister in free India. The credit for making a law and creating the necessary atmosphere to wipe out 'Untouchability' goes to Ambedkar.

SHOULD NOT HINDU, WHO SEEK JUSTICE, GIVE JUSTICE?

The 'untouchables' are Hindus. Therefore, the doors of temples should be open to them. If the Hindus can touch the Christians and the Muslims, why should they not touch the people who are themselves Hindus and who worship the Hindu Gods? This was Ambedkar's argument. He gave a call that people who practise and support 'untouchability' should be punished. Some people argued that the 'untouchables' were not yet fit for equality. The Hindus say that they want independence and democracy. How can a people who have temple upon all the libertise of a backward group aspire to democracy? Ambedkar argued like this and thundered that these people had no right to speak of justice and democracy.

In 1927 there was a big conference. It resolved that there should be no cast differences in the Hindu Dharma and that people of all castes should be allowed to work as priests in temples. The Chowdar Tank dispute went to the court. The court decided that tanks are public property. The 'untouchables' who have been subjected to humiliation for hundreds of years should find justice. For this purpose Ambedkar indicated a few clear steps. No section of the Hindus should be kept out of temples.

There should be more representatives of the 'untouchables' in the legislatures. These representatives should not be nominated by the government. They should be elected by the people. The government should employ the 'untouchalbes' in larger numbers the army and the police department.

A Fearless, Firm Mind: Those who suffer in the Hindu Society should get justice.

This was Ambedkar's rocklike decision. He was prepared to oppose anybody to reach his goal. The British Government invited several Indian leaders to discuss the problems of India.

The conferences were held in London; they were called the 'Round Table Conference'. Gandhiji also took part in them. At the Round Table Conference Ambedkar spoke angrily against the government. He said that the backward sections did not enjoy equality with other sections, even under the British Government; the British had just followed the ways of the other Hindus. This was a time when Gandhiji was very popular in India. Millions of people followed his footsteps with devotion. Ambedkar openly opposed Gandhiji's views on how justice should be secured for the 'untouchables'. He supported the views which seemed right to him. Ambedkar secured for the Harijans (the 'untouchables') 'separate electorates' at the Second Round Table Conference in 1931. As a result, the Harijans could elect their representatives separately.

AFTER RESIGNATION AS A MINISTER

In 1952, he was defeated by a Congress candidate in the election for the Lok Sabha. The entire country was shocked by his defeat.

Later he was elected to the Rajya Sabha. Whenever he felt that the government had not done justice to the Harijans he criticised it sharply. In 1953 the government brought a bill before the parliament. According to this bill those who practised 'untouchablity' would be punished; imprisonment, imposition of fines, dismissal from employment and withdrawal of licence to follow a profession - these were the forms of punishment.

To the Path of the Buddha: Soon after the framing of the Constitution, Ambedkar's mind turned towards Buddha. His mind was thirsting for peace and justice. He attended the Buddhist Conference in Ceylon (Sri Lanka) in 1950. The bitterness of his mind was ever on the increase. In spite of it, he was not willing to embrace the Christian or the Muslim faith. Finally, Ambedkar decided to become a Buddhist. This was a great decision in his life, a decision taken after deep thought.

A Neglected Message from Dr. Ambedkar to OBCs

An article was published recently in Marathi local magazine by Suhas Sonwane based on daily Loksatta. The following is a gist of it, translated from Marathi.

Mr. Baba Saheb Gawande, the founder president of an Organization of Marathas from Bombay called "Maratha Mandir" was a close friend of Dr. Ambedkar. Mr. Gawande asked Dr. Ambedkar, who was then a Law Minister in Nehru Cabinet in 1947, for a message for the Maratha people to be published in the Souvenir of "Maratha Mandir". Ambedkar declined saying that he had no relation with the Organization or the Marathas, but on persistent insistence, a message was given and published in the souvenir on 23rd March 1947. Unfortunately that special issue is not available in the office of the Organization today, but was made available by Shri Vijay Survade recently and was undocumented till now.

Dr. Ambedkar said:

> "This principle will apply not only to Marathas but all Backward Castes. If they do not wish to be under the thumb of others they should concentrate on two things, one is politics and the other is education."
>
> "One thing I like to impress on you is that the community can live in peace only when it has enough moral but indirect pressure over the rulers. Even if a community is numerically weak, it can keep its pressure over the rulers and create its dominance as is seen by the example of status of present day Brahmins in India. It is essential that such a pressure is maintained, as without it, the aims and policies of the state can not have proper direction, on which depends the development and progress of the state."
>
> "At the same time, it must not be forgotten that education is also important. Not only elementary education but higher education is most essential to keep ahead in competition of communities in their progress."
>
> "Higher education, in my opinion, means that education, which can enable you to occupy the strategically important places in State administration. Brahmins had to face a lot of opposition and obstacles, but they are overcoming these and progressing ahead."
>
> "I can not forget, rather I am sad, that many people do not realize that the Caste system is existing in

India for centuries because of inequality and a wide gulf of difference in education, and they have forgotten that it is likely to continue for some centuries to come. This gulf between the education of Brahmins and non-Brahmins will not end just by primary and secondary education. The difference in status between these can only be reduced by higher education. Some non-Brahmins must get highly educated and occupy the strategically important places, which has remained the monopoly of Brahmins since long. I think this is the duty of the State. If the Govt. can not do it, institutions like "Maratha Mandir" must undertake this task."

"I must emphasize one point here that middle class tries to compare itself with the highly educated and well placed and well to do community, whereas lower class all over the world has same fault. The middle class is not as liberal as upper one, and has no ideology as lower one, which makes it enemy of both the classes. The middle class Marathas of Maharashtra also have this fault. They have only two ways out, either to join hands with upper classes and prevent the lower classes from progress, and the other is to join hands with lower classes and both together destroy the upper class power coming against the progress of both.

There was a time, they used to be with lower classes, now they seem to be with the upper class. It is for them to decide which way to go. The future of not only Indian masses but also their own future depends upon what decision the Maratha leaders take. As a matter of fact it all should be left to the skill and wisdom of the leaders of Marathas. But there seems to be a lack of such wise leadership among the Marathas."

What he said about Marathas, equally applies to all OBCs, and still holds true after half a century. Dr. Ambedkar wrote much to educate the OBCs. It is only now that OBCs are awakening gradually. It must not be forgotten that the future of this country depends on them.

WORKS AGAINST COMMUNISM

Marx has given scientific explanation of religion, and that it is "Religion is the Opium of the people". But "it can not lead people who suffer difficulties to overcome the difficulties. It only allows them to anaesthetize themselves, thereby, Religion changes material struggle into a kind of spiritual comfort. It transforms real needs to hopes of an illusory world." It apparently equate religion with God, and as Science has disproved the existence of God, and as so called religious ethics comes from the will of God, it has no meaning.

Secondly, only Marxism holds that, ultimately, rooting out private ownership will remove all evil. Though Socialism has brought liberation of masses, still people believe in religion. This is because of legacy of feudalism, influence of capitalism, imperialism, beurocratism.

Lastly it outline the line of action not only for their own country but for the whole world. It appears, as if, the Communist party of China thinks it necessary to form a united front with "patriotic religious believers to oppose the reactionary forces at home and abroad and to carry out socialist revolution and modernization". These are bound to expound Marxism through "research into religion and into its history, doctrine and present circumstances." This propaganda one wishes to do with "unhurried discussion to reason things out" by criticizing religion but not the people who follow or preach it, except the "criminals". Of course they do not forget to assign the power of final judgment to a few persons as they say that all this must be according to the "theories, plans and policies of Party Central".

They, however, admit that there were "religious wrongs", but blame the "Gang of four" with their "ultra leftist" attitude for these religious wrongs. Further claiming that State is not controlling Religion.

There is such a vast literature by Dr. Ambedkar in favour of Buddhism and against Communism, that only quoting from Ambedkar, who has already thought over Communism for years before giving Buddhism to the multitudes of Indian masses, will answer all points raised before. One thing needs to be remembered is that Ambedkar's views are nearly fifty years old, and are still valid. They do not mention Mao, as his theories had not then come into prominence, but what he says about communism in general should also apply to Maoism too.

The very fact that "The Gang of Four" can become successful in capturing power and do the things, against the "real" Marxism, proves the fact that there is some inherent weaknesses in Marxism.

PREREQUISITES OF COMMUNISM

Dr. Ambedkar avers that there are certain prerequisites for the Marxism to succeed. These are the society should be a "Free society", meaning it should give importance to an Individual over the society and that it should be based on equality, fraternity and liberty. [Ambedkar, "India and the Prerequisites of Communism", (W&S vol. 3,), p.95] These have been brought to China by Buddhism and to Russia by Christianity. The absence of these factors in caste ridden Indian society could not foster the growth of Marxism in India, and that is why Marx failed in Hindu India. Marx could not properly evaluate the importance of caste or its influence on Indian masses. Because, Marx failed here, his followers in India talk of "Class" and not of "Caste". That is the reason, the movement of Marx in India was and still is in the hands of oppressor class.

RESIDUE OF MARXISM

Marx expounded his theories about 150 years ago. Most of Marxism is demolished during these years. But what remains of the Karl Marx, Dr. Ambedkar feels, is a residue of fire, small but still very important. The residue in his opinion, consists of four items:

1. The function of philosophy is to reconstruct the world and not to waste its time in explaining the origin of the world.
2. That there is a conflict of interest between class and class.
3. That private ownership of property brings power to one class and sorrow to another through exploitation.

4. That it is necessary for the good of society that the sorrow be removed by the abolition of private property.

Comparison between Buddha and Karl Marx

Taking the points form the Marxian Creed which have survived Dr. Ambedkar compares the Buddha and Karl Marx. He feels that, on the first point there is complete agreement between the Buddha and Karl Marx. That language is different but the meaning is the same. If for misery one reads exploitation Buddha is not away form Marx.

On the question of private property, Dr. Ambedkar quotes the illuminating extract from a dialogue between Buddha and Ananda, Buddha saying avarice is because of possession, which in turn is because of tenacity. Not only Buddha prohibited private property in Sangha, he put more restrictions and "rules are far more rigorous than are to be found in Communism in Russia".

Means to Achieve Goals

Dr. Ambedkar, then, examines the means to achieve the goals. Having summarized Buddha's tenets, he feels that, it is clear that the means adopted by the Buddha were to convert a man by changing his moral disposition to follow the path voluntarily. The means adopted by the Communists are equally clear, short and swift. They are (1) Violence and (2) Dictatorship of the Proletariat.

The Communists say that there are the only two means of establishing Communism. The first is violence. Nothing short of it will be suffice to break up the existing system. The other is Dictatorship of the Proletariat. Nothing short of it will be suffice to continue the new system. It is now clear what are the similarities and differences between Buddha and Karl Marx. The differences are about the means. The end is common to both. The Bhikshu Sangha had the most democratic constitution. The Buddha was only one of the Bhikkus. At the most he was like a Prime Minister among members of the Cabinet. He was never a dictator. Twice before his death be was asked to appoint some one as the head of the Sangha to control it. But each time he refused saying that the Dhamma is the Supreme Commander of the Sangha. He refused to be a dictator and refused to appoint a dictator.

Can the Communists say that in achieving their valuable they have not destroyed other valuable ends? They have destroyed private property. Assuming that this is a valuable end can the Communists say that they have not destroyed other valuable end in the process of achieving it? How many people have they killed for achieving their end. Has human life no value? Could they not have taken property without taking the life of the owner?

Dictatorship is often defined as absence of liberty or absence of Parliamentary Government. Both interpretations are not quite clear. There is no liberty even when there is Parliamentary Government. For law means want of liberty. The difference between Dictatorship and Parliamentary Government lies in this. In Parliamentary Government every citizen has a right to criticize the restraint on liberty imposed by the Government. In Parliamentary Government you have a duty and a right; the duty to obey the law and right to criticize it. In Dictatorship you have only duty to obey but no right to criticize it.

We must now consider whose means are more lasting. One has to chose between Government by force and Government by moral disposition. As Burke has said force cannot be a lasting means. In his speech on conciliation with America he uttered this memorable warning:

> "First, Sir, permit me to observe, that the use of force alone is but temporary. It may subdue for a moment: But it does not remove the necessity of subduing again; and a nation is not governed which is perpetually to be conquered."
>
> "The next objection is its uncertainty. Terror is not always the effect of force, and an armament is not a victory. If you do not succeed, you are without resource, for, conciliation failing, force remains; but force failing, no further hope of reconciliation is left. Power and authority are sometimes bought by kindness; but they can never be begged as alms by an impoverished and defeated violence.

> A further objection to force is, that you impair the object by your very endeavours to preserve it. The thing you fought for is the thing which you recover, but depreciated, sunk, wasted and consumed in the contest."

Withering away of State

Dr. Ambedkar also discusses the Communist theory of "withering away of the state". He says, The Communists themselves admit that their theory of the State as a permanent dictatorship is a weakness in their political philosophy. They take shelter under the plea that the State will ultimately wither away. There are two questions which they have to answer. (1) When will it wither away? (2) What will take the place of the State when it withers away? To the first question they can give no definite time.

Though the second question is more important than the first, Dr. Ambedkar feels, the Communists have no satisfactory answer to the question what would take the place of the State when it withers away. Will it be succeed by Anarchy? If so, he feels, the building up of the Communist State is an useless effort. If it cannot be sustained except by force and if it results in anarchy when the force holding it together is withdrawn what good is the Communist State. He therefore avers that, the only thing which could sustain it after force is withdrawn is Religion. He observes:

> "But to the Communists, Religion is anathema. Their hatred to Religion is so deep seated that they will not even discriminate between religions which are helpful to Communism and religions which are not. The Communists have carried their hatred of Christianity to Buddhism without waiting to examine the difference between the two."

Charges against Christianity

Dr. Ambedkar discusses two charges against Christianity levelled by the Communists. Surprisingly, the same charges are levelled by Chinese Research Scholars in the same terminology. Ambedkar answers these charges as he observes:

> "Their first charge against Christianity was that they made people worship other worldliness and made them suffer poverty in this world. As can be seen from quotations from Buddhism in the earlier part of this tract such a charge cannot be levelled against Buddhism."

Dr. Ambedkar then answers the second charge as follows:

> "The second charge levelled by the Communists against Christianity cannot be levelled against Buddhism. This charge is summed up in the statement that Religion is the opium of the people. This charge is based upon the Sermon on the Mount which is to be found in the Bible. The Sermon on the Mount sublimates poverty and weakness. It promises heaven to the poor and the weak. There is no Sermon on the Mount to be found in the Buddha's teachings. His teaching is to acquire wealth." [Ibid. p.460]

He then gives the Buddha's Sermon on the subject to Anathapindika one of his disciples, wherein Buddha describes how wealth should be acquired justly and legitimately.

Dr. Ambedkar concludes the discussion by observing:

> The Russians are proud of their communism. But they forget that the wonder of all wonders is that the Buddha established Communism so far as the Sangha was concerned without dictatorship. It may be that it was a communism on a very small scale but it was communism without dictatorship, a miracle which Lenin failed to do.

The Buddha's method was different. His method was to change the mind of man: to alter his disposition: so that whatever man does, he does it voluntarily without the use of force or compulsion. His main means to alter the disposition of men was his Dhamma and the constant preaching of his Dhamma. The Buddha's way not to force people to do what they did not like to do although it was good for them. His way was to alter the disposition of men so that they would do voluntarily what they would not otherwise to do.

> "It has been claimed that the Communist Dictatorship in Russia has wonderful achievements to its credit. There can be no denial of it. That is why I say that a Russian Dictatorship would be good for all backward countries. But this his no argument for permanent Dictatorships. Humanity does not only want economic values, it also wants spiritual values to be retained. Permanent Dictatorship has paid no attention to spiritual values and does not seem to intend to. Carlyle called Political Economy a Pig Philosophy. Carlyle was of course wrong. For man needs material comforts. But the Communist Philosophy seems to be equally wrong for the aim of their philosophy seems to be fatten pigs as though men are no better than pigs. Man must grow materially as well as spiritually. Society has been aiming to lay a new foundation was summarized by the French Revolution in three words. Fraternity, Liberty and Equality. The French Revolution was welcomed because of this slogan. It failed to produce equality. We welcome the Russian Revolution because it aims to produce equality. But it cannot be too much emphasized that in producing equality society cannot afford to sacrifice fraternity or liberty.

Equality will be of no value without fraternity or liberty. It seems that the three can coexist only if one follows the way of the Buddha. Communism can give one but not all.

Tests of Religion

In his memorable treatise, "Buddha and future of His Religion", after comparing Buddhism with Hinduism, while comparing Buddhism with other non-hindu religions, Dr. Ambedkar concludes by enumerating the tests a religion must pass:

1. That society must have either the sanction of law or the sanction of morality to hold it together. Without either society is sure to go pieces. In all societies law plays a very small part. It is intended to keep the minority

within the range of social discipline. The majority is left and has to be left to sustain its social life by the postulates and sanction of morality. Religion in the sense of morality, must therefore, remain the governing principle in every society.

2. That religion as defined in the first proposition must be in accord with science. Religion is bound to lose it respect and therefore become the subject of ridicule and thereby not merely lose its force as a governing principle of life but might in course of time disintegrated and lapse if it is not in accordance with science. In other words, religion if it is to function, must be in accordance with reason which is merely another name for science.
3. That religion as a code of social morality, must recognize the fundamental tenets of liberty, equality and fraternity. Unless a religion recognizes these three fundamental principles of social life religion will be doomed.
4. That religion must not sanctify or ennoble poverty. Renunciation of riches by those who have it may be a blessed state. But poverty can never be. To declare poverty to be a blessed state is to pervert religion, to perpetuate vice crime, to consent to make earth a living hell."

Dr. Ambedkar asks, which religion fulfils these requirements today, reminding that the days of the Mahatmas are gone and the world cannot have a new Religion. It will have to make its choice from existing religions. Some of the religions might satisfy one or two tests but Buddhism is the only religion satisfying all tests. He observes:

"So far as I know the only religion which satisfies all these tests is Buddhism. In other words Buddhism is the only religion which the world can have. If the new world-which be it realized is very different from the old-must have a religion-and the new world needs religion for more than the old world did-then it can only be religion of the Buddha."

"Could the Buddha answer Karl Marx?"

Admitting that all this may sound very strange, because most of writers on Buddha have propagated the idea that the only thing Buddha taught was Ahimsa. It is true Buddha taught Ahimsa, he says, he does not want to minimize its importance, because it is a great doctrine and the world can not be saved without it. He further observes:

> "What I wish to emphasize is that Buddha taught many other things besides Ahimsa. He taught as a part of religion, social freedom, intellectual freedom, economic freedom and political freedom. He taught equality, equality not between man and man only but between man and woman. It would be difficult to find a religious teacher to compare with Buddha whose teachings embrace so many aspects of the social life of a people whose doctrines are so modern and whose main concern was to give salvation to man in his life on earth and not to promise it to him in heaven after he is dead."

Dr. Ambedkar says many divergent views expressed about Buddha's teachings, including Samadhi, Vippasana, Esoterism etc. are because the authors are not students of Buddhism, but of history or anthropology. He asks "Did the Buddha have no social message?" If pressed for an answer, the Buddhist scholars admit that Buddha taught: Ahimsa and Peace. But the real questions are seldom asked and replied. These are: Did the Buddha teach: Justice, Love, Liberty, Equality, Fraternity, and "Could the Buddha answer Karl Marx?" He further avers that "My answer is that the Buddha has a social message. He answers all these questions. But they have been buried by modern authors."

QUEST FOR DISTRIBUTIVE JUSTICE

Bhimrao Ambedkar (1891-1956) who was a dominating figure and active organiser of the dalits during the anti-colonial struggle against the British in India. His concept of distributive justice was based on the idea of a casteless society. This is of course a vast topic, and in order to make it manageable, let us concentrate on certain aspects of his theory, namely, the critique of domination and oppression of dalits, and their exclusion from the rights of citizenship.

Ambedkar's main claim is that a society based on the caste system cannot be a 'real' community because it violates the respect and dignity of individuals. His critique of a caste-ridden society raises some interesting questions about the limits of the theory and practice of citizenship and liberal politics in India. Intention here is to analyse his ideas on equality and justice in the way they complement other themes and concepts in his work. Since many arguments were are part of a larger project, the numerous simplifications may be regarded as tentative and provisional.

To develop the setting for the discussion on distributive justice, In section I Ambedkar's critiques of both the rule of the Indian National Congress and Brahmin domination of society place him in an uneasy position within the discourse of nationalism. In Section II, the views of Gandhi and Ambedkar on equality and distributive justice, which reflect the differences in their approach towards the abolition of the caste system. In Section III, critical examination of three components of Ambedkar's theory of distributive justice. Having done this, a brief work or in the final section to argue that while Ambedkar believed both in the basic tenets of liberal politics and a casteless society, the principles behind the one often contradict those behind the other.

Some of the questions raised in this account are: first why did Ambedkar differ from other nationalist leaders in his analysis of Indian society? What is the concept of Swaraj in Ambedkar's account of Brahmin domination? How did Ambedkar resolve, if he ever did, the idea of separate electorates with a conception of distributive justice in the struggle for the liberation of dalits? But in focusing on Ambedkar, some might object to have ignored many other arguments presented in favour of liberation. Before looking at possible answers to these questions let us give some reasons why it is important to look at Ambedkar from this perspective. There are three contemporary debates to which this essay will make a contribution.

First, consider the claims made by the historians of the freedom movement led by the Indian National Congress. The view that the national movement is a 'popular, multi-class movement' is grounded on the assumption that the entire world of political action can be comprehended through the categories of imperialism, nationalism and communalism. As a corollary to the above, there is the assumption that the concept of nationalism has a deeper significance and therefore it resists multiplicity and retains its indissolubility despite every attempt to resolve it into subdivisions such as region, class, caste and gender.

Of course, recent history writings, represented for example by the historians of the subaltern school, question these assumptions to a large extent. But it is surprising how often one reads about 'subaltern' protests without encountering the name of Ambedkar, and his efforts to improve the condition of the dalits. Moreover, these critiques of colonial discourse valorise indigenous communities; this makes impossible sympathetic evaluations of many movements for women's rights and lower-caste protests which might have utilised aspects of colonial policies and western ideologies.

It is argued that the question of the identity and existence of the nation was addressed by Ambedkar in opposing there elite-led nationalist project. What was the nation, what was national oppression and the way to overcome it, was a common question. What is interesting is his answer which focuses on the oppressive character of the Hindu community based on the principles of the caste system. By arguing for the rights and basic needs of the dalits, he challenges the assumptions of both nationalist politics and indigenous communitarian politics. By choosing to discuss Ambedkar, we hope to point towards histories not neatly preoccupied with anti-colonial nationalism; once ensnared within the 'particularism' of national politics, these leaders found it difficult to maintain focus on social disadvantage as the main fulcrum around which politics should be organised.

The second problem which arises in focusing on Ambedkar is of locating him in the debate on modernity and tradition. Of the various streams which responded to colonialism, Ambedkar could be inaccurately placed, in the category of 'modernists'. This response, as described by Bhikhu Parekh, viewed Hindu society as "beyond hope and their salvation lay in radically restructuring it along modern or European lines". The modernist programme for the "regeneration of India consisted in creating and using a strong, interventionist, democratic, secular and centralised state to recreate society". Although they covered a wide spectrum, the proponents of this view were united in their belief that the state stood for modernity and society for tradition.

Ambedkar articulates the theme of modernity by claiming that individualist forms of organisation typically replace communitarian ones like the caste system in modern society. He shares much with his contemporaries in the liberal tradition on this project. However, he goes further because he envisions the reconstruction of our existence embedded in social relations characterised by caste groups. Despite his belief in the project of modernity, he departs from other exponents of this tradition by giving new arguments for certain concepts like equality and distributive justice in the colonial context and by adopting a critical position on the European experience. The prospect of moulding India or its institutions in the image of the British had no appeal for Ambedkar. For how else could he turn to Dhamma?

This point is raised because it is of great importance in the current debate on modernity and tradition in political science. Some scholars question this dichotomy by arguing that "a transformed version of this "traditional" structure had become a vehicle for representative and parliamentary democracy and was functioning as a democratising force". Caste, according to this view, "was anti-caste, in that the horizontal mobilisation of larger lower caste communities was gaining them power, status and wealth which allowed them to challenge and overturn the hierarchy of caste as ritual rank... In this sense, "traditional" structures and communities of sentiment, identity and action seemed to us by no means irrelevant even to competitive democratic politics and the realisation of egalitarian values."

Now this is very different from what Ambedkar wished to achieve by questioning this dichotomy; he saw the caste system as a serious obstacle in the path of democracy. According to him, democracy lies not in the form of government but in terms of association between the people who form that society. Because

Indian society is divided and graded on the basis of the caste system, it is not democratic.

The third problem is to explore how questions of caste have entered into formulations of both Indian and Hindu nationalism. According to Gail Omvedt, even before Veer Savarkar developed a coherent Hindu ideology during the 1920s equating 'Hinduism' and 'nationalism', "the dominant elite ideological trend by the end of the 19th century was that of a revitalised Hinduism equated with nationalism". This is the most difficult area to explore. Ambedkar's relationship to the national movement was complicated and problematic. The fundamental error, Ambedkar believed, was to fail to see the danger from the views of, not of the orthodox Hindu, whom he had given up years before as hopeless, but of Gandhi and the Congress. Why could he not isolate the obscurantist and parochial current in this confrontation?

4

INDIAN SOCIETY: AMBEDKAR'S ANALYSIS

INTRODUCTION

The first question which arises is: Why did Ambedkar not endorse the nationalist discourse of this period? There are several answers to this. One explanation for this is given by Omvedt when she writes: "It is impossible to conceptualise the Dalit movement in India in the absence of Ambedkar, it is equally difficult to imagine, sociologically, Ambedkar coming of any other region than the Marathi-speaking areas of British presidency". Let us explore this a little bit more.

Omvedt refers to the existence of an important tradition of anti-caste movement in Maharashtra that needs to be seen as part of the response to industrialisation and urbanisation. This was the site of the radical movement of Jotiba Phule's Satyashodhak Samaj, and from the time of Tilak, it had also provided a strong base for Hindu revivalism in the form of a Hindu Mahasabha. In fact, the Indian National Congress held its first session in 1885 in Bombay.

There was another reason for Ambedkar's critical position on nationalist politics. He was a Mahar, the largest untouchable caste in Maharashtra. His actions, then, according to Zelliot, "were moulded not only by his own personal background, and achievements, and the Maharashtrian thinking of his day, but also by his status as an untouchable". This group he came from had begun social and political movements before he assumed a position of leadership. Behind this identification with a non-

Brahmin group lay the logic of a movement that was essentially anti-caste and not simply a movement for 'untouchability removal' or 'self-reform'. This is not to say that the Mahar movement in the later 19th century was an isolated movement but only to suggest that all these influences constantly streaming in are employed by Ambedkar in a new sense and directed towards a new solution.

To what extent does his work, in this political scenario, represent more than a resuscitation of known and traditional ideas and to what extent does it deviate from the traditional mode and contain new and original thought? There is no doubt that Ambedkar's writings chiefly captured the political tradition of their time: the philosophical views of that time must be at least in part responsible for his dissatisfaction with the nationalist discourse - the new political mood after the Montague-Chelmsford Reforms; an awakening among the minorities for safeguarding their interests in relation to the Hindu majority which pointed towards wider political participation in the national movement. Yet, his thesis does not fit in with the dominant discourse on nationalism. One of the reasons behind Ambedkar's verdict on the national movement and its leaders, was their general indifference to caste issues. The intelligentsia, as part of the Congress leadership, organised first as social reformers against the British, and also organised as nationalists to challenge many aspects of Indian tradition. But they remained very ambiguous towards removal of the caste system. Linked to the debate on social and political reform was the issue of class. Many communist leaders analysed caste in a mechanical class framework and sought to override traditional identities rather than reinterpret them.

Therefore, a plausible explanation could be found in his own solution for liberating the dalits. Ambedkar realised that the identification of Indian culture with Hinduism is incorrect. Because he believed that absorption into Hinduism meant the acceptance of Hindu leadership in the national movement, he felt it would be wiser to take chances with a religion which has many safeguards. At first, he tried to assert the path of radical autonomy, encouraged the dalits to form their own organisations and to deal independently with some basic issues. It means that the dalits themselves, "would have to redefine and reconstitute their relations with the whole of Hindu society". But if the dalits were not Hindus, what were they? In fact, a non-Hindu choice seems to have led him finally, to identify with Buddhism.

At the theoretical level, Ambedkar's language turned out to be singularly open to misconstruals. It was not easy for many to accept the Indian National Congress, social reform organisations and the Hindu Mahasabha as irreconcilable opponents of the dalits; neither was it easy to accept the praise accorded by Ambedkar to the British state for raising the status of untouchables. Even more open to misunderstanding was Ambedkar's critique of nationalism: whereas Ambedkar attacked the Congress for their failure to recognise caste issues, he was erroneously taken to reject nationalism altogether. He was supposed to be not only anti-national but to advocate a separatist policy which was anti-sectarian as well. Opposed by both traditionalists and Congress leaders, Ambedkar reserved his most bitter attack for Gandhi's reformism.

DISTRIBUTIVE JUSTICE: DEBATE WITH GANDHI

The conflict between Gandhi and Ambedkar in terms of their ideological difference on the caste system. Both the thinkers approach the matter from quite different angles. There are real and serious disagreements between them, especially regarding the conclusions that each of them draws from their premises.

Gandhi had two arguments against untouchability: the unity or the political argument and the ethical argument.

As a leader working for a national goal, Gandhi argued for removing injustices faced by 'untouchables' because he felt the need to weave the divergent interests in India into a unified opposition to the British; he argued for pursuing this course of reform without challenging the social fabric of Indian society. He emphasised that a political separation of untouchables from the rest of the Hindu population would reduce Hindu plurality vis-a-vis other minority groups, in part, the Muslims.

The ethical argument is premised on the view that Hindu society must rest on moral consensus, that political conflict can only be kept within bounds if there is a moral consensus on the caste system. Gandhi's ethical argument rested on two claims. First, he claimed that the heart of the caste Hindu could be changed by applying moral pressures within the framework of the Hindu tradition. Second, there was an obligation on the caste Hindu to be individually responsible towards the lower caste groups. In his conception of the moral or perfect society, Gandhi maintained that its enduring basis can only be the moral calibre of the individuals who constitute it.

Although Gandhi's views changed over the years, he always believed in the varnashrama dharma, the divinely ordained division of society into four defined groups according to duty: Brahmin, Kshatriya, Vaishya, Sudra. In an exchange of views on this problem, he said:

> I do not believe the caste system even as distinguished from varnashrama to be an 'odious and vicious' dogma. It has its limitations and defects but there is nothing sinful about it, as there is about untouchability, and, if it is a bye-product of the caste system, it is only in the same sense that an ugly growth is of a body or weeds of a crop. It is wrong to destroy caste because of the outcaste, as it would be to destroy a body because of an ugly growth in it, or of a crop because of its weeds...

Later, he distinguished between caste and varna. In his response to Ambedkar's undelivered speech titled: 'Annihilation of Caste' (1936), he said:

> Caste has nothing to do with religion... it is harmful both to spiritual and national growth. Varna and Ashram are institutions which have nothing to do with castes. The law of varna teaches us that we have each one of us to earn our bread by following the ancestral calling. It defines not our rights but our duties... The callings of a Brahmin- spiritual teacher- and a scavenger are equal, and at one time their due performance carries equal merit before god and seems to have carried identical reward before man.

To this Ambedkar replied, questioning the logical conclusions of his doctrine: "When can a calling be deemed to have become an ancestral calling so as to make it binding on a man? Must man follow his ancestral calling even if it does not suit his capacities, even when it has ceased to be profitable? Must a man live by his ancestral calling even if he finds it to be immoral?"

Following arguments from justice, rather than arguments for unity, Ambedkar states that existing inequalities cannot be morally defended: to avoid the morally illegitimate exclusion of untouchables one would have to differentiate conceptually and practically between different levels of citizenship.

Ambedkar proposed these arguments when he came into conflict with the Congress, and with Gandhi in particular, on two occasions - the temple entry attempts and separate electorates. Ambedkar put forward arguments based on the principle of liberal equality and distributive justice to sustain his case. Equality meant not the equal status of varnas, but equal social, political and economic opportunity for all.

At first, he made several attempts to gain religious and social rights for the untouchables, by using the Gandhian technique of satyagraha; drinking water from a public tank in Mahad (1927), temple entry to the Parvati temple at Poona (1929), and then the Kala Ram temple at Nasik (1930-35). The failure of temple entry movements demonstrated, according to Ambedkar, that the untouchables were not really a part of Hindu society and would never be accepted as equals by Hindus within that framework. It was quite obvious that this low threshold concept of a legal conception of equality allows for different degrees of political participation. In short, it does not allow for a corresponding conception of political citizenship. Thus, from a position of questioning the brahmanical social order, Ambedkar moved towards its rejection: raising the issue of conversion by the untouchables in 1935.

But there was another reason. The second occasion was the Round Table Conference held in 1930 at London, where both leaders confronted each other on the issue of the political rights of depressed classes.

Earlier, in the 'Evidence before the Southborough Committee on Franchise' (1919), Ambedkar (invited as a delegate of the depressed classes) had argued eloquently for uniform franchise, for securing access for the depressed classes to the public sphere-to public wells, roads, schools, temples, and cremation grounds-and for special provisions for their adequate representation of their interests and opinions.

Untouchability constitutes a definite set of interests which the untouchables alone can speak for. Hence, it is evident that we must find the untouchables to represent their grievances which are their interests, and secondly, we must find them in such members as will constitute a force sufficient to claim redress.

After the Round Table Conference, (where he argued against a general territorial electorate for the untouchables), the communal award of 1932 gave the depressed classes, a double vote, one in a special constituency and one in the general electorate - a decision which appeared to recognise untouchables as a minority group outside of Hinduism. Gandhi's response was to enter fast unto death on September 20, 1932. He expressed his argument on the grounds for unity between the two:

A heart understanding between the two, the greatest opportunity of repentance and reparation on the part of the suppressors... I would therefore favour widest possible franchise for the suppressed and establish a convention between the two sections for securing proper election of representatives of the suppressed.

Under great pressure from other political leaders, Ambedkar relented. However, the Poona Pact, which followed, recognised untouchables as a political category across British India by providing reservations of seats for the depressed classes in the central legislature and in the provincial legislature. Admittedly, all of these changes had hardly any effect on the economic conditions of the untouchables, but it did set in motion an important process of transformation at the level of ideology.

LIMITS OF AMBEDKAR'S QUEST FOR LIBERATION

In a limited sense, Ambedkar's conception of equality and justice derive from the liberal vision and tradition. But given the context of the colonial state, he departs from that tradition and innovates thinking about justice in a remarkably novel way. There are three components of Ambedkar's theory of distributive justice:

(a) equality of opportunity for all citizens

(b) critique of Hindu society based on an autonomous ideology, and

(c) establishment of a casteless society by removing oppression and domination.

Ambedkar accepted a legal and social conception of equality, which call the formal principle of a liberal conception of equality. It entails the elimination of arbitrary advantages in a social and economic system, irrespective of whether the inequality results from one's choice or that of another.

What he also found desirable was the idea of equality of opportunity for all human beings in the social and political sphere. It was further linked to his argument for more abundant political and civil liberty for dalits. On his account this requires that any government treat all those in its charge as equals, that is, as entitled to equal concern and respect. This idea of equality of opportunity as an example of the maximisation of equal liberty. In this view, to demand equality of opportunity is to demand the removal of obstacles that stand in the way of an individual realising his potential.

Ambedkar's initial programmes attempt to integrate the dalits into society and politics through 'modern' political institutions. He put his faith in the constitution and the legislative process, as well as the representative bodies to correct social and economic injustice. Ambedkar's ideal for the low caste groups was to raise their educational standard so that they may overcome the social disadvantages imposed by their birth, and be in a position to use political power in resolving problems of injustice. His adaptation of western concepts is reflected in the way he used to justify political rights of the dalits based on democracy, fraternity and liberty, in Marathi speeches; he conveyed the implication of these concepts in a single word, manuski which means 'humanness'.

While Ambedkar saw the prescriptive uses of the concept of equality in moral and political arguments as quite useful, he was conscious of the inequality of treatment based on caste and tradition. To bring about a more substantial equality must involve treating people differently which is contrary to the formal principle. For such reasons he advocated a separatist policy for the dalits which might accentuate caste distinctions at an initial stage but eventually make these identities unimportant. Therefore, Ambedkar insisted on the right to take into account the special claims of certain communities which had for centuries been excluded from position of equality and respect.

Departing fundamentally from the individualist premise of the equality principle he proposes:

(1) A theory of rights as legal entitlements casting obligations on the members of civil society. The 'untouchables' had a set of rights and the state a duty to eradicate discriminatory practices. Norms of nondiscrimination apply not only to government but also to civil society-corporations, schools, places of worship, etc.

Where the rights theorists of the 17th and 18th century tended to regard right as a faculty of possession, Ambedkar encourages us to stress the relational aspect of rights. The important point here is that these rights are put forward as important elements or vital ingredients in a fully realised human life. The core argument is that members of the group suffer because they are neither accorded the same respect nor afforded the same opportunities as other persons or groups. They are prevented from realising their capacities, in other words, they are not treated with full respect and dignity.

(2) The basic human needs of the dalits were not only material (wealth, occupational mobility) but non-material; all have the right to be human and the right to live with dignity and self-respect. Although, he stressed the need for reservation in representative institutions, this is only to acquire equality in other

goods. For such reasons, he extended his theory to cover such goods as self-respect, power and honour.

Therefore, Ambedkar accepted the premise of equality but advocated group-based politics to achieve that goal. The first is constitutive and the second derivative. Ambedkar eloquently pleaded the case the necessary priority of community claims over individual rights on the grounds that these departures from formal equality could be justified in the following way:

The Anti-discriminatory Theme: The anti-discriminatory principle's main purpose is to prevent private practices and legal procedures from stigmatising the individuals involved. This was viewed as necessary given that structural forms of oppression against the dalits were well entrenched. To remedy this social malaise Ambedkar raises the possibilities for political participation of dalits through reservations. It was his view that a legislature 'mainly composed of high caste men, will not pass a law removing untouchability, sanctioning inter-caste marriages, removing the ban of the use of public streets, public temples, public schools.'

The Reparation Theme: The other idea was that of historic injustice suffered by the dalits. This theme was proposed to offset the systematic and cumulative deprivations suffered by lower castes in the past. Ambedkar argues that some oppressive cultural practices and social institutions result in injustice and accumulated disabilities for untouchables.

He was aware of the conceptual incoherence these themes gave rise to when applied to policy issues. But this is a derivative political position. In fact, he was to warn of the possibility that these special claims might eat the general rule of equality altogether. Unlike anyone else, he pursued the argument that "the constitution should not only declare that we shall have specific rights that every community will have, but that the constitution should provide ways and means by which we shall be protected in the exercise of these rights".

The second component of Ambedkar's theory of distributive justice was the construction of an 'autonomous' ideology opposed in fundamental respects to the traditional ideology of varna. The central problem, for him, in this regard was the formulation of a counter-ideology which can bring about radical social change; he was concerned to fight for a new society based on equal concern for all. This is evident from his critique of the Hindu community on the following basis:

(1) the community as unequal;

(2) the community as based on segregation both territorial and ideological;

(3) the closed nature of the community; and

(4) the distinction between the public and private sphere.

The first aspect of his critique was directed at the theory of 'chaturvarnya' which makes the principle of graded inequality 'the basis for determining the terms of associated life as between the four varnas'. This is not merely notional, but legal and penal: under this system the sudra is subjected to innumerable ignominies and disabilities so as to prevent him from raising above the conditions fixed for him by law.

The second aspect draws attention to the permanent segregation of people in the Hindu community based on the ideological principle of purity and impurity. He rejects the territorial segregation which accompanies this. While distinguishing between the rights of untouchables and the pure he raises some fundamental questions of citizenship: "But the impurity of the 50-60 million of the untouchables of India, quite unlike the impurity arising from birth, death, etc., is permanent: The Hindus who touch them and become polluted thereby can become pure by undergoing purificatory ceremonies. But there is nothing which can make the untouchables purer... It is a case of permanent, hereditary stain which nothing can cleanse".

The third aspect of his critique is directed at the nature of closed religious communities without entry points. In 'Mr. Gandhi and the Emancipation of Untouchables' (1945), he points out that the legislative majorities and minorities are political categories which are fluid subject to the process of party formation and electoral practices. But the Hindu and the untouchable relationship cannot be captured by these categories. Their difference is that 'they are separated by a fundamental and deadly antagonism'. Hindus and untouchables are not fluid categories but they are 'fixed as permanent communities'.

He argues against nationalist attempts to define what it means to have equal opportunities - in terms of having the same distribution of results for major social groups in the public shaper. He revealed the inequality in the social sphere arising out of the nature of closed religious communities, because "most people do not realise that society can practise tyranny and oppression against an individual in far greater degree than a government can... What punishment in the penal code is comparable in its magnitude and its severity to excommunication?"

On the basis of these propositions, Ambedkar's solution for the dalits - the establishment of a casteless society - went beyond the liberal framework he was located in.

From a liberal point of view, Ambedkar was arguing for an individual's freedom to associate; to form communities and to live by their own terms based on equal concern. A corollary of this is that the individuals should be free to dissociate from such communities.

Again, his view placed great weight on the nature of communities as voluntary associations. But, since membership is determined by birth in a Hindu community, rather than by deliberate choice, it is a coercive association. There is no option of entry for those born outside-even though groups might seek to redefine their boundaries. While superficially attractive, the liberal view of the self as a totally unencumbered and radically free subject seemed plagued with difficulties.

This eventually led Ambedkar to locate the distinction between a (voluntary) political community within which an individual exercises his legal rights, and a (coercive) cultural community within which individuals could not even formulate their aims. People who have the same rights to citizenship may not have the same cultural rights. A political community, argued Ambedkar, may not be coextensive with one cultural community, as is envisaged by the nation state. For Ambedkar the two forms of community do not always coincide. This distinction leads him to argue that individuals are free to leave-to renounce-membership and to reconstitute their own community. Here Ambedkar was mistaken in his assertions about liberalism's implications: there was no good reason for any liberal to support him in this. But, it is this very justification that inspired him to seek conversion to Buddhism.

In Ambedkar's opinion the transition from British to Hindu masters signified no emancipatory potential for the masses. The fight for a national cause, according to him, misconstrues the role of Swaraj: "In the fight for Swaraj, you fight with the whole nation on your side. In this, you have to fight against the whole nation and that too, on your own... In my opinion, only when the Hindu society becomes a casteless society that it can hope to have strength enough to defend itself. Without such internal strength, Swaraj for Hindus may turn out to be only a step towards slavery."

It is this total programme of societal transformation which constituted his conception of Swaraj. Swaraj was not just freedom from the British, it was a freedom based on distributive justice.

Ambedkar's critical dialogue with some Congress leaders and his struggles to reform Hindu society occurred within a colonial context. His struggle is not with faith but with false brahmanical beliefs, not with religion but with Brahmin domination of Indian society. He portrays the nature of the caste system in our society in particular using it to show that Hinduism was incapable of establishing a just political and social order. His view differed from other nationalist leaders and social reformers in that he never claimed higher caste status for untouchables, nor did he ever invoke another claim - that untouchables were pre-Aryan, the original settlers of the land or claimed spiritual equality for lower castes within the Hindu tradition. And most importantly his reforms were not directed towards the caste- Hindus. Unlike other critiques of Brahmin domination and caste hierarchy which focus on the unity argument, Ambedkar's critique provides a justice argument against the caste system.

Most nationalists argued that their country was fragmented, deeply divided into a large number of castes, sub-castes and local communities; that is why the Hindus had failed to develop a sense of mutual concern and social compassion. Ambedkar's theory of caste oppression focuses not only the distributive paradigm (allocation of material goods such as resources, income, wealth or the distribution of social positions, such as jobs) as many contemporary liberal theories do, but also brings out the issues of decision-making (representative institutions for the dalits) division of labour (occupational mobility), and culture that bear on distributive justice but were often ignored in national assessments of their social structure.

This argument was premised on two views:

(a) the problems of dalits would always have a particularity that could not be subsumed under class or national mobilisation;

(b) the status of the dalits was 'irreversible' if they remained isolated within Hinduism. Therefore, he formulated Dalit liberation in terms of two solutions-political assertion through separate electorates and ideological liberation from Hinduism by converting to Buddhism.

Unfortunately, the very cogency and persuasiveness of his arguments raise questions as to the broader contours of his thesis. Dissatisfied with the dominant proposals for the reform of the caste system, Ambedkar undertakes a recovery of Buddhism as a religion that relates to individuals with dignity and respect.

However, Ambedkar's point that Buddhism provides the needed theoretical framework to understand Indian politics has its weaknesses. Indeed, by spending considerable energy exploring key conceptions in Buddhism such as Ahimsa, rebirth, karma, etc., Ambedkar leaves us wondering how helpful Buddhism is if the terminology is so open to interpretation.

Behind this solution lay the laudable ideal that responsibility for removing group identity status lies with the dalits themselves, not with the larger dominant society. But it is an explanation that completely ignores the pernicious effects of casteism in the Indian social fabric.

On the flip side, Ambedkar's 'self-help' ideology perpetuates the mythical notion of a 'monolithic' Dalit community which made it possible for them to confront other parties. But this political legitimisation also pre-empts questions of interest differentiation among the dalits.

This takes us to my final observations. All this is not to deny that in his critique of the caste system, Ambedkar is clearly arguing for expanding the rights of citizenship to the 'untouchables'. At a more substantive level he is pushing the case for a casteless society without oppression. How was this possible in practical politics?

These two perspectives are contradictory if the objectives they focus upon - the promotion of political and social equality, the abolition of the caste system - are conceived as aims in themselves.

But unlike the abolition of the caste system, in Ambedkar's writings, that liberal politics with their emphasis on rights, equality of concern and respect, or freedom to associate can sensibly be defended as more than an instrumental objective. He believed that the more an individual's rights are restricted due to his caste location-for example by constricting the mobility in occupation, of residence, of religion, etc.-the less possibility is there of social and distributive justice.

The principles underlying the caste system unlock the mystery to the inegalitarian distributive outcomes in other spheres. It is an important consideration and one that plays a key role in what is regarded as the only cogent justification for removing caste system in Ambedkar's work.

He poses the question whether separation, in some fashion, from the larger body politic, may produce more tangible results than have previous strategies (Gandhi's and Shinde's) aimed at integrating them into the system. Hence, his arguments for separate electorates for dalits should be seen as derivative; equal opportunity in liberal politics was not his ultimate goal. In fact, he wishes to achieve much more.

In the most general sense, the Dalit community is reconstructed by analysing the structural antagonism and conflict within the Hindu community: the idea of shared meanings, of normative frames and cultural values is questioned. By developing a theory of oppression of the untouchables by locating their exploitation, marginalisation and powerlessness, he highlights the structural and institutional relations that delimit the lives of the dalits. He also gives prominence to their cultural oppression which means how the dominant meanings of our society stereotype one group.

Ambedkar always thought his account of the role of caste system and its ultimate demise was superior to any other. And as history has shown, he was too optimistic in his predictions and not clear enough in this vision. However, mistaken he was in this analysis and however short-sighted he might appear to many scholars, with respect to the discourse of nationalism, the chief application of Ambedkar's political thought may be seen today to reside in his reflections on social and distributive justice. The subsequent course of Indian politics was to prove him correct; it was not the nation state but its opposite, - irreconcilable political clashes between religious communities and caste-wars that would become the order of the day.

5

PHILOSOPHY OF HINDUISM AND BUDDHISM

INTRODUCTION

Inequality is the soul of Hinduism. To the Untouchables, Hinduism is a veritable chamber of horrors. The iron law of caste, the heartless law of karma and the senseless law of status by birth are veritable instruments of torture, which Hinduism has forged against the Untouchables.

Hinduism and Buddhism: There is a great difference between Buddhism and Hinduism. Buddhism means casteless society based on equal rights. Hinduism on the other hand is primarily based on caste system; a system which encourages aloofness, inequality and exploitation.

Unlike Hinduism, Buddhism lays no emphasis on the attainment of heaven. Nor it is necessary. To be happy in the present life, one should practice the ethics of morality, non violence (ahimsa), equality and universal brotherhood. This is an eternal truth taught by the Buddha. It is quite wrong to hold that man is not a factor in the making of history. Man is necessary to rub two pieces of flint to make fire. Man is a factor in the making of history and the environmental forces, whether impersonal or social, if they are, they are the first and not the last things.

Achievements: Nothing valuable in this world is achieved except by great efforts. All great things in the world were achieved by patient industry and by undergoing toil and tribulations.

Ahimsa: Ahımsa Permo Dharma is an extreme Doctrine. It is a Jaina Doctrine. It is not Buddhist Doctrine. Buddha meant to make a distinction between 'will to kill' and 'need to kill'. What he banned was killing where there was nothing but the will to kill. Buddha made a distinction between principle and Rule. He did not make Ahimsa a matter of Rule. He enunciated it as a matter of \Principle or way of life. A Principle leaves you freedom to act. A rule does not. Rule either breaks you or you break the rule.

Ambition: One should always cherish some ambition to do something in the world. They alone rise who strive.

Anarchy: In anarchy and dictatorship, liberty is lost.

Appeasement: Appeasement means buying off the aggressor by conniving at his acts of murder, arson and loot against innocent victims of his displeasure. Appeasement sets no limits to the demands and aspirations of the aggressor.

Army: The ultimate guarantee of the independence of a country is a safe army-an army on which you can rely to fight for the country at all times and in any eventuality. A safe army is better than a safe border.

Back to Nature: The call of back to nature means back to nakedness, back to squalor, back to poverty and back to ignorance for the vast mass of people.

Buddhism: I prefer Buddhism because it gives three principles in combination, which no other religion does. Buddhism teaches Prajna (understanding as against superstition and supernaturalism), Karuna (love), and Samata (equality). This is what man wants for a good and happy life.

Buddhist Culture: Even though Buddhism is almost extinct in India, yet it has given birth to a culture, which is far better and richer than the Brahminic culture. When the question of the National Flag and the National Emblem was being considered by the Constituent Assembly we could not find any suitable symbol from the Brahminic culture. Ultimately, the Buddhist culture came to our rescue and we accepted the Wheel of Law (Dhamma-Chakra) as the National Symbol.

Caste and Class: Caste System is not merely a division of labour. It is also a division of labourers. It is an hierarchy in which the divisions of labourers are graded one above the other.

Caste has killed public spirit. Caste has destroyed the sense of public charity. Caste has made public opinion impossible. Virtue has become caste ridden and morality has become caste bound. There is no sympathy to the deserving. There is no appreciation of the meritorious. There cannot be a more degrading system of social organisation than the Chaturvarna. It is the system which deadens, paralyses and cripples the people from helpful activity. Caste in the hands of the orthodox has been a powerful weapon for persecuting the reforms and for killing all reform.

These castes are anti-national. In the first place because they bring about separation in social life. They are anti-national also because they generate jealousy and antipathy between caste and caste.

The Caste system is a system which is infested with the spirit of isolation and in fact it makes isolation of one Caste from another a virtue. There is isolation in the class system. But it does not make isolation virtue nor does it prohibit social intercourse. The class system, it is true produces groups, but they are not akin to Caste groups. The groups in the class system are only non-social while the Castes in the Castes system are in their mutual relations definitively and positively antisocial.

Practically speaking, in a class structure, there is on the one hand, tyranny, vanity, pride, arrogance, greed selfishness and on the other insecurity, poverty, degradation, loss of liberty, self reliance, independence dignity and self-respect. The group setup prevents an individual from acquiring consistency of mind, which is possible only when society has common ideals, common models.

The group setup leads to stratification of classes. Those who are masters remain masters and those who are born in slavery remain slaves. Owners remain owners and workers remain workers. The privileged remain privileged and the serfs remain serfs.

Constitution: I feel that the Constitution is workable; it is flexible and it is strong enough to hold the country together both in peacetime and in wartime. Indeed, if I may say so, if things go wrong under the new constitution the reason will not be that we had a bad Constitution. What we will have to say is that Man was vile.

Courage: The secret of freedom is courage and courage is born in combination of individuals into a party.

Culture: It is true that man shares the constitution and functions of animals, nutritive, reproductive etc. But these are not distinctively human functions. The distinctively human function is reason, the purpose of which is to enable man to observe, meditate, cogitate, study and discover the beauties of the universe and enrich his life and control the animal elements in his life.

What divides the brute from man is culture. Culture is not possible for the brute but it is essential for man.

The aim of human society must be to enable every person to lead a life of culture which means the cultivation of the mind as distinguished from the satisfaction of mere physical wants.

While the ultimate goal of a brute's life is reached once his physical appetites are satisfied, the ultimate goal of a man's existence is not reached unless and until he has fully cultivated his mind.

Democracy: Political Democracy rests on four premises which may be set out in the following terms: (i) The individual is an end in himself. (ii) That the individual has certain inalienable rights, which must be guaranteed to him by the Constitution. (iii) That the individual shall not be required to relinquish any of his constitutional rights as a precondition precedent to the receipt of a privilege. (iv) That the State shall not delegate powers to private persons to govern others.

The soul of Democracy is the doctrine of one man, one value. Democracy is a form and method of government whereby revolutionary changes in the economic and social life of the people are brought about without bloodshed. Democracy is not merely a form of Government. It is primarily a mode of associated living of conjoined communicated experience. It is essentially an attitude of respect and reverence towards fellowmen. Democracy is incompatible and inconsistent with isolation and exclusiveness, resulting in the distinction between the privileged and the unprivileged. Democracy cannot work without friction unless there is fellow feeling among those who constitute the State.

The first thing required for the successful working of democracy is that there must be no glaring inequalities and there must be neither an oppressed class nor a suppressed class. The second thing required is the existence of opposition to show whether the Govt. is going wrong.

The third thing is equality before law and in administration. The fourth is the observance of constitutional morality. The fifth point is the functioning of moral order in society, for moral is taken for granted in the democracy. The sixth thing is the requirement of public conscience. A democratic Government can remain democratic only if it is worked by two parties? a party in power and a party in opposition.

Despotism: To have popular government run by a single party is to let democracy become a mere form for despotism to play its part from behind it. Despotism does not cease to be despotism because it is elective. Nor does despotism become agreeable because despots belong to our own kindred.

Dhamma: According to the Buddha, Dhamma consists of Prajna and Karuna. Prajna is understanding. The Buddha made Prajna one of the two comer stones of His Dhamma because he did not wish to leave any room for superstition. Karuna is love. Because, without it society can neither live nor grow, that is why the Buddha made it the second cornerstone of his Dhamma. A unique amalgam of Prajna and Karuna is the Dhamma of the Buddha. In Dhamma there is no place for prayers, pilgrimages, rituals, ceremonies or sacrifices. Dhamma is righteousness, which means right relations between man and man in all sphere of life.

Duty: Blessed are those who are awakened to their duty to those among whom they are born. The duty must be performed; let the efforts be successful or not; let the work be appreciated or not. When a man's sincerity of purpose and capacity are proved even his enemies come to respect him.

Education: Give up the idea that parents give 'Janma' to the child and not destiny (karma). They can mould the destiny of their children by giving them education. Knowledge is the foundation of a man's life. Education is as necessary for females as it is for males. If one's education is detrimental to the welfare of the poor, the educated man is a curse to the society. Character is more important than education.

Ethics and Economics: History shows that where ethics and economics come in conflict, victory is always with economics. Vested interests have never been known to have willingly divested themselves unless there was sufficient force to compel them.

Equality: Equality may be a fiction but nonetheless one must accept it as a governing principle.

Fate: Do not believe in fate. Believe in your strength.

Force: Force, it cannot be denied, is the medicine of the body politic and must be administered when the body politic becomes sick. But just because force is the medicine of the body politic, it cannot be allowed to become its daily bread.

Fraternity: Fraternity is the name for the disposition of an individual to treat men as the object of reverence and love and the desire to be in unity with his fellow beings.

Freedom: Freedom of the nation, if it is to be a reality, must vouchsafe the freedom of the different classes comprised in it, particularly of those who are treated as the servile classes.

Glory: Glory to those who devote their time, talents and their all to the annihilation of slavery. Glory to those who would keep on their struggle for the liberation of the enslaved in spite of heavy odds, carping humiliations, storms and dangers till the down trodden secure their human rights.

Great Man: A great man must be motivated by the dynamics of a social purpose and must act as the scourge and the scavenger of the society.

Happiness: Poverty gives rise to sorrow. But removal of poverty does not necessarily give rise to happiness. Not high standard of living but a standard of culture is what gives happiness.

Hero-worship: Bhakti (hero-worship) in religion may be a road to salvation of the self. But in politics, bhakti or hero-worship is a sure road to degradation and to eventual dictatorship. Hero-worship in the sense of expressing our unbounded admiration is one thing. To obey the hero is a totally different kind of hero worship. There is nothing wrong in the former while the latter is no doubt a most pernicious thing. The former is only man's respect for everything which is noble and of which the Great Man is only an embodiment. The former is consistent with respect, but the latter is a sign of debasement.

PHILOSOPHY OF HINDUISM

What is the philosophy of Hinduism? This is a question which arises in its logical sequence. But apart from its logical sequence its importance is such that it can never be omitted from consideration. Without it no one can understand the aims and ideals of Hinduism. It is obvious that such a study must be preceded by a certain amount of what may be called clearing of the ground and defining of the terms involved.

At the outset it may be asked what does this proposed title comprehend? Is this title of the Philosophy of Hinduism of the same nature as that of the Philosophy of Religion? One does not have a clear idea of what is meant by Philosophy of Religion. This is probably due to two facts. In the first place while religion is something definite, there is nothing definite as to what is to be included in the term philosophy. In the second place Philosophy and Religion have been adversaries if not actual antagonists as may be seen from the story of the philosopher and the theologian.

According to the story, the two were engaged in disputation and the theologian accused the philosopher that he was "like a blind man in a dark room, looking for a black cat which was not there". In reply the philosopher charged the theologian saying that "he was like a blind man in the dark room, looking for a black cat which was not there but he declared to have found there". Perhaps it is the unhappy choice of the title - Philosophy of Religion-which is responsible for causing confusion in the matter of the exact definition of its field. The nearest approach to an intelligible statement as to the exact subject matter of Philosophy of Religion can be perhaps in Prof. Pringle-Pattison who observes:

> "A few words may be useful at the outset as an indication of what we commonly mean by the Philosophy of Religion. Plato described philosophy long ago as the synoptic view of things. That is to say, it is the attempt to see things together-to keep all the main features of the world in view, and to grasp them in their relation to one another as parts of one whole. Only thus can we acquire a sense of proportion and estimate aright the significance of any particular range of facts for our ultimate conclusions about the nature of the world-process and the world-ground. Accordingly, the philosophy of any particular department of experience, the Philosophy of Religion, the Philosophy of Art, the Philosophy of Law, is to be taken as meaning an analysis and interpretation of the experience in question in its bearing upon our view of man and the world in which he lives. And when the facts upon which we concentrate are so universal, and in their nature so remarkable, as those disclosed by the history of religion-the philosophy of man's religious experience-cannot but exercise a determining influence upon our general philosophical conclusions. In fact with many writers the particular discussion tends to merge in the more general."
>
> "The facts with which a philosophy of religion has to deal are supplied by the history of religion, in the most comprehensive sense of that term. As Tiele puts it, "all religions of the civilised and uncivilised world, dead and living", is a 'historical and psychological phenomenon' in all its manifestations. These facts, it should be noted, constitute the data of the philosophy of religion; they do not themselves constitute a 'philosophy' or, in Tiele's use of the term, a 'science' of religion. 'If, he says, I have minutely described all the religions in existence, their doctrines, myths and customs, the observances they inculcate, and the

organisation of their adherents, tracing the different religions from their origin to their bloom and decay, I have merely.

Collected the materials with which the science of religion works'. 'The historical record, however complete, is not enough; pure history is not philosophy. To achieve a philosophy of religion we should be able to discover in the varied manifestations a common principle to whose roots in human nature we can point, whose evolution we can trace by intelligible-stages from lower to higher and more adequate forms, as well as its intimate relations with the other main factors in human civilisation".

If this is Philosophy of Religion it then it is merely a different name for that department of study, which is called comparative religion with the added aim of discovering a common principle in the varied manifestations of religion. Whatever be the scope and value of such a study, the title Philosophy of Religion to denote something quite different from the sense and aim given to it by Prof. Pringle-Pattison.

It meant teachings as it did when people spoke of the philosophy of Socrates or the philosophy of Plato. In another sense it meant critical reason used in passing judgements upon things and events. Proceeding on this basis Philosophy of Religion is not a merely descriptive science. But should be regarded as being both descriptive as well as normative. In so far as it deals with the teachings of a Religion, Philosophy of Religion becomes a descriptive science.

A study of the Philosophy of Religion me involves the determination of three dimensions. They are like the unknown quantities contained as factors in a product. One must ascertain and define these dimensions of the Philosophy of Religion if an examination of it is to be fruitful.

Of the three dimensions, Religion is the first. One must therefore define what he understands by religion in order to avoid argument being directed at cross-purposes. This is particularly necessary in the case of Religion for the reason that there is no agreement as to its exact definition. This is no place to enter upon an elaborate consideration of this question.

The word Religion is being used to mean Theology. This will perhaps be insufficient for the purposes of definition. For there are different kinds of Theologies. Historically there have been two Theologies spoken of from ancient times. Mythical theology and Civil theology. The Greeks who distinguished them gave each a definite content. By Mythical theology they meant the tales of gods and their doings told in or implied by current imaginative literature.

Civil theology according to them consisted of the knowledge of the various feasts and fasts of the State Calendar and the ritual appropriate to them. Here it means theology natural theology which is-the doctrine of God and the divine, as an integral part of the theory of nature. As traditionally understood there are three thesis which 'natural theology' propounds. (1) That God exists and is the author of what we call nature or universe (2) That God controls all the events which make nature and (3) God exercises a government over mankind in accordance with his sovereign moral law.

As Revealed Theology-spontaneous self disclosure of divine reality-which may be distinguished from Natural theology. But this distinction does not really matter. For as has been pointed out that a revelation may either "leave the results won by Natural theology standing without modifications, merely supplementing them by further knowledge not attainable by unassisted human effort" or it "may transform Natural theology in such a way that all the truths of natural theology would acquire richer and deeper meaning when seen in the light of a true revelation." But the view that a genuine natural theology and a genuine revelation theology might stand in real contradiction may be safely excluded as not being possible.

Taking the three thesis of theology namely: (1) the existence of God, (2) God's providential government of the universe and (3) God's moral government of mankind, Religion to mean the propounding of an ideal scheme of divine governance the aim and object of which is to make the social order in which men live a moral order. This is what one understand by Religion and this is the sense in which shall be used "The Term Religion".

The traditional usage of religion had grown up gradually in the course of many centuries, and reflected habits of thought, characteristic of very diverse stages of man's intellectual and moral development. No conception of the nature of the gods could possibly afford the clue to all parts of that motley complex of rites and ceremonies which the later paganism had received by inheritance, from a series of ancestors in every state of culture from pure savagery upwards. The record of the religious thought of mankind, as it is embodied in religious institutions, resembles the geological record of the history of the earth's crust; the new and the old are preserved side by side, or rather layer upon layer.

We have seen a religion growing up from stage to stage, from the simplest childish prayers to the highest metaphysical abstractions. In the majority of the hymns of the Veda we might recognise the childhood; in the Brahmanas and their sacrificial, domestic and moral ordinances the busy manhood; in the Upanishads the old age of the Vedic religion. We could have well understood if, with the historical progress of the Indian mind, they had discarded the purely childish prayers as soon as they had arrived at the maturity of the Brahamans; and if, when the vanity of sacrifices and the real character of the old god's had once been recognised, they would have been superseded by the more exalted religion of the Upanishads.

But it was not so. Every religious thought that had once found expression in India that had once been handed down as a sacred heirloom was preserved, and the thoughts of the three historical periods, the childhood, the manhood, and the old age of the Indian nation, were made to do permanent service in the three stages of the life of every individual. Thus alone can we explain how the same sacred code, the Veda, contains not only the records of different phases of religious thought, but of doctrines which we may call almost diametrically opposed to each other.

But this difficulty is not so great in the case of Religions which are positive religions. The fundamental characteristic of positive Religions, is that they have not grown up like primitive religions, under the action of unconscious forces operating silently from age to age, but trace their origin to the teaching of great religious innovators, who spoke as the organs of a divine revelation. Being the result of conscious formulations the philosophy of a religion which is positive is easy to find and easy to state. Hinduism like Judaism, Christianity and Islam is in the main a positive religion. One does not have to search for its scheme of divine governance. It is not like an unwritten constitution. On the Hindu scheme of divine governance is enshrined in a written constitution and any one who cares to know it will find it laid bare in that Sacred Book called the Manusmriti, a divine Code which lays down the rules which govern the religious, ritualistic and social life of the Hindus in minute detail and which must be regarded as the Bible of the Hindus and containing the philosophy of Hinduism.

The third dimension in the philosophy of religion is the criterion to be adopted for judging the value of the ideal scheme of divine governance for which a given Religion stands. Religion must be put on its trial. By what criterion shall it be judged? That leads to the definition of the norm. Of the three dimensions this third one is the most difficult one to be ascertained and defined.

Unfortunately the question does not appear to have been tackled although much has been written on the philosophy of Religion and certainly no method has been found for satisfactorily dealing with the problem. One is left to one's own method for determining the issue.

It is safe to proceed on the view that to know the philosophy of any movement or any institution one must study the revolutions which the movement or the institution has undergone. Revolution is the mother of philosophy and if it is not the mother of philosophy it is a lamp which illuminates philosophy. Religion is no exception to this rule. Therefore it seems quite evident that the best method to ascertain the criterion by which to judge the philosophy of Religion is to study the Revolutions which religion has undergone.

Students of History are familiar with one Religious Revolution. That Revolution was concerned with the sphere of Religion and the extent of its authority. There was a time when Religion had covered the whole field of human knowledge and claimed infallibility for what it taught. It covered astronomy and taught a theory of the universe according to which the earth is at rest in the centre of the universe, while the sun, moon, planets and system of fixed stars revolve round it each in its own sphere.

It included biology and geology and propounded the view that the growth of life on the earth had been created all at once and had contained from the time of creation onwards, all the heavenly bodies that it now contains and all kinds of animals of plants. It claimed medicine to be its province and taught that disease was either a divine visitation as punishment for sin or it was the work of demons and that it could be cured by the intervention of saints, either in person or through their holy relics; or by prayers or pilgrimages; or (when due to demons) by exorcism and by treatment which the demons (and the patient) found disgusting. It also claimed physiology and psychology to be its domain and taught that the body and soul were two distinct substances.

Bit by bit this vast Empire of Religion was destroyed. The Copernican Revolution freed astronomy from the domination of Religion. The Darwinian Revolution freed biology and geology from the trammels of Religion. The authority of theology in medicine is not yet completely destroyed. Its intervention in medical questions still continues. Opinion on such subjects as birth control, abortion and sterilisation of the defective are still influenced by theological dogmas. Psychology has not completely freed itself from its entanglements. None the less Darwinism was such a severe blow that the authority of theology was shattered all over to such an extent that it never afterwards made any serious effort to remain its lost empire.

It is quite natural that this disruption of the Empire of Religion should be treated as a great Revolution. It is the result of the warfare which science waged against theology for 400 years, in which many pitched battles were fought between the two and the excitement caused by them was so great that nobody could fail to be impressed by the revolution that was blazing on. There is no doubt that this religious revolution has been a great blessing. It has established freedom of thought.

It has enabled society "to assume control of itself, making its own the world it once shared with superstition, facing undaunted the things of its former fears, and so carving out for itself, from the realm of mystery in which it lies, a sphere of unhampered action and a field of independent thought". The process of secularisation is not only welcomed by scientists for making civilisation-as distinguished from culture-possible, even Religious men and women have come to feel that much of what theology taught was unnecessary and a mere hindrance to the religious life and that this chopping of its wild growth was a welcome process.

But for ascertaining the norm for judging the philosophy of Religion we must turn to another and a different kind of Revolution which Religion has undergone. That Revolution touches the nature and content of ruling conceptions of the relations of God to man, of Society to man and of man to man. How great this revolution was can be seen from the differences which divide savage society from civilized society.

Strange as it may seem no systematic study of this Religious Revolution has so far been made. None the less this Revolution is so great and so immense that it has brought about a complete transformation in the nature of Religion as it is taken to be by savage society and by civilised society although very few seem to be aware of it.

To begin with the comparison between savage society and civilised society. In the religion of the savage one is struck by the presence of two things. First is the performance of rites and ceremonies, the practice of magic or tabu and the worship of fetish or totem. The second thing that is noticeable is that the rites, ceremonies, magic, tabu, totem and fetish are conspicuous by their connection with certain occasions. These occasions are chiefly those, which represent the crises of human life. The events such as birth, the birth of the first born, attaining manhood, reaching puberty, marriage, sickness, death and war are the usual occasions which are marked out for the performance of rites and ceremonies, the use of magic and the worship of the totem.

Students of the origin and history of Religion have sought to explain the origin and substance of religion by reference to either magic, tabu and totem and the rites and ceremonies connected therewith, and have deemed the occasions with which they are connected as of no account. Consequently we have theories explaining religion as having arisen in magic or as having arisen in fetishism. Nothing can be a greater error than this.

It is true that savage society practices magic, believes in tabu and worships the totem. But it is wrong to suppose that these constitute the religion or form the source of religion. To take such a view is to elevate what is incidental to the position of the principal. The principal thing in the Religion of the savage are the elemental facts of human existence such as life, death, birth, marriage etc. Magic, tabu, totem are things which are incidental. Magic, tabu, totem, fetish etc., are not the ends. They are only the means.

The end is life and the preservation of life. Magic, tabu etc., are resorted to by the savage society not for their own sake but to conserve life and to exercise evil influences from doing harm to life.

Thus understood the religion of the savage society was concerned with life and the preservation of life and it is these life processes which constitute the substance and source of the religion of the savage society.

So great was the concern of the savage society for life and the preservation of life that it made them the basis of its religion. So central were the life processes in the religion of the savage society that everything, which affected them, became part of its religion. The ceremonies of the savage society were not only concerned with the events of birth, attaining of manhood, puberty, marriage, sickness, death and war they were also concerned with food. Among pastoral peoples the flocks and herds are sacred.

Among agricultural peoples seedtime and harvest are marked by ceremonials performed with some reference to the growth and the preservation of the crops. Likewise drought, pestilence, and other strange, irregular phenomena of nature occasion the performance of ceremonials. Why should such occasions as harvest and famine be accompanied by religious ceremonies? Why is magic, tabu, totem be of such importance to the savage.

The only answer is that they all affect the preservation of life. The process of life and its preservation form the main purpose. Life and preservation of life is the core and centre of the Religion of the savage society. As pointed out by Prof. Crawley the religion of the savage begins and ends with the affirmation and conservation of life.

In life and preservation of life consists the religion of the savage. What is however true of the religion of the savage is true of all religions wherever they are found for the simple reason that constitutes the essence of religion. It is true that in the present day society with its theological refinements this essence of religion has become hidden from view and is even forgotten. But that life and the preservation of life constitute the essence of religion even in the present day society is beyond question. This is well illustrated by Prof. Crowley. When speaking of the religious life of man in the present day society, he says how:

> "A man's religion does not enter into his professional or social hours, his scientific or artistic moments; practically its chief claims are settled on one day in the week from which ordinary worldly concerns are excluded. In fact, his life is in two parts; but the moiety with which religion is concerned is the elemental. Serious thinking on ultimate questions of life and death is, roughly speaking, the essence of his Sabbath; add to this the habit of prayer, giving the thanks at meals, and the subconscious feeling that birth and death, continuation and marriage are rightly solemnised by religion, while business and pleasure may possibly be consecrated, but only metaphorically or by an overflow of religious feeling."

Comparing this description of the religious concerns of the man in the present day society with that of the savage, who can deny that the religion is essentially the same, both in theory and practice whether one speaks of the religion of the savage society or of the civilised society.

It is therefore clear that savage and civilised societies agree in one respect. In both the central interests of religion-namely in the life processes by which individuals are preserved and the race maintained-are the same. In this there is no real difference between the two. But they differ in two other important respects. In the first place in the religion of the savage society there is no trace of the idea of God. In the second place in the religion of the savage society there is no bond between morality and Religion. In the savage society there is religion without God. In the savage society there is morality but it is independent of Religion.

How and when the idea of God became fused in Religion it is not possible to say. It may be that the idea of God had its origin in the worship of the Great Man in Society, the Hero-giving rise to theism-with its faith in its living God. It may be that the idea of God came into existence as a result of the purely philosophical speculation upon the problem as to who created life-giving rise to Deism-with its belief in God as Architect of the Universe. In any case the idea of God is not integral to Religion. How it got fused into Religion it is difficult to explain. With regard to the relation between Religion and Morality this much may be safely said. Though the relation between God and Religion is not quite integral, the relation between Religion and morality is. Both religion and morality are connected with the same elemental facts of human existence-namely life, death, birth and marriage. Religion consecrates these life processes while morality furnishes rules for their preservation.

Religion in consecrating the elemental facts and processes of life came to consecrate also the rules laid down by Society for their preservation. Looked at from this point it is easily explained why the bond between Religion and Morality took place. It was more intimate and more natural than the bond between Religion and God. But when exactly this fusion between Religion and Morality took place it is not easy to say. Be that as it may, the fact remains that the religion of the Civilised Society differs from that of the Savage Society into two important features. In civilised society God comes in the scheme of Religion. In civilised society morality becomes sanctified by Religion.

This is the first stage in the Religious Revolution. This Religious Revolution must not be supposed to have been ended here with the emergence of these two new features in the development of religion. The two ideas having become part of the constitution of the Religion of the Civilised Society have undergone further changes which have revolutionized their meaning and their moral significance. The second stage of the Religious Revolution marks a very radical change. The contrast is so big that civilized society has become split into two, antique society and modern society, so that instead of speaking of the religion of the civilised society it becomes necessary to speak of the religion of antique society as against the religion of modern society.

The religious revolution, which marks off antique society from modern society, is far greater than the religious revolution, which divides savage society from civilised society. Its dimensions will be obvious from the differences it has brought about in the conceptions regarding the relations between God, Society and Man. The first point of difference relates to the composition of society. Every human being, without choice on his own part, but simply in virtue of his birth and upbringing, becomes a member of what we call a natural society. He belongs that is to a certain family and a certain nation. This membership lays upon him definite obligations and duties which he is called upon to fulfil as a matter of course and on pain of social penalties and disabilities while at the same time it confers upon him certain social rights and advantages. In this respect the ancient and modern worlds are alike. But in the words of Prof. Smith:

> "There is this important difference, that the tribal or national societies of the ancient world were not strictly natural in the modern sense of the word, for the gods had their part and place in them equally with men. The circle into which a man was born was not simply a group of kinsfolk and fellow citizens, but embraced also certain divine beings, the gods of the family and of the state, which to the ancient mind were as much a part of the particular community with which they stood connected as the human members of the social circle. The relation between the gods of antiquity and their worshippers was expressed in the language of human relationship, and this language was not taken in a figurative sense but with strict literally. If a god

> was spoken of as father and his worshippers as his offspring, the meaning was that the worshippers were literally of his stock, that he and they made up one natural family with reciprocal family duties to one another. Or, again, if the god was addressed as king, and worshippers called themselves his servants, they meant that the supreme guidance of the state was actually in his hands, and accordingly the organisation of the state included provision for consulting his will and obtaining his direction in all weighty matters, also provision for approaching him as king with due homage and tribute.
>
> "Thus a man was born into a fixed relation to certain gods as surely as he was born into relation to his fellow men; and his religion, that is, the part of conduct which was determined by his relation to the gods, was simply one side of the general scheme of conduct prescribed for him by his position as a member of society. There was no separation between the spheres of religion and of ordinary life. Every social act had a reference to the gods as well as to men, for the social body was not made up of men only, but of gods and men."

Thus in ancient Society men and their Gods formed a social and political as well as a religious whole. Religion was founded on kinship between the God and his worshippers. Modern Society has eliminated God from its composition. It consists of men only.

The second point of difference between antique and modern society relates to the bond between God and Society. In the antique world the various communities "believed in the existence of many Gods, for they accepted as real the Gods of their enemies as well as their own, but they did not worship the strange Gods from whom they had no favour to expect, and on whom their gifts and offerings would have been thrown away. Each group had its own God, or perhaps a God and Goddess, to whom the other Gods bore no relation whatever."

The God of the antique society was an exclusive God. God was owned by and bound to one singly community. This is largely to be accounted for by "the share taken by the Gods in the feuds and wars of their worshippers. The enemies of the God and the enemies of his people are identical; even in the Old Testament `the enemies of Jehovah' are originally nothing else than the enemies of Israel. In battle each God fights for his own people, and to his aid success is ascribed; Chemosh gives victory to Moab and Asshyr to Assyria; and often the divine image or symbol accompanies the host to battle. When the ark was brought into the camp of Israel, the Philistines said, "Gods are come into the camp; who can deliver us from their own practice, for when David defeated them at Baalperazirm, part of the booty consisted in their idols which had been carried into the field.

When the Carthaginians, in their treaty with Phillip of Macedon, speak of "the Gods that take part in the campaign," they doubtless refer to the inmates of the sacred tent which was pitched in time of war beside the tent of the general, and before which prisoners were sacrificed after a victory. Similarly an Arabic poet says, "Yaguth went forth with us against Morad"; that is, the image of the God Yaguth was carried into the fray". This fact had produced solidarity between God and the community.

> "Hence, on the principle of solidarity between Gods and their worshippers, the particularism characteristic of political society could not but reappear in the sphere of religion. In the same measure as the God of a clan or town had indisputable claim to the reverence and service of the community to which he belonged, he was necessarily an enemy to their enemies and a stranger to those to whom they were strangers".

God had become attached to a community, and the community had become attached to their God. God had become the God of the Community and the Community had become the chosen community of the God.

This view had two consequences. Antique Society never came to conceive that God could be universal God, the God of all. Antique Society never could conceive that there was any such thing as humanity in general.

The third point of difference between ancient and modern society, has reference to the conception of the fatherhood of God. In the antique Society God was the Father of his people but the basis of this conception of Fatherhood was deemed to be physical.

"In heathen religions the Fatherhood of the Gods is physical fatherhood. Among the Greeks, for example, the idea that the Gods fashioned men out of clay, as potters fashion images, is relatively modern. The older conception is that the races of men have Gods for their ancestors, or are the children of the earth, the common mother of Gods and men, so that men are really of the stock or kin of the Gods.

That the same conception was familiar to the older Semites appears from the Bible. Jeremiah describes idolaters as saying to a stock, Thou art my father; and to a stone, Thou has brought me forth. In the ancient poem, Num. xxi. 29, The Moabites are called the sons and daughters of Chemosh, and at a much more recent date the prophet Malachi calls a heathen woman "the daughter of a strange God". These phrases are doubtless accommodations to the language, which the heathen neighbours of Israel used about themselves. In Syria and Palestine each clan, or even complex of clans forming a small independent people, traced back its origin to a great first father; and they indicate that, just as in Greece this father or progenitor of the race was commonly identified with the God of the race. With this it accords that in the judgment of most modern enquirers several names of deities appear in the old genealogies of nations in the Book of Genesis.

Edom, for example, the progenitor of the Edomites, was identified by the Hebrews with Esau the brother of Jacob, but to the heathen he was a God, as appears from the theophorous proper name Obededom, "worshipper of Edom", the extant fragments of Phoenician and Babylonian cosmogonies date from a time when tribal religion and the connection of individual Gods with particular kindreds was forgotten or had fallen into the background. But in a generalized form the notion that men are the offspring of the Gods still held its ground. In the

Phoenician cosmogony of Philo Bablius it does so in a confused shape, due to the authors euhemerism, that is, to his theory that deities are nothing more than deified men who had been great benefactors to their species.

Again, in the Chaldaean legend preserved by Berosus, the belief that men are of the blood of the Gods is expressed in a form too crude not to be very ancient; for animals as well as men are said to have been formed out of clay mingled with the blood of a decapitated deity." This conception of blood kinship of Gods and men had one important consequence. To the antique world God was a human being and as such was not capable of absolute virtue and absolute goodness. God shared the physical nature of man and was afflicted with the passions infirmities and vices to which man was subject. The God of the antique world had all the wants and appetites of man and he often indulged in the vices in which many revelled. Worshipers had to implore God not to lead them into temptations.

In modern Society the idea of divine fatherhood has become entirely dissociated from the physical basis of natural fatherhood. In its place man is conceived to be created in the image of God; he is not deemed to be begotten by God. This change in the conception of the fatherhood of God looked at from its moral aspect has made a tremendous difference in the nature of God as a Governor of the Universe. God with his physical basis was not capable of absolute good and absolute virtue. With God wanting in righteousness the universe could not insist on righteousness as an immutable principle. This dissociation of God from physical contact with man has made it possible for God to be conceived of as capable of absolute good and absolute virtue.

The fourth point of difference relates to the part religion plays when a change of nationality takes place.

In the antique world there could be no change of nationality unless it was accompanied by a change of Religion. In the antique world, "It was impossible for an individual to change his religion without changing his nationality, and a whole community could hardly change its religion at all without being absorbed into another stock or nation. Religions like political ties were transmitted from father to son; for a man could not choose a new God at will; the Gods of his fathers were the only deities on whom he could count as friendly and ready to accept his homage, unless he forswore his own kindred and was received into a new circle of civil as well as religious life."

How change of religion was a condition precedent to a Social fusion is well illustrated by the dialogue between Naomi and Ruth in the Old Testament.

> "Thy Sister" says Naomi to Ruth, "is gone back unto her people and unto her Gods"; and Ruth replies, "Thy people shall be my people and thy God my God."

It is quite clear that in the ancient world a change of nationality involved a change of cult. Social fusion meant religious fusion.

In modern society abandonment of religion or acceptance of another is not necessary for social fusion. This is best illustrated by what is in modern terminology and naturalisation, whereby the citizen of one state abandons his citizenship of the state and becomes a citizen of new state. In this process of naturalisation religion has no place. One can have a social fusion which is another name for naturalisation without undergoing a religious fusion.

To distinguish modern society from antique society it is not enough to say that Modern Society consists of men only. It must be added that it consists of men who are worshippers of different Gods.

The fifth point of difference relates to the necessity of knowledge as to the nature of God as part of religion.

> "From the antique point of view, indeed the question what the Gods are in themselves is not a religious but a speculative one; what is requisite to religion is a practical acquaintance with the rules on which the deity acts and on which he expects his worshippers to frame their conduct-what in Kings xvii. 26 is called the "manner" or rather the "customary law" (misphat) of the God of the land. This is true even of the religion of Israel. When the prophets speak of the knowledge of the laws and principles of His government in Israel,

> and a summary expression for religion as a whole is "the knowledge and fear of Jehovah," i.e. the knowledge of what Jehovah prescribes, combined with a reverent obedience. An extreme scepticism towards all religious speculation is recommended in the Book of Ecclesiastes as the proper attitude of piety, for no amount of discussion can carry a man beyond the plain rule, to "fear God and keep His Commandments". This counsel the author puts into the mouth of Solomon, and so represents it, not unjustly, as summing up the old view of religion, which in more modern days had unfortunately begun to be undermined."

The sixth point of difference relates to the place of belief in Religion. In ancient Society:

> "Ritual and practical usages were, strictly speaking, the sum total of ancient religions. Religion in primitive times was not a system of belief with practical applications; it was a body of fixed traditional practices, to which every member of society conformed as a matter of courage. Men would not be men if they agreed to do certain things without having a reason for their action; but in ancient religion the reason was not first formulated as a doctrine and then expressed in practice, but conversely, practice preceded doctrinal theory. Men form general rule of conduct before they begin to express general principles in words; political institutions are older than political theories and in like manner religious institutions are older than religious theories.
>
> This analogy is not arbitrarily chosen, for in fact the parallelism in ancient society between religious and political institutions is complete. In each sphere great importance was attached to form and precedent, but the explanation why the precedent was followed consisted merely of legend as to its first establishment. That the precedent, once established, was authoritative did not appear to require any proof. The rules of society were based on precedent, and the continued

existence of the society was sufficient reason why a precedent once set should continue to be followed."

The seventh point of difference relates to the place of individual conviction in Religion. In ancient Society:

> "Religion was a part of the organized social life into which a man was born, and to which he conformed through life in the same unconscious way in which men fall into any habitual practice of the society in which they live. Men took the Gods and their worship for granted, just as they took the other usages of the state for granted, and if they reason or speculated about them, they did so on the presupposition that the traditional usages were fixed things, behind which their reasoning must not go, and which no reasoning could be allowed to overturn. To us modern's religion is above all a matter of individual conviction and reasoned belief, but to the ancients it was a part of the citizen's public life, reduced to fixed forms, which he was not bound to understand and was not at liberty to criticize or to neglect. Religious nonconformity was an offence against the state; for if sacred tradition was tampered with the bases of society were undermined, and the favour of the Gods was forfeited. But so long as the prescribed forms were duly observed, a man was recognized as truly pious, and no one asked how his religion was rooted in his heart or affected his reason. Like political duty, of which indeed it was a part, religion was entirely comprehended in the observance of certain fixed rules of outward conduct."

The eighth point of difference pertains to the relation of God to Society and man, of Society to Man in the matter of God's Providence. First as to the difference in the relation of God to Society. In this connection three points may be noted. The faith of the antique world "Sought nothing higher than a condition of physical bien ere.... The good things desired of the Gods were the blessings of earthly life, not spiritual but carnal things." What the antique societies asked and believed themselves to receive from their God lay mainly in the following things:

> "Abundant harvests, help against their enemies and counsel by oracles or soothsayers in matters of natural difficulty." In the antique world
>
> "Religion was not the affair of the individual but of the Community.... It was the community, and not the individual, that was sure of the permanent and the unfailing hand of the deity." Next as to the difference in the relation of God to man.
>
> "It was not the business of the Gods of heathenish to watch, by a series of special providence, over the welfare of every individual. It is true that individuals laid their private affairs before the Gods, and asked with prayers and views for strictly personal blessings. But they did this just as they might crave a personal boon from a king, or as a son craves a boon from a father, without expecting to get all that was asked. What the Gods might do in this way was done as a matter of personal favour, and was not part of their proper function as heads of the community."
>
> "The Gods watched over a man's civic life, they gave him his share in public benefits, the annual largess of the harvest and the vintage, national peace or victory over enemies, and so forth, but they were not sure helpers in every private need, and above all they would not help him in matters that were against the interests of the community as a whole. There was therefore a whole region of possible needs and desires for which religion could and would do nothing." Next the difference in the attitude of God and Society to man.
>
> In the antique world Society was indifferent to individual welfare. God as no doubt bound to Society. But "the compact between the God and his worshippers was not held to pledge the deity to make the private cares of each member of the Community his own."

> "The benefits expected of God were of a public character affecting the whole community, especially fruitful seasons, increase of flocks of herds and success in war. So long as community flourished the fact that an individual was miserable reflected no discredit on divine providence."

On the contrary the antique world looked upon the misery of a man as proof.

"That the sufferer was an evildoer, justly hateful to the Gods. Such a man was out of place among the happy and the prosperous crowd that assembled on feast days before the alter." It is in accordance with this view that the leper and the mourner were shut out from the exercise of religion as well as from the privileges of social life and their food was not brought into the house of God.

As for conflict between individual and individual and between society and the individual God had no concern. In the antique world:

> "It was not expected that God should always be busy righting human affairs. In ordinary matters it was men's business to help themselves and their own kins folk, though the sense that the God was always near, and could be called upon at need, was a moral force continually working in some degree for the maintenance of social righteousness and order. The strength of this moral force was indeed very uncertain, for it was always possible for the evildoer to flatter himself that his offence would be overlooked." In the antique world man did not ask God to be righteous to him.

> "Whether in civil or in profane matters, the habit of the old world was to think much of the community and little of the individual life, and no one felt this to be unjust even though it bore hardly on himself. The God was the God of the national or of the tribe, and he knew and cared for the individual only as a member of the community."

That was the attitude that man in the antique world took of his own private misfortune. Man came to rejoice before his God and "in rejoicing before his God man rejoiced with and for the welfare of his kindred, his neighbours and his country, and, in renewing by solemn act of worship the bond that united him to God, he also renewed the bonds of family, social and national obligation." Man in the antique world did not call upon his maker to be righteous to him.

Such is this other Revolution in Religion. There have thus been two Religious Revolutions. One was an external Revolution. The other was an internal Revolution. The External Revolution was concerned with the field within which the authority of Religion was to prevail. The Internal Revolution had to do with the changes in Religion as a scheme of divine Governance for human society. The External Revolution was not really a Religious Revolution at all. It was a revolt of science against the extra territorial jurisdiction assumed by Religion over a field which did not belong. The Internal Revolution was a real Revolution or may be compared to any other political Revolution, such as the French Revolution or the Russian Revolution. It involved a constitutional change. By this Revolution the Scheme of divine governance came to be altered, amended and reconstituted.

How profound have been the changes which this internal Revolution, has made in the antique scheme of divine governance can be easily seen. By this Revolution God has ceased to be a member of a community. Thereby he has become impartial. God has ceased to be the Father of Man in the physical sense of the word. He has become the creator of the Universe. The breaking of this blood bond has made it possible to hold that God is good. By this Revolution man has ceased to be a blind worshipper of God doing nothing but obeying his commands. Thereby man has become a responsible person required to justify his belief in God's commandments by his conviction. By this Revolution God has ceased to be merely the protector of Society and social interests in gross have ceased to be the centre of the divine Order. Society and man have changed places as centres of this divine order. It is man who has become the centre of it.

All this analysis of the Revolution in the Ruling concepts of Religion as a scheme of divine governance had one purpose namely to discover the norm for evaluating the philosophy of a Religion. The impatient reader may not ask where are these norms and what are they? The reader may not have found the norms specified by their names in the foregoing discussion. But he could not have failed to notice that the whole of this Religious Revolution was raging around the norms for judging what is right and what is wrong. If he has not, let it be made explicit what has been implicit in the whole of this discussion. We began with the distinction between antique society and modern society as has been pointed out they differed in the type of divine governance they accepted as their Religious ideals.

At one end of the Revolution was the antique society with its Religious ideal in which the end was Society. At the other end of the Revolution is the modern Society with its Religious ideal in which the end is the individual. To put the same fact in terms of the norm it can be said that the norm or the criterion, for judging right and wrong in the Antique Society was utility while the norm or the criterion for judging right and wrong in the modern Society is Justice. The Religious Revolution was not thus a revolution in the religious organization of Society resulting in the shifting of the centre-from society to the individual-it was a revolution in the norms.

Some may demur to the norms suggested. It may be that it is a new way of reaching them. But there is no doubt that they are the real norms by which to judge the philosophy of religion. In the first place the norm must enable people to judge what is right and wrong in the conduct of men. In the second place the norm must be appropriate to current notion of what constitutes the moral good. From both these points of view they appear to be the true norms. They enable us to judge what is right and wrong. They are appropriate to the society which adopted them. Utility as a criterion was appropriate to the antique world in which society being the end, the moral good was held to be something which had social utility.

Justice as a criterion became appropriate to the Modern World in which individual being the end, the moral good was held to be something which does justice to the individual. There may be controversy as to which of the two norms is morally superior. But there can not be any serious controversy that these are not the norms. If it is said that these norms are not transcendental enough; the reply is that if a norm whereby one is to judge the philosophy of religion must be Godly, it must also be earthly. At any rate these are the norms propose to be adopt in examining the philosophy of Hinduism.

This is a long detour. But it was a necessary preliminary to any inquiry into the main question. However, when one begins the inquiry one meets with an initial difficulty. The Hindu is not prepared to face the inquiry. He either argues that religion is of no importance or he takes shelter behind the view-fostered by the study of comparative Religion-that all religions are good. There is no doubt that both these views are mistaken and untenable.

Religion as a social force cannot be ignored. Religion has been aptly described by Hebert Spencer as "the weft which everywhere crosses the warp of history". This is true of every Society. But Religion has not only crossed everywhere the warp of Indian History it forms the warp and woof of the Hindu mind. The life of the Hindu is regulated by Religion at every moment of his life. It orders him how during life he should conduct himself and how on death his body shall be disposed of. It tells him how and when he shall indulge in his sexual impulses. It tells him what ceremonies are to be performed when a child is born-how he should name, how he should cut the hair on its head, how he should perform its first feeding.

It tells him what occupation he can take to, what woman he should marry. It tells him with whom he should dine and what food he should eat, what vegetables are lawful and what are forbidden. It tells how he should spend his day, how many times he should eat, how many times he should pray. There is no act of the Hindu which is not covered or ordained by Religion. It seems strange that the educated Hindus should come to look upon it as though it was a matter of indifference.

Besides, Religion is a social force. As has been pointed out Religion stands for a scheme of divine governance. The scheme becomes an ideal for society to follow. The ideal may be nonexistent in the sense that it is something which is constructed. But although nonexistent, it is real. For an ideal it has full operative force which is inherent in every ideal. Those who deny the importance of religion not only forget this, they also fail to realize how great is the potency and sanction that lies behind a religious ideal as compound with that of a purely secular ideal. This is probably due to the lag which one sees between the real and the ideal which is always present whether the ideal is religious or secular. But the relative potency of the two ideals is to be measured by another test-namely their power to override the practical instincts of man.

The ideal is concerned with something that is remote. The practical instincts of man are concerned with the immediate present. Now placed as against the force of the practical instincts of man the two ideals show their difference in an unmistaken manner. The practical instincts of man do yield to the prescriptions of a religious ideal however much the two are opposed to each other. The practical instincts of man do not on the other hand yield to the secular ideal if the two are in conflict. This means that a religious ideal has a hold on mankind, irrespective of an earthly gain. This can never be said of a purely secular ideal. Its power depends upon its power to confer material benefit. This shows how great the difference in the potency and sanction of the two ideals is over the human mind. A religious ideal never fails to work so long as there is faith in that ideal. To ignore religion is to ignore a live wire.

Again to hold that all religions are true and good is to cherish a belief which is positively and demonstrably wrong. This belief, one is sorry to say, is the result of what is known as the study of comparative religion. Comparative religion has done one great service to humanity. It has broken down the claim and arrogance of revealed religions as being the only true and good religions of study. While it is true that comparative religion has abrogated the capricious distinction between true and false religions based on purely arbitrary and a priori considerations, it has brought in its wake some false notions about religion. The most harmful one is the one mentioned namely that all religions are equally good and that there is no necessity of discriminating between them. Nothing can be a greater error than this. Religion is an institution or an influence and like all social influences and institutions, it may help or it may harm a society which is in its grip. As pointed out by Prof. Tiele religion is "one of the mightiest motors in the history of mankind, which formed as well as tore asunder nations, united as well as divided empires, which sanctioned the most atrocious and barbarous deeds, the most libinous customs, inspired the most admirable acts of heroism, self renunciation, and devotion, which occasioned the most sanguinary wars, rebellions and persecutions, as well as brought about the freedom, happiness and peace of nations-at one time a partisan of tyranny, at another breaking its chains, now calling into existence and fostering a new and brilliant civilization, then the deadly foe to progress, science and art."

A force which shows such a strange contrast in its result can be accepted as good without examining the form it takes and the ideal it serves. Everything depends upon what social ideal a given religion as a divine scheme of governance hold out. This is a question which is not avowed by the science of comparative religion. Indeed it begins where comparative religion ends. The Hindu is merely trying to avoid it by saying that although religions are many they are equally good. For they are not.

However much the Hindu may seek to burke the inquiry into the philosophy of Hinduism there is no escape. He must face it.

Now to begin with the subject let us to apply both the tests, the test of justice and the test of utility to judge the philosophy of Hinduism. First I will apply the test of justice. Before doing so principle of gustic needs to be explained.

No one has expounded it better than Professor Bergbon As interpreted by him the principle of justice is a compendious one and includes most of the other principles which have become the foundation of a moral order. Justice has always evoked ideas of equality, of proportion of "compensation". Equity signifies equality. Rules and regulations, right and righteousness are concerned with equality in value. If all men are equal, all men are of the same essence and the common essence entitled them to the same fundamental rights and to equal liberty.

In short justice is simply another name for liberty, equality and fraternity.

Which of these tenets does Hinduism recognize? Let us take the question one by one.

In the scheme of Manu the Brahmin is placed at the first in rank. Below him is the Kshatriya. Below Kshatriya is the Vaishya. Below Vaishya is the Sudra and Below Sudra is the Ati-Sudra (the Untouchables). This system of rank and gradation is, simply another way of enunciating the principle of inequality so that it may be truly said that Hinduism does not recognize equality. This inequality in status is not merely the inequality that one sees in the warrant of precedence prescribed for a ceremonial gathering at a King's Court. It is a permanent social relationship among the classes to be observed- to be enforced- at all times in all places and for all purposes. It will take too long to show how in every phase of life Manu has introduced and made inequality the vital force of life. But it will illustrate it by taking a few examples such as slavery, marriage and Rule of Law.

Manu recognizes Slavery. But he confined it to the Sudras. Only Sudras could be made slaves of the three higher classes. But the higher classes could not be the slaves of the Sudra.

But evidently practice differed from the law of Manu and not only Sudras happened to become slaves but members of the other three classes also become slaves. When this was discovered to be the case a new rule was enacted by a Successor of Manu namely Narada. This new rule of Narada runs as follows:

"In the inverse order of the four castes slavery is not ordained except where a man violates the duties peculiar to his caste. Slavery (in that respect) is analogous to the condition of a wife."

Recognition of slavery was bad enough. But if the rule of slavery had been left free to take its own course it would have had at least one beneficial effect. It would have been a levelling force. The foundation of caste would have been destroyed. For under it a Brahmin might have become the slave of the Untouchable and the Untouchable would have become the master of the Brahmin. But it was seen that unfettered slavery was an equalitarian principle and an attempt was made to nullify it. Manu and his successors therefore while recognising slavery ordains that it shall not be recognised in its inverse order to the Varna System. That means that a Brahmin may become the slave of another Brahmin. But he shall not be the slave of a person of another Varna i.e. of the Kshatriya, Vaishya, Sudra, or Ati-Sudra. On the other hand a Brahmin may hold as his slave any one belonging to the four Varnas. A Kshatriya can have a Kshatriya, Vaisha, Sudra and Ati-Sudra as his slaves but not one who is a Brahmin. A Vaishya can have a Vaishya, Sudra and Ati-Sudra as his slaves but not one who is a Brahmin or a Kshatriya. A Sudra can hold a Sudra and Ati-sudra can hold an Ati-Sudra as his slave but not one who is a Brahmin, Kshatriya, Vaishya or Sudra.

Challenge Conversion and Hindu Response: Again at a moment of history of our ancient nation when the Hindu foundation of the nation is being challenged and sought to be undermined. But never before in our history has the challenge been as dangerously deceptive, pernicious, and sophisticated as it is now. It is therefore difficult to respond to this challenge since it cannot be easily perceived.

Hence, the response to this challenge and the implicit threat has to be well thought out and profound, but as before in our history, the response to be fruitful has to be designed and structured by the confluence of spiritual guidance and political resolve. Such a confluence has been the fundamental basis of our past responses to such challenges in history, from the installation by rishis of Adi Raja Prithu as King of Bharatvarsh, Chanakya's founding of the Mauryan kingdom, the establishment of the Vijayanagaram empire at Hampi by Sringeri Shankaracharya, to inspiring the fighting armies of Shivaji by Swami Ramdass. Even Mahatma Gandhi and Jayaprakash Narayan in their respective struggles for independence of the nation from colonialism, and for the restoration of democracy in a nation that was drowned in the darkness of the Emergency, had followed this unique Hindu model of spiritually guiding a political movement without seeking the fruits of office for themselves. The Hindu foundation of modern India is why India has been and is even today referred to, in India and abroad, as Hindustan. Hindustan is defined as a nation of Hindus and those who accept that their ancestors are Hindus. The concept also includes refugee minorities who accept the core values of the Hindu culture and therefore recognised as a part of the Hindustan nation. Thus, when the Dwarka Mutt Shankaracharya gave the arriving Parsi refugees in Sanjaan [Kutch coast] a five-point requirement for settling in the country, they readily accepted and have not deviated from it even today.

These five points were: Giving up Persian language and adopting Gujarati; wearing Indian clothes instead of Persian; treating the cow as sacred; reciting some select Sanskrit shlokas in their marriage ceremony; and laying down of weapons. Despite being the smallest minority, with disproportionate share in offices of power and national wealth, and perhaps also the wealthiest community, there is and has been no tension or conflict between Hindus and Parsis.

Today Hindus despite de facto in power and in the organs of the state, are victims of that same targeting, but of course in a very subtle and sophisticated manner. In furthering the objective of this targeting, Islam and Christianity, more so the latter, have been able to leverage the influence of prominent Hindus themselves.

Parsis and Jews do not threaten the Hindu character of the nation. They do not seek to proselytise or convert Hindus by monetary inducements or by obscurantist preachings such as curing persons who convert, of incurable terminal diseases. But on the other hand, the preachings of the religious leaders of Islam and Christianity in India, altogether for a thousand years, had targeted Hindus and sought the religious conversions to their faiths by creating deprivation and loss of self-esteem, through the abuse of the power of the state against Hindus.

They were not subtle about it. For example, in 1545, King John III of Portugal gave a command to the then Governor of Goa that neither public nor private 'idols' of Hindu heathens be tolerated on the island of Goa and that severe punishment be meted out to those who persist in keeping them. Thereafter, a terrible inquisition followed during which Hindus were killed, brutalised and their temples razed to the ground. Still we must not forget only a minority of Hindus converted to Christianity.

No other religious community other than Hindus suffered such prolonged and atrocious persecution and survived as a religion of a vast majority on their own soil. Let us not forget this defiance in our past.

Today Hindus despite de facto in power and in the organs of the state, are victims of that same targeting, but of course in a very subtle and sophisticated manner. In furthering the objective of this targeting, Islam and Christianity, more so the latter, have been able to leverage the influence of prominent Hindus themselves, who wittingly for money or unwittingly because of a programmed mindset of being defensive about being a Hindu [thereby ready to ape the West] are tools of this targeting.

What is the nature and scope of this targeting, and is there a way for us to end it by conciliation with Christians and Muslims? In other words, can we seek to end religious conversion in India today by the ancient Hindu way of shashtrarthas as Hindu saints did, as for example Adi Sankara did with Buddhism and Uttara Mimamsa theologies and Azhwars and Nayanars saints in the south did with Jainism? Will indeed Christians and Muslims recognise the sanctity of shashtrarthas?

There is a serious problem here because as an interesting study of Sarah Claerhout and Jakob De Roover titled: The Question of Conversion in India [Economic and Political Weekly, July 9, 2005] concludes, Hindus and Christians have fundamentally different and mutually exclusive concepts of religion and thus also in their approaches to the question of conversion. Hence, say the authors, for Hindus and Christians to dialogue on conversion would be fruitless because they will have "great difficulties making sense of each other's statements and arguments". This is because Hindus do not consider any religion as wholly false, and as Gandhiji put it, all religions have some errors in them. Since all religions lead to God, hence there is no need for forcing a conversion. Christians [and Muslims] think that their's is the only true religion, and it is God's work to convert heathens and kafirs to their only true religion. Therefore, either Hindus will have to capitulate on this question by permitting religious conversion in India, or in the alternative be united and assertive to ensure that laws are enacted and effectively enforced against religious conversion of Hindus. There is no third way.

It is urgent now that Hindus be mobilised to assertively oppose any further conversion from Hinduism to any other non-Indian religion. There is no room for indifference here. This is because that status quo is damaging to the Hindu faith, since the Christian missionaries and Muslim mullahs are already fully at work, funds being no constraint, to convert Hindus. If conversions are not explicitly opposed, then Hindus are implicitly acquiescing in the atrocity. There is a fundamental disconnect between the religious outlook of Hindus and the Christians and Muslims which makes it impossible for a fruitful debate and mutual understanding on the question of religious conversion.

Reflect on the past trends: In 1000 A.D., Muslims and Christians in undivided India were in negligible numbers. By 1400, they had become 3.5 per cent of the subcontinent. In 1700, they rose to 11 per cent, and by 1891 to 13 per cent. By the time of Partition, they were 23 per cent, and today in South Asia, the Christian and Muslim population is 36 per cent. What will it be in 2050 or 2150? This is an extraordinary rise, which has continued even after freedom from British colonial rule. De facto power in the hands of Hindu majority has not changed the attitude of the proselytisers, only their strategy has changed and become invisible for most Hindus. And those Hindus who have been in power in government have been soft on this issue entrapped by the lack of a Hindu mindset and bloc voting by the Muslims and Christians.

Even the most secular Hindus should however worry about this demographic trend, because secularism is itself under threat, if the Hindus lose their majority share in population. That is why even Gandhiji and Dr. Ambedkar [no Hindu fundamentalists but highly regarded secularists], during the freedom struggle had stoutly opposed religious conversions. In Mahatma's interview given to The Hindu in 1931.

Legal definition of "Hindu"

Hindu Law: India's Constitution does not give a definition of the term Hindu, but it does define to whom the "Hindu Law" applies. It has to do this because in spite of its pretence to secularism, the Indian Constitution allows Muslims, Christians and Parsis a separate Personal Law. In a way, this separate treatment of different communities merely continues the communal autonomy of castes and sects accepted in pre-modern Hindu states, but it exposes the credibility deficit of Indian secularism. At any rate, the situation is that Personal Law is divided on the basis of religion, and that one of the legal subsystems is called Hindu Law.

Article 25 (2)(b) of the Constitution stipulates that "the reference to Hindus shall be construed as including a reference to persons professing the Sikh, Jain or Buddhist religion". The Hindu Marriage Act of 1955 goes in greater detail to define this "legal Hindu", by stipulating in Section 2 that the Act applies:

(a) To any person who is a Hindu by religion in any of its forms and developments, including a Viashaiva, a Lingayat or a follower of the Brahmo, Prarthana or Arya Samaj.

(b) To any person who is a Buddhist, Jain or Sikh by religion.

(c) To any other person domiciled in the territories to which this Act extends who is not a Muslim, Christian, Parsi or Jew by religion.

This definition of the "legal Hindu", though explicitly not equating him with the "Hindu by religion", is exactly coterminous with the original Islamic use of the term Hindu: all Indian Pagans are legally Hindus. The Buddhists, Jains and Sikhs are explicitly included in the "Hindus by law" but separated from the "Hindus by religion": at this point, the law follows the usage established by Western scholars, contrary to the original usage.

Note that the changes in Hindu Law imposed by an Act of Parliament (on top of the very existence of separate Hindu and Muslim Law regimes) constitute a further measure of communal inequality. The secular government would not dare to touch the other religion-based law systems, as has repeatedly been shown in the past decades regarding items of Christian and Muslim Personal Law. An interference in Hindu Law by a national legislative body only makes sense in an avowedly Hindu state; in a sense, therefore, the Hindu Marriage Act constitutes an admission by Jawaharlal Nehru that ultimately India is a Hindu state.

Semi-Hindus: Separatist Sikhs have at times criticized the inclusion of the Sikhs in the "legal Hindu" category. When Law Minister Dr. Bhimrao Ambedkar first introduced the Hindu Code Bill in 1951, Sikh spokesman Sardar Hukum Singh regarded the Bill as "a dubious attempt on the part of the Hindus to absorb the Sikhs". Dr. Ambedkar replied: "The application of the Hindu Code to Sikhs, Buddhists and Jains was a historical development and it would be too late, sociologically, to object to it. When the Buddha differed from the Vedic Brahmins, he did so only in matters of creed, but left the Hindu legal framework intact. He did not propound a separate law for his followers. The same was the case with Mahavir and the ten Sikh gurus. The Privy Council had as early as 1830 laid down that the Sikhs were governed by the Hindu law."

This at once explains why Ambedkar's neo-Buddhist followers have not objected to their inclusion in the "legal Hindu" category. On the contrary, this inclusion later served to justify their inclusion in reservation schemes and other benefits for Hindu ex-Untouchables: as Untouchability was a problem of Hindu society, it was reasonable that special benefits for this section of Hindu society only apply to ex-Untouchable members of the Hindu, or at least the "legal Hindu" category.

When the Ramakrishna Mission went to court to have itself declared a non-Hindu minority (in order to escape the legal anti-Hindu discriminations esp. in education), it claimed that its members could legally still be treated as Hindus in matters of marriage and inheritance, even while being recognized as non-Hindus in the religious sense. In effect, the Ramakrishnaites wanted to have the same status as Sikhs and Buddhists: legal recognition as "legal Hindus and religious non-Hindus". They rightly understood that the law has created a category of semi-Hindus who have no separate traditions of personal law but have nevertheless a separate religious identity entitling them to the privileges accorded to the minorities.

The Indian laws make a distinction between what we may call the "Hindu in the broad sense", to whom Hindu Law applies, and who is coterminous with the Hindu of Persian-Islamic usage, viz. every Indian Pagan; and the "Hindu in the narrow sense", a category which may not include Buddhism and Sikhism. Though the law does not mention them, the tribal traditions are also taken to fall partly (except for a measure of accomplished sanskritization) outside this narrow category. Of course, the claims by different groups of belonging to this broad-Hindu but non-narrow-Hindu category should be considered separately and on their own merits, e.g. Buddhism's claim to a distinct identity does not imply an endorsement of Sikhism's claim to the same. The debate over whether certain communities come under the definition of Hinduism is largely a debate over whether it is the narrow or the broad definition that should be considered as the "true" definition.

The Scheduled Castes: A contentious point, esp. since the institution and expansion of caste-based reservation schemes, is the religious factor in defining the Scheduled Castes, the former Untouchables. The legal situation is as follows: "The Constitution (Scheduled Castes) Order 1950 said in so many words that a non-Hindu could never be a Scheduled Caste (even if belonging to a particular caste included in the official list of Scheduled Castes).

By an amendment introduced in 1956, it was provided that only a Hindu or a Sikh could be a Scheduled Caste. The Scheduled Caste law is, thus, clearly religion-based and its religious basis has generated abundant case law. The Supreme Court has held that a Scheduled Caste Hindu on ceasing to be a Hindu also ceases to be a Scheduled Caste and, should he ever reconvert to Hinduism, he will also regain forthwith the Scheduled Caste status."

Meanwhile, Buddhists have also been explicitly included (and had already been implicitly treated) as belonging to the Hindu category in this regard, i.e. entitled to Scheduled Caste status if belonging to such a caste. Jains need no mention here, as they belong to the Vaishya upper castes; but the rare Scheduled Caste convert to Jainism would likewise remain entitled to benefits earmarked for the Scheduled Castes.

In contemporary anti-Hindu polemic, chiefly by Christian missionaries, and here by the Muslim chairman of the Minorities'

Commission (an intrinsically anti-Hindu institution), it is frequently claimed that: "This law has been clearly designed with the object of preventing low caste Hindus, even if disgruntled with religion-based social inequalities, from converting to Christianity or Islam."

If this seems plausible, and is hence repeated faithfully in most Western publications, it is nonetheless untrue. The Government of India Act (1935), enacted by the British who had other concerns, already excluded Christian converts from the Scheduled Castes category. This was done after consultation with the missionaries, who were honest enough to acknowledge this as the obvious implication of their own boast that conversion brought freedom from caste disabilities. As long as Christians and Muslims propagate the notion that their own religion is egalitarian and caste-free, it is only logical that converts have to give up their Scheduled Caste status. Today, all while propagating the necessary connection between Hinduism and caste disabilities, the Churches are clamouring for the recognition of their SC converts as "Dalit Christians". If they haven't had their way so far, it is mainly due to the opposition not from the Hindutva forces but from the neo-Buddhists and the legitimate Scheduled Castes themselves. At the time of writing, the legal position remains that only followers of Indic religions are classified by caste, with the concomitant legal benefits in case of low castes.

The Scheduled Tribes: The Scheduled Tribes as such are not mentioned in the context of defining the borders of the Hindu community, for "tribal" is only recognized in law as a sociological rather than a religious category. A Christian tribal is consequently still entitled to all the special privileges of Scheduled Tribe status. Or to put it in Tahir Mahmood's partisan language:

> "The law on Scheduled Tribes is, on the contrary, wholly free from religious shackles. The 'No non-Hindu please' clause of the Constitution (Scheduled Castes) Order 1950 has no parallel in the Constitution (Scheduled Tribe) Order 1950. Nor is there any judicial decision saying that all Scheduled Tribes are born Hindus. Any change of religion on the part of a member

> of a Scheduled Tribe does not legally alter his or her Scheduled Tribe status. The modem Hindu code of 1955-56 does not apply to Scheduled Tribes. In respect of several tribal communities there have been judicial decisions specifically affirming that the four Hindu law enactments of 1955-56 do not extend to the Scheduled Tribes."

This means, for example, that customary marriage systems including polygamy (abolished in the Hindu Marriage Act) are condoned in the case of tribals. There is undeniably a contradiction here, for the Hindu Marriage Act had defined the legal Hindu as including (apart from Hindus in the narrow sense, Buddhists, Jains and Sikhs) "any other person domiciled in the territories to which this Act extends who is not a Muslim, Christian, Parsi or Jew by religion". In spite of that definition, Indian law in general treats tribals as non-Hindus.

The 1991 census also separated tribal religion from Hinduism. It divided the population into eight different categories: Hindus, Muslim, Christians, Sikhs, Buddhists, Jains, "Other Religions and Persuasions", and "Religion non stated". In appendix, the "other religions and persuasions" are detailed, and about 60 tribal religions are specified. The prevalent academic and mediatic dicourse takes this line further, e.g. by redefining the sanskritization of the tribals (the gradual adoption of elements of Sanskritic civilization, which has been a natural and ongoing process since many centuries) as "conversion to Hinduism", on the same footing as "conversion to Christianity"; and by describing Hindu social activists working in tribal areas as a kind of missionaries, outsiders propagating a religion that is quite foreign to the tribals. So, against the historical definition of "Hindu" which includes all Indian Pagans, and against the specific definition in the Hindu Marriage Act, which is coterminous with the historical definition, official India treats tribal religions as separate from Hinduism.

DOES HINDUISM RECOGNISE FRATERNITY?

There are two forces prevalent in Society. Individualism and Fraternity. Individualism is ever present. Every individual is ever asking "I and my neighbours, are we all brothers, are we even fiftieth cousins, am I their keeper, why should I do right to them" and under the pressure of his own particular interests acting as though he was an end to himself, thereby developing a non-social and even an antisocial self. Fraternity is a force of opposite character. Fraternity is another name for fellow feeling. It consists in a sentiment which leads an individual to identify himself with the good of others whereby "the good of others becomes to him a thing naturally and necessarily to be attended to like any of the physical conditions of our existence". It is because of this sentiment of fraternity that the individual does not "bring himself to think of the rest of his fellow-creatures as struggling rivals with him for the means of happiness, whom he must desire to see defeated in their object in order that he may succeed in his own." Individualism would produce anarchy. It is only fraternity, which prevents it and helps to sustain the moral order among men. Of this there can be no doubt.

How does this sentiment of Fraternity of fellow feeling arise? J. S. Mill says that this sentiment is a natural sentiment.

> "The social state is at once so natural, so necessary, and so habitual to man, that, except in some unusual circumstances or by an effort of voluntary abstraction he never conceives himself otherwise than as a member of a body; and this association is riveted more and more, as mankind are further removed from the state of savage independence. Any condition, therefore, which is essential to a state of society, becomes more and more an inseparable part of every person's conception of the state of things which he is born into, and which is the destiny of a human being.
>
> Now, society between human beings, except in the relation of master and slave, is manifestly impossible on any other footing than that the interests of all are to be consulted. Society between equals can only exist on the understanding that the interests of all are to be regarded equally. And since in all states of civilisation, every person, except an absolute monarch, has equals, every one is obliged to live on these

terms with some body; and in every age some advance is made towards a state in which it will be impossible to live permanently on other terms with any body. In this way people grow up unable to conceive as possible to them a state of total disregard of other people's interests."

Does this sentiment of fellow feeling find a place among the Hindus? The following facts throw a flood of light on this question.

The first fact that strikes one is the number of castes. No body has made an exact computation of their number. But it is estimated that total is not less than 2000. It might be 3000. This is not the only distressing aspect of this fact. There are others. Castes are divided into sub-castes. Their number is legion. The total population of the Brahmin Caste is about core and a half. But there are 1886 sub-castes of the Brahmin Caste. In the Punjab alone the Saraswat Brahmins of the Province of Punjab are divided into 469 sub-castes. The Kayasthas of Punjab are divided into 590 sub-castes. One could go on giving figures to show this infinite process of splitting social life into small fragments.

The third aspect of this splitting process is the infinitely small fragments into which the Castes are split. Some of the Baniya sub-castes can count no more than 100 families. They are so inter related they find extremely difficult to marry within their castes without transgressing the rules of consanguinity. It is noteworthy what small excuses suffice to bring about this splitting. Equally noteworthy is the hierarchical character of the Caste System. Castes form an hierarchy in which one caste is at the top and is the highest, another at the bottom and it is the lowest and in between there are castes every one of which is at once above some castes and below some castes. The caste system is a system of gradation in which every caste except the highest and the lowest has a priority and precedence over some other castes.

How is this precedence or this superiority determined? This order of superiority and inferiority or this insubordination is determined by rules: (1) which are connected with religious rites and (2) which are connected with commensuality.

Religion as a basis of Rules of precedence manifests itself in three ways. Firstly through religious ceremonies, secondly through incantations that accompany the religious ceremonies and thirdly through the position of the priest.

Beginning with the ceremonies as a source of rules of precedence it should be noted that the Hindu Scriptures prescribe sixteen religious ceremonies. Although those are Hindu ceremonies every Hindu Caste cannot by right claim to perform all the sixteen ceremonies. Few can claim the right to perform all. Some are allowed to perform certain ceremonies; some are not allowed to perform certain of the ceremonies. For instance take the ceremony of Upanayan, wearing of the sacred thread. Some castes can't. Precedence follows this distinction in the matter of right to perform the ceremonies. A caste which can claim to perform all the ceremonies is higher in status than the caste which has a right to perform a few.

Turning to the Mantras, it is another source for rules of precedence. According to the Hindu Religion the same ceremony can be performed in two different ways: (1) Vedokta and (2) Puranokta. In the Vedokta form the ceremonies are performed with Mantras (incantations) from the Vedas. In the Puranokta form the ceremony is performed with Mantras (incantations) from the Puranas.

Hindu Religious Scriptures fall into two distinct categories: (1) The Vedas which are four, and (2) the Puranas which are eighteen. Although they are all respected as scriptures they do not all have the same sanctity. The Vedas have the highest sanctity and the Puranas have the lowest sanctity. The way the Mantras give rise to social precedence will be obvious if it is borne in mind that not every caste is entitled to have the ceremony performed in the Vedokta form.

Three castes may well claim the right to the performance of one of the sixteen ceremonies. But it will be that one of it is entitled to perform it in the Vedokta form, another in the Puranokta form. Precedence goes with the kind of Mantra that a caste is entitled to use in the performance of a religious ceremony. A caste which is entitled to use Vedic Mantras is superior to a caste which is entitled to use only Puranokta Mantras.

Taking the priest as a second source of precedence connected with Religion, Hinduism requires the instrumentality of a priest for the derivation of the full benefit from the performance of a religious ceremony. The priest appointed by the scripture is the Brahmin. A Brahmin therefore is indispensable. But the scriptures do not require-that a Brahmin shall accept the invitation of any and every Hindu irrespective of his caste to officiate at a religious ceremony. The invitation of which caste he will accept and of which he will refuse is a matter left to the wishes of the Brahmin. By long and well-established custom it is now settled at which caste he will officiate and at which caste he will not. This fact has become the basis of precedence as between castes. The caste at which a Brahmin will officiate is held as superior to a caste at whose religious functions a Brahmin will not officiate.

There is no sharing among Hindus of joys and sorrows involved in the vital facts of life. Everything is separate and exclusive. The Hindu is separate and exclusive all through his life. A foreigner coming to India will not find men crying Hindu Pani (water for Hindus) and Musalman Pani (water for Musalmans). He will find Brahmin Coffee

This view of the caste is due to taking the separate aspects of caste separately. One must take them in conjunction. The resultant social utility or distillate of caste can be ascertained only by putting together the separate aspects of caste and judge them in their combination. Following this line of attacking the problem, the following conclusions follow:

(1) Caste divides Labourers

(2) Caste disassociates work from interest

(3) Caste disconnects intelligence from manual labour

(4) Caste devitalises by denying to him the right to cultivate vital interest and

(5) Caste prevents mobilisation. Caste System is not merely division of labour.

Civilised society undoubtedly needs division of labour. But in no civilised society is division of labour accompanied by this unnatural division of labourers into watertight compartments.

Caste System is not merely a division of labourers, which is quite different from division of labour it is an hierarchy in which the divisions of labourers are graded one above the other. In no other country is the division of labour accompanied by this gradation of labourers. There is also a third point of criticism against this view of the Caste System. This division of labour is not spontaneous, it is not based on natural aptitudes. Social and individual efficiency requires us to develop the capacity of an individual to the point of competency to chose and to make his own career. This principle is violated in the Caste System in so far as it involves an attempt to appoint tasks to individuals in advance, selected not on the basis of trained original capacities, but on that of the social status of the parents.

Looked at from another point of view this stratification of occupations which is the result of the Caste System is positively pernicious. Industry is never static. It undergoes rapid and abrupt changes. With such changes an individual must be free to change his occupations. Without such freedom to adjust himself to changing circumstances it would be impossible for him to gain his livelihood. Now the Caste System will not allow Hindus to take occupations where they are wanted if they do not belong to them by heredity. If a Hindu is seen to starve rather than take to new occupations not assigned to his Caste, the reason is to be found in the Caste System. By not permitting readjustment of occupations, caste becomes a direct cause of much of the unemployment we see in the country.

As a form of division of labour the Caste System suffers from another serious defect. The division of labour brought about by the Caste System is not a division based on choice. Individual sentiment, individual preference has no place in it. It is based on the dogma of predestination. Considerations of social efficiency would compel us to recognise that the greatest evil in the industrial system is not so much poverty and the suffering that it involves, as the fact that so many persons have callings which make no appeal to those who are engaged in them.

Such callings constantly provoke one to aversion, ill will and the desire to evade. There are many occupations in India which on account of the fact that they are regarded as degraded by the Hindus provoke those who are engaged in it to aversion. There is a constant desire to evade and escape from such occupations which arises solely because of the blighting effect which they produce upon those who follow them owing to the slight and stigma cast upon them by the Hindu religion.

The second mischief it dose is to dissociate intelligence from work and create contempt for labour. The theory of the Caste is that a Brahmin who is permitted to cultivate his intellect is not permitted to labour, indeed is taught to look down upon labour. While the Sudra who is required to labour is not permitted to cultivate his intelligence. The disastrous consequences of this have been well portrayed by Mr. R.C.Dutt. Wealth without education and wealth is brutal. Each is necessary to every one. They are necessary for the growth of a man.

That the Brahmin should cultivate knowledge, Kshatriya should bear arms, the Vaishya should trade and that the Sudra should serve is presented as a theory of mutual interdependence found in the family. It is asked why should the Sudra need trouble to acquire wealth when the three Varnas are there to support him; Why need the Sudra bother to take to education when the Brahmin to whom he can go when the occasion for reading or writing arises; Why need the Sudra worry to arm himself because there is the Kshatriya to protect him?

The theory of Chaturvarnya understood in this sense may be said to look upon the Sudra as the ward and the three Varnas as his guardians. Thus interpreted it is a simple and alluring theory. Assuming this to be the correct view of the underlying conception of Chaturvarnya it seems to me that the system is neither foolproof nor knave-proof. What is to happen if the Brahmins, Vaishyas and Kshatriyas fail to pursue knowledge, to engage in economic enterprises and to be efficient soldiers which are their respective functions? Contrary-wise, suppose that they discharge their functions but flout their duty to the Sudra or to one another? What is to happen to the Sudra if the three classes refuse to support him on fair terms or combine to keep him down? Who is to safeguard the interests of the Sudra or for the matter of that of the Vaishya and Kshatriya when the person who is trying to take advantage of his ignorance is the Brahmin? Who is to defend the liberty of the Sudra or that of the Brahmin and the Vaishya, when the person who is robbing him of is the Kshatriya?

Interdependence of one class on another class is inevitable. Even dependence of one class upon another may sometimes become allowable. But why make one person depend upon another in the matter of his vital needs? Education every one must have. Means of defence every one must have. These are the paramount requirements of every man for his self-preservation. How can the fact that his neighbour is educated and armed, help a man who is uneducated and disarmed. The whole theory is absurd. These are the questions which the defenders of Chaturvarnya do not seem to be troubled about. But they are very pertinent questions. Assuming their conception of Chaturvarnya that the relationship between the different classes is that of ward and guardian is the real conception underlying Chaturvarnya, it must be admitted that it makes no provision to safeguard the interests of the ward from the misdeeds of the guardian.

Whether the relationship of guardian and ward was the real underlying conception on which Chaturvarnya was based there is no doubt that in practice the relation was that of master and servant. The three classes, Brahmins, Kshatriyas and Vaishyas although not very happy in their mutual relationship managed to work by compromise. The Brahmin flattered the Kshatriya and both let the Vaishya live in order to be able to live upon him. But the three agreed to beat down the Sudra. He was not allowed to acquire wealth lest he should be independent of the three Varnas. He was prohibited from acquiring knowledge lest he should keep a steady vigil regarding his interests. He was prohibited from bearing arms lest he should have the means to rebel against their authority. That this is how the Sudras were treated by the Trayavarnikas is evidenced by the Laws of Manu. There is no code of laws more infamous regarding social rights than the Laws of Manu.

Any instance from anywhere of social injustice must pale before it. Why have the mass of people tolerated the social evils to which they have been subjected? There have been social revolutions in other countries of the world. Why have there not been social revolutions in India is a question which has incessantly troubled many. There is only one answer, it is that the lower classes of Hindus have been completely disabled for direct action on account of this wretched system of Chaturvarnya. They could not bear arms and without arms they could not rebel. They were all ploughmen or rather condemned to be ploughmen and they were not allowed to convert their ploughshares into swords. They had no bayonets and therefore everyone who chose ploughs did sit upon them. On account of the Chaturvarnya they could receive no education. They could not think out or know the way to their salvation. They were condemned to be lowly and not knowing the way of escape and not having the means of escape, they became reconciled to eternal servitude which they accepted as their inescapable fate.

It is true that even in Europe the strong has not shrunk from the exploitation, nay the spoliation of the weak but in Europe, the strong have never contrived to make the weak helpless against exploitation so shamelessly as was the case in India among the Hindus. Social war has been raging between the strong and the weak far more violently in Europe than it has ever been in India. Yet the weak in Europe has had in him freedom of military service his physical weapon, in suffrage his political weapon and in education his moral weapon. Three weapons for emancipation were never withheld by the strong from the weak in Europe. All these weapons were however denied to the masses in India by Chaturvarnya.

There cannot be a more degrading system of social organisation than Chaturvarnya. It is the system, which deadens, paralyses and cripples the people from helpful activity. This is no exaggeration. History bears ample evidence. There is only one period in Indian history, which is a period of freedom, greatness and glory. That is the period of the Maurya Empire. At all other times the country suffered from defeat and darkness. But the Maurya period was a period when Chaturvarnya was completely annihilated, when the Sudras, who constituted the mass of the people came into their own and became the rulers of the country. The period of defeat and darkness is the period when Chaturvarnya flourished to the damnation of the greater part of the people of the country.

Caste prevents mobilisation. Occasions arise when society must mobilise all its resources to one end in order to save itself from a catastrophe. To take a catastrophe like war, Society must mobilise all its resources for militarization. Every one must do war. Every one must be a soldier. Is this possible under the theory of caste? Obviously not. Indeed the destiny of a defeat which has been the lot of India throughout history is due to caste. Caste prevented general mobilisation. Or the extent of mobilisation was of a very limited character. Only the Kshatriyas were expected to fight. The rest the Brahmins and the Vaishyas were not armed and the Sudras who formed the large majority of the country were disarmed. The result was that once the small class of Kshatriyas were defeated by a foreign foe, the whole country fell at his feet. It could offer no resistance. It was not capable of resistance. Indian wars have been mostly wars of single battles or single campaigns. This was due to the fact that once the Kshatriyas fell everything fell. Why? Simply because there was no general mobilisation and the theory deeply imbedded in the psychology of the people.

If these conclusions are sound, how can a philosophy which dissects society in fragments, which dissociates work from interest, which disconnects intelligence from labour, which expropriates the rights of man to interests vital to life and which prevented society from mobilising resources for common action in the hour of danger, be said to satisfy the test of Social Utility.

The Philosophy of Hinduism therefore neither satisfies the test of social utility nor does it satisfy the test of individual justice.

The result of this analysis is so odd that it will surprise many. Astonished some may even say that if the conclusions are so odd then there must be something wrong in the analysis of the philosophy of Hinduism. To those who refuse to accept this analysis because they do not have a correct notion what is central in the philosophy of Hinduism. If they do they will feel no surprise at the conclusions.

This matter is so important that it needs to be explained. It may be recalled that the foregoing analysis of the religious revolution showed that religious ideals as forms of divine governance for human Society fall into two classes, one in which Society is the centre and the other in which the Individual is the centre. The same analysis showed that for the former the appropriate test of what is good and what is right i.e. the test of the moral order is utility while for the latter the test is justice.

Now the reason why the philosophy of Hinduism does not answer the test either of utility or of justice is because the religious ideal of Hinduism for divine governance of human society is an ideal, which falls into a separate class by itself. It is an ideal in which the individual is not the centre. The centre of the ideal is neither individual nor society. It is a class-the class of Supermen called Brahmins. Those who will bear the dominant and devastating fact in mind will understand why the philosophy of Hinduism is not founded on individual justice or social utility. The philosophy of Hinduism is founded on a totally different principle. To the question what is right and what is good the answer, which the philosophy of Hinduism gives, is remarkable. It holds that to be right and good the act must serve the interest of this class of supermen, namely, the Brahmins. Oscar Wilde said that to be intelligible is to be found out. Manu is neither afraid nor ashamed of being found out. Indeed Manu does not leave it to be found out. He expresses his view in resonant and majestic notes as who are the Supermen and anything which serves the interest of the Supermen is alone entitled to be called right and good.

6

VIEWS OF THE AMBEDKAR

INTRODUCTION

Although Indian society is fragmented into castes, there has been some change due to the movement of Dr. Ambedkar and other reformers. Some of his followers have benefited in terms of education and wealth due to his efforts. However, the change is not striking, and many are still subjected to hatred and perish in poverty. Caste-based violence continues to be an all pervading phenomenon. Even after the abolition of untouchability by law, practices, such as inhuman treatment, raping untouchable women and so forth, still occur in India. The situation at the time of Dr. Ambedkar was worse, and he personally experienced the caste system in its most inhuman form, being born into and brought up in an untouchable family.

A few seminal experiences awakened him to reality of the caste system. The first took place in Goregaon when Dr. Ambedkar was a boy of nine. He was to visit his father along with his brother. The location of his father's work place was far from the railway station, and no cart man was willing to take them on a bullock cart. One cart man agreed with the condition that the boys would have to drive the cart while he would sit behind. Throughout this escapade which lasted through the night, the boys went hungry because they could not get pure water to drink, even though they had plenty of food. Their inability to get water was of course due to the fact that untouchables were barred from using public wells. This incident had a very important place in Dr. Ambedkar's life and it left an indelible impression on his mind.

His worst experience of the caste system took place in Baroda when he was to become the Military Secretary to the Baroda State. He could not get accommodation in Baroda because he was an untouchable, though highly educated. He found a quarter in a Parsi boarding house and assumed a Parsi name. At work, the Brahman clerks and subordinates kept their distance and threw files and papers on him to avoid his touch. Even in the club, he was only allowed to sit in the corner and was not allowed to take part in games. No clear assignment was given to him, though he was a Military Secretary. When the Parsis discovered his identity, they besieged his boarding house and threatened to beat him. Eventually, the owner expelled him and he had to leave Baroda.

The third seminal experience took place in Chalisgaon, where no horse carriage driver was willing to take Dr. Ambedkar from the railway station to the place where a meeting was to be held. After a long wait, a carriage was finally brought. The driver and he were the only two occupants of the carriage. The carriage had not gone 200 paces when there was almost a collision with a motor car. Dr. Ambedkar was surprised that the driver, who was paid for hire every day, should have been so inexperienced. The accident was averted only because of the loud shout of a policeman. They somehow arrived at the culvert on a river. Around it there were no walls as there are on a bridge.

The carriage was thrown down on the stone pavement of the culvert, and the horse and the carriage fell down from the culvert into the river. So heavy was the fall that Dr. Ambedkar was knocked senseless. As a result of this he received several injuries. His leg was fractured and he was disabled for several days. On inquiry, Dr. Ambedkar was told the real facts. The delay at the railway station was due to the fact that the carriage drivers were not prepared to drive with a passenger who was an untouchable. They felt it was beneath their dignity. The Mahar untouchables could not tolerate that their leader should walk to their quarters. A compromise was therefore arrived at: the owner of a carriage would give it on hire but not drive. Although they could not find someone to drive it, the Mahars thought this to be a happy solution, evidently forgetting that the safety of the passenger was more important than the maintenance of his dignity. It was then that Dr. Ambedkar learned that even a menial Hindu carriage driver looked upon himself as superior to any untouchable even if that person be a barrister-at-law like Dr. Ambedkar.

There are many more incidences such as these from Dr. Ambedkar's life. These few, however, are sufficient for any person to understand the suffering experienced due to the practice of untouchability and caste. Many people in contemporary India still suffer from this system of graded inequality. They are living the life of degraded human beings.

Dr. Ambedkar's Analysis of Caste: Understanding the origin, genesis and mechanism of caste in India is a very complex problem. Many able minds have tried to penetrate it, including Dr. Ambedkar who began work on this issue as early as 1916. He attempted to link the many chains in the history of India in order to show how the caste system evolved. In Dr. Ambedkar's understanding, the prime factor responsible for the evolution of the system of untouchability was the religious persecution of Buddhists, while other social-psychological factors are secondary. The existence of caste in India is due to the notion of inequality imposed by religion, which gives rise to social and cultural practices and prejudices. If these social and cultural practices cease, caste could be annihilated. This is a simple formulation of the quite complex issue of caste.

The life and work of the Buddha marks the flowering of the axial period in India in the sixth century BC. This period was one of great turmoil as smaller tribal societies were transforming into larger settled ones and eventually mighty empires. It has been shown that these smaller, pre-imperial societies were not based on a graded system of inequality or caste. This is not to say that there was no class system. Further, these societies often exhibited unethical and immoral aspects, like incest, alcoholism, war mongering, and the savage practice of ritual sacrifice. Thus the revolutionary role of the Buddha was in first clearly proclaiming that the happiness of humans and society lies in ethics and not in rituals. Dr. Ambedkar understood the Buddha's awakening under the bodhi tree as a true revolution. "It was as great a revolution as the French

Revolution. Though it began as a religious revolution, it became more than a religious revolution. It became a social and political revolution."

The Buddha's revolution which culminated in the emergence of the mighty empire of Ashoka (r. 270-232 B. C.) further strengthened the Buddhist world view based on liberty, equality, and fraternity; a universal message that went beyond the Indian subcontinent. Under Ashoka, equality of punishment irrespective of the social standing of the criminal emerged. The priestly class was given the same treatment as that of the common people. Although Ashoka prevented worship of clan deities (kula devata) which served as the basis of income for the Brahmins, he was ecumenical and promoted inter-religious tolerance. He did not persecute the Brahmins, yet the Brahmans lost their social prestige as the majority of the people abandoned the animal sacrifices that the Brahmans officiated. The rule of law was established, and even animals received good treatment, as noted by the famous Chinese pilgrim, Hsuan Tsang.

In Revolution and Counter revolution in Ancient India, Dr. Ambedkar described that after the establishment of the rule of law, the Brahmins lived as a depressed class for the nearly 140 years of the Mauryan Empire. Pushyamitra Sunga of the Samvedi Brahmin clan then conspired to destroy Buddhism as the state religion and to make the Brahmins the sovereign rulers of India with the political power of the state behind it through murdering Ashoka's grandson, Emperor Brhadratha, in 185 B.C. After his accession, Pushyamitra launched a violent and virulent campaign of persecution against Buddhists and Buddhism. Thus, the counter-revolution against Buddhism began with the emergence of the Brahmins under the Sunga Dynasty.

At the same time, various major Brahmanical texts were written in order to counter Buddhism. According to Dr. Ambedkar, these texts are the true sources of inequality and were largely post-Mauryan developments. For example, Dr. Ambedkar showed that the Code of Manu (Manusmriti) was written by Sumati Bharagava after Psuhyamitra's revolt in 185 B.C. The Code of Manu, which served as the law of inequality, was drafted and enforced with the newly acquired state power by the Brahmins, while the myth of the first cosmic being Purusha, which tells of the divine origin of caste, was interpolated into the Rig-Veda. According to Dr. Ambedkar, the Manusmriti, the Bhagavad Gita, Shankaracharya's Vedanta, the Mahabharata, the Ramayana and the Puranas are all post-Mauryan texts which serve as sources of inequality.

It should be noted, however, that the Buddhists of ancient India did not accept this worldview all at once-perhaps they never did as is evident from the continuous struggle between the Brahmans and the untouchables (former Buddhists) of modern India. The hatred and contempt preached by the Brahmins was directed against Buddhists in particular and not against other groups. After the Mauryan Period, most Indians who had upheld Buddhism slipped back into Brahmanised Hinduism.

Other Indians who did not became untouchables, like the "Broken Men." The "Broken Men", according to Dr. Ambedkar, were the remaining peoples of broken and defeated tribal groups of ancient India. Dr. Ambedkar wrote about this concept of "Broken Men" and how they came into being when the primitive societies were breaking up and transforming into the larger settled societies of imperial India. Brahmanism never tried to absorb these Buddhists into the caste system but rather shut them right out of it by making them untouchables and all that they stood for, like no education, no means of economic development, etc. Untouchability was thus only born sometime around 400 A.D., as these "Broken Men" were not able to abandon beef eating when cow killing was made a capital offence by the Gupta kings. In this way, the cow politics of present day India has its roots in the counter-revolution of the Brahmans against the Buddhists. Untouchability was thus born out of the struggle for supremacy between Buddhism and Brahmanism on a variety of levels from political power to social convention.

This is not to say that Buddhism was destroyed all at once. The struggle went on until the Muslim invasion in 1200 C.E. The Muslim invasions played a decisive role as the Muslim invaders killed Buddhist monks or caused them to flee India. According to Dr. Ambedkar, "Religion like any other ideology can be attained only by propaganda. If propaganda fails, religion must disappear. The priestly class, however detestable it may be, is necessary to the sustenance of religion. For it is by its propaganda that religion is kept up. Without the priestly class religion must disappear." Due to this onslaught, the Buddhist Sangha in India underwent a great change in its composition. A disorganized system of married clergy with families who were called aryas developed.

They took the place of the bhikkhus and began to cater to the religious needs of the general community. They eventually attained the status of bhikkhus through the performance of some sacraments. They officiated at religious ceremonies, but at the same time, in addition to their profession of priesthood, they earned their livelihood through such avocations as masonry, painting, sculpting, gold smithing, and carpentry. These artisan-priests, who were in later times larger in number than the bhikkhus, became the religious guides of the people. Their avocations left them little time and desire for the acquisition of learning, for deep thinking, or for devotion to meditation and other spiritual exercises. They could not be expected to raise Buddhism to a higher position through their endeavours, nor could they check its course towards ruin through the introduction of salutary reforms. It is obvious that this new Buddhist priesthood had neither prestige nor learning and was a poor match for the rival Brahmins.

The upheaval caused by the Muslim invaders in the Buddhist Community lasted for a while. However, the Muslims did not destroy or challenge its principles or doctrines, which governed the spiritual life of the people. On the other hand, the Brahmanic invasion changed the principles which Buddhism had preached for centuries as universal ones of a spiritual life. According to Dr. Ambedkar, the Brahmanic invasion of Buddhist India is significant but usually neglected by the historians of India. Buddhist India is not a myth or construction of Dr. Ambedkar. This is supported by material evidence (Rhys Davids 1903). However, the concept of Vedic India or the Golden Vedic Age is truly a construction of recent times by Hindu Nationalists. The neo-Brahmanism of the post-Mauryan period brought the real changes in the political and social structure.

Through the medieval and colonial periods, the struggle against Brahmanism continued, though it was very much weakened due to the forces of time. The saint-poets of the 14th century onwards, such as Kabir, Nanadnar, Chokamela, and Tukaram, came from untouchable castes or backward classes and reflect "Buddhist" sentiments. Their teaching is marked with anti-caste and anti-Brahmanistic ideas. They ridiculed the Vedas and the religious texts of the Brahminism. They praised the ideals of liberty, equality and fraternity. This influenced Untouchables in south India who also realized in the beginning of the twentieth century that they were Buddhists and began their now well documented movement (G. Aloysius, 2004).

This deep-seated caste based hatred is responsible for most of the problems and evils in India today, including the degradation of women. The creative energy of the country is imprisoned in the caste system. The life and mission of Dr. Ambedkar was to annihilate caste and create a new society based on the principles of liberty, equality, and fraternity. He also knew that the solution lies in making people aware of their social history and why they are condemned to such a life. He wanted to usher India into an era of enlightenment, or "Right Enlightenment". (Nanda, 2002). This enlightened vision is the preface and key to everything else in conquering ignorance (the origin of suffering) and in the higher life (the end of suffering). For developing this enlightened vision, Dr. Ambedkar felt one needs to realize and understand the law of causality (paticca samuppada) or dhamma, "This is, that is; with the arising of this, that arises. This is not, that is not. With the cessation of this, that ceases."

DR. AMBEDKAR'S "AWAKENED" VISION

The New Buddhism: Dr. Ambedkar likened Indian society to an orange. If one removes the artificial rind of Hinduism, what remains is a fragmented society with mutually conflicting groups called the castes that run into 6000 in kind. Ambedkar did not strive for positional change in the whole system of graded inequality. He wanted to bring structural change to Indian society. He concluded that the contemporary state of degradation in India was due to the triumph of Brahmanism over Buddhism-the victory of a world view which sanctifies a graded inequality amongst living beings over one which prizes ethical conduct towards all such beings. David Brazier in his thought-provoking book, The New Buddhism, raises some very important points by questioning what the real project of the Buddha was after his enlightenment. He stresses that the Buddha had a vision of an ideal society which he shared with his disciples and thus awakened them to the reality of the world. This vision he termed as bodhi, that is, awakened vision. This vision of an awakened society moved the Buddha to turn the wheel of the Dhamma and to express his enlightenment experience to others to make this awakened society a reality.

Dr. Ambedkar also challenged traditional Buddhist positions and views. While he accepted that the Buddha was centrally concerned with suffering and the end of suffering, he did not define suffering based on the traditional eight types of suffering. His set of sufferings includes suffering due to humans' own wrongdoing and suffering due to inequality to other humans. In The Buddha and His Dhamma, he reformulates the life and teachings of the Buddha so that they can speak to contemporary Indian society and modern world. For him, the function of the Dhamma is two fold. That is to purify one's mind and to reconstruct world. In short, the purpose of the Dhamma is to transform an individual into a Buddha and to transform the world into a sangha. In the preface to The Buddha and His Dhamma, Dr. Ambedkar speaks of the purpose of the Dhamma as the creation of Dhamma Rajya, an ideal society based on liberty, equality and fraternity. It is clear that Dr. Ambedkar was trying to revive the Buddha's original project of the reconstruction of world. He called this vision Navayana or the "New Buddhism," which is a universal model applicable to all societies.

Steps Towards an Awakened Society: In the early years, Dr. Ambedkar was still struggling with his spirituality and slowly defining for himself this awakened vision. Therefore, most of his work for the liberation of his people came within a framework of activism concerning laws, committees, and commissions in the British India. For example, he gave evidence before the Southborough Committee for franchise and representation to the Indian legislatures in 1919. This was his first successful campaign without any mandate from his people. He successfully gained representation for depressed classes in the legislative assembly in Bombay. He was invited to participate in the Round Table Conference during 1932-1934 in order to discuss the future constitution of India, which he subsequently drafted. At this conference, he clashed with Gandhi, who denied the independent political rights of untouchables by deliberately trying to keep them in the fold of Hinduism. He also submitted a memorandum to the Cabinet Mission Plan in 1946 on behalf of the All India Scheduled Caste Federation (AISCF) in order to guarantee civil and political rights for them in free India.

The limited effect of such work within the system led Dr. Ambedkar to increasingly work outside of it as well. He began initiating mass protest movements, such as the Mahad Water Tank Movement (1927), and the Kalaram Temple Entry Movement (1934). He consciously created conditions for the illiterate people around him to become aware of the reality of the caste system. These conditions included writing books addressing various issues, editing several newspapers, launching political parties, and forming social organizations.

After clashing with Gandhi on the issue of the political empowerment of untouchables, Dr. Ambedkar realized the futility of changing the minds of the high caste Hindus. Although Gandhi outwardly showed his commitment to the untouchables, his real purpose appears to have been political. He wanted to ensure numerical power to Hindus (i.e. high-caste Hindus) vis-a-vis Muslims. These events led Ambedkar to renounce the systemic container of Hinduism. On May 30-31, 1936 at Dadar in Mumbai, he delivered a lengthy speech entitled "What way Liberty?" In this historic speech, he detailed the path leading towards liberty and gave a call to conversion. He did not make it clear as to which religion he was going to convert. However, at the end of this speech, he gave a clarion call to his people, which echoed the teaching of the Buddha, to "be your own light and refuge":

While thinking over what message should I give you on this occasion, I recollected the message given by the Lord Buddha to his Bhikkhu Sangha just before his mahaparinirvana and which has been quoted in Mahaparinibbana Sutta:

> "Once the Bhagwan, after having recovered from illness, was resting on a seat under a tree and his disciple venerable Ananda went to the Buddha. Having saluted, he sat beside him and said, 'I have seen the Lord in illness as well as in happiness. But from the present illness of the Lord, my body has become heavy like lead, my mind is not is peace. I cannot concentrate on the Dhamma, but I feel consolation and satisfaction that the Lord will not attain the parinibbana until a message is given to the Sangha.'"
>
> "Then the Lord replied, 'Ananda! What does the Sangha expect from me? Ananda, I have preached the Dhamma with an open heart, without concealing anything. The Tathagata has not kept anything concealed as some other teachers do. So Ananda, what more can the Tathagata tell the Bhikkhu Sangha. So Ananda, be self illuminating like the sun. Do not be dependent for light like the Earth. Believe in yourself, do not be dependent on others. Be truthful. Always take refuge in the truth and do not surrender to anyone.'"

I also take refuge in the words of the Buddha to be your own guide. Take refuge in your own reason. Do not listen to the advice of others. Do not succumb to others. Be truthful and take refuge in the truth. Never surrender to anything. If you keep in mind this message of Lord Buddha at this juncture, I am sure, your decision will not be wrong.

In order to realize an awakened society, Dr. Ambedkar saw than an inner revolution among his people needed to take place in tandem with the social and political work of gaining equal rights for untouchables. This internal revolution he found in the act of conversion from the dependency and subservience of being an untouchable in Hinduism to the independence and empowerment of a Buddhist identity and complete development as a human being. In this way, Dr. Ambedkar began to develop a vision for his people in order to make them realize the importance of the Buddha Dhamma. He saw that religious reformation is often a precursor to political emancipation. In his Annihilation of Caste, he cited such examples in the revolutions of Protestant Europe, the first Mauryan ruler Chandragupta, and the contemporary revolution of Guru Nanak and the Sikhs in Punjab. He concluded that the emancipation of the mind is a necessary preliminary for the political emancipation of the people.

DR. AMBEDKAR'S VISION OF DHAMMA AND PRACTICE

Vision of Dhamma: Dhamma is the perfection of life: In The Buddha and His Dhamma, Dr. Ambedkar describes the path of the bodhisattva and presents the sublime teaching of non-attachment through quotes from the dialogue between the Buddha and Subhuti in the Diamond Sutra. In this sutra, the six perfections (paramita) of giving, morality, patience, energy, meditation, and wisdom are taught as not only practices for the individual but also ones to instigate others to do.

Dhamma is to Live in Nibbana: Dr. Ambedkar strongly affirmed the nature of Nibbana as experienced here in this life and in this world. He wrote that the Buddha clearly rejected notions of Nibbana held by other schools of thought at the time. Specifically, the Buddha saw that the Brahmanistic and Upanishadic notions of the salvation of a soul made Nibbana into a goal achieved after death. Dr. Ambedkar quotes the famous Fire Sermon (Adittapariyaya Sutta, S.iv.19) to show how the Buddha's notion of the extinction of the passions, and not physical death, made Nibbana into a much more practical this-worldly goal. Nibbana or "awakened vision" tells one of the difficulties in the realization of the Eight-Fold Path. The chief of these difficulties are the five fetters (samyojana) or five underlying tendencies (anusaya). The third fetter of dependence on the efficacy of rites and ceremonies is especially important in this context. Dr. Ambedkar felt that no good resolutions, however firm, will lead to anything unless we shed ritualism. By ritualism, he meant the belief that outward acts associated with priestly power and holy ceremony can afford one assistance of some kind. It is only when we have overcome our ties to salvific ritual, that humans can be said to have fairly entered the stream of liberation and have a chance to sooner or later win victory. Dhamma is Karma-the instrument of moral order: Dr. Ambedkar clearly stated that the moral order or the world (kamma niyama) does not depend on a creator god or any other gods. The moral order may be good or bad but this depends on humans and nothing else. The Buddha discovered that the world (loka) revolves due to karma. There are three worlds: the sensual world, the form-ish world, and the formless world. The state of Nibbana, where the law of karma is not operative, is a way of being and acting beyond these worlds. However, the world in which most of us live most of the time is the world of sensual pleasures. The mental states in the sensual world are destructive because enormous strife and suffering come about due to competition for sensual desires. This world is made up of sounds, forms, colours, tastes, tactile objects, ideas, concepts etc. Sometimes, the ideas or concepts are just imposed by society, such as caste or graded inequality in India.

Caste as a consciousness comes into being due to social practices and conventions and is wrong view (miccha ditthi). It is a mental and social conditioning whereby the individual is crushed. Individuals have little or no choice. Clearly, this goes against the Buddha's teaching of karma and the power of intention (cetana). The intention or mental state behind an action indicates its moral quality and action per se does not determine the nature of karma. As mental states precede actions by body and speech, positive mental states lead to positive actions of body and speech and negative mental states lead to negative actions of body and speech. Thus, the law of karma emphasizes personal responsibility and positive action, not passivity to harmful social conventions. In this way, it clearly does not support that the idea that birth in a lower caste is the deserved result of one's unwholesome past actions.

Practice-purification of mind, body and speech by meditation and morality

Thus Dr. Ambedkar made it explicit that purification of mind, body and speech is the Dhamma. Dr. Ambedkar emphasized the training of mind in meditation, as did the Buddha, for developing intention or thought, which leads to right states of consciousness. He paraphrases the Sallekha Sutta (M.i.40):

You are to expunge by resolving that, though others may be harmful, you will be harmless.

That though others may kill, you will never kill.

That though others may steal, you will not.

That though others may not lead the higher life, you will.

That though others may lie, traduce, denounce, or prattle, you will not.

That though others may be covetous, you will covet not.

That though others may be malignant, you will not be malignant.

That though others may be given over to wrong views, wrong aims, wrong speech, wrong actions, and wrong concentration, you must follow (the Noble Eightfold Path in) right outlook, right aims, right speech, right actions, right mode of livelihood, right effort, right mindfulness and right concentration.

That though others are wrong about the truth and wrong about deliverance, you will be right about truth and right about deliverance.

That though others may be possessed by sloth and torpor, you will free yourselves therefrom.

That though others may be puffed up, you will be humble-minded.

That though others may be perplexed by doubts, you will be free from them.

That though others may harbour wrath, malevolence, envy, jealousy, niggardliness, avarice, hypocrisy, deceit, imperviousness, arrogance, forwardness, association with bad friends, slackness, unbelief, shamelessness, unscrupulousness, lack of instruction, inertness, bewilderment, and unwisdom, you will be the reverse of all these things.

That though others may clutch at and hug the temporal nor loose their hold thereon, you will clutch and hug the things that are not temporal, and will ensue renunciation.

I say it is the development of thought which is so efficacious for right states of consciousness, not to speak of act and speech. And therefore, Cunda, there must be developed the thought to all the foregoing resolves I have detailed.

This sutta can be interpreted as one's own resolve to transform oneself into a Buddha even when the world around is steeped with various vices.

Morality & Ethics (sila)-the bridge between the individual and the social or the foundation of a just society.

The highest realization in Buddhism is the emancipation of the mind, which Dr. Ambedkar also understood as liberty. The antithesis of liberty is slavery. According to the Buddha, there are two kinds of slavery: inner and outer. A certain deity asked the Buddha:

The inner tangle and the outer tangle:

This generation is entangled in a tangle.

And so I ask of Gautama this question:

Who succeeds in disentangling this tangle?

The Buddha replied:

When a wise man, established in Virtue

Develops Consciousness and Understanding

Then as a Bhikkhu ardent and sagacious

He succeeds in disentangling this tangle.

Liberty is freedom from any control and in return demands no will to control others. The ethics of Buddhism ensures this freedom from control. Therefore, sila is the foundation of a just society. It is universal and not marked with sectarian feeling. If it does, it will only protect the "group interest," and according to Dr. Ambedkar will become antisocial. Sila is right or ethical behaviour by one person towards another. Thus Dr. Ambedkar wrote that religion is personal, while Dhamma as the practice of sila is interpersonal. Therefore, society cannot do without Dhamma or righteousness.

In this way, Dr. Ambedkar clearly shows an understanding of the difference between the type of morality belonging to personal power and threat and the type belonging to collective power and personal responsibility. He makes the observation that the former type belongs to religion, which is concerned with the relation between humans and God. This type of morality helps to maintain peace and order and "is attached and detached as the occasion requires" to protect the interests of a particular group (Sangharakshita, 1986:156). In the latter understanding of morality, Ambedkar speaks not of religion but of Dhamma:

> Morality is Dhamma and Dhamma is Morality. Morality and Dhamma arise from the direct necessity for man to love man. It is not to please God that man has to be moral. It is for his own good that man has to love man. (Sangharakshita, 1986:156)

This Dhamma is the universal morality which protects the weak from the strong and which safeguards the growth of the individual. It gives common models, standards, and rules. Finally, it ensures that liberty and equality can be established.

> The only remedy lies in making fraternity universally effective. What is fraternity? It is nothing but another name for the brotherhood of men which is another name for morality. This is why the Buddha preached that Dhamma is morality and as Dhamma is sacred so is morality. (Sangharakshita, 1986:157)

This morality, however, is not just a set of ideals, but part of the threefold training of the mind in morality, concentration, and wisdom. For Dr. Ambedkar, training in sila is formalized for non-monastics in the practice of the five basic precepts (pancasila) and the "taking of refuge" in a ceremony called diksha. In the institutionalization of the diksha ceremony for untouchables converting to Buddhism, Ambedkar included taking the five precepts as well as twenty-two additional vows. Dr. Ambedkar made this ceremony of taking refuge central to his vision of a new Buddhist identity for the lay Buddhist movement he led among untouchables. He recognized the fundamental need of a very conscious statement of Buddhist identity for his community as it renounced Hinduism and embraced Buddhism. In order to face the oppressive system of caste society in India, this new Buddhist identity could not be fuzzy or passive, especially since there was no monastic order to lead and defend the community. He also felt a strong lay community was imperative to re-establishing a proper ordained community in India, since he saw the existing monastic order, especially in Theravada countries, as corrupt.

DR. AMBEDKAR'S MOVEMENT FOR JUSTICE

Just Society through a Model Society (Sangha) of Just People: The vision of an awakened society led the Buddha to set in motion the Wheel of the Dhamma. The Buddha set in motion the wheel of the Dhamma when he awakened five disciples in Sarnath. According to Dr. Ambedkar, the Buddha organized the Bhikku Sangha to make this just society a living reality and to set a model for the society to imitate.

But the blessed Lord also knew that merely preaching the Dhamma to the common man would not result in the creation of that ideal society based on righteousness. An ideal must be practical and must be shown to be practicable. Then and then only people strive after it and realize it. To create this striving, it is necessary to have a picture of a society working on the basis of the ideal and thereby proving to the common man that the ideal was not impracticable but on the other hand realizable. The Sangha is a model of a society realizing the Dhamma preached by the blessed Lord. (BAWS XI, 434)

According to Dr. Ambedkar, the code of the bhikkhu, the patimokkha, was formulated to make the sangha an ideal society. Thus, the bhikkhu must always be seen as subordinate to and enfolded into the sangha or ideal society. The training of a bhikkhu/bhikkhuni is aimed at making him/her a perfect citizen of the ideal society. In another sense, the rules of the monastic are not meant for making a perfect being, but for creating a servant of the society who will be committed to end suffering and living the ideals of Liberty, Equality and Fraternity. The monastic should not be indifferent to the suffering of lay people.

She/he must fight for establishing an ideal society.

Since the Buddha established the sangha in order to lay the foundation of an awakened society, he preached his Dhamma to all without distinction, to monastic as well as to lay people. Ambedkar felt there was no difference between the monastic and a lay person as far as the practice of the Dhamma goes. The distinction, however, is in the degree of involvement in the preaching and propagating of the Dhamma, essentially of time and commitment. Monastics are the full-timers, having neither the worldly responsibilities of marriage nor private property. On the other hand, lay persons are the part-timers, ensconced in worldly duties. As the full-timers have no private property, the part-timers have had to support them with dana. The part-timers have mainly given alms, and provided abodes and robes to the full-timers. The Buddha put in place these dependencies, which are also freedoms, as a check and balance mechanism to ensure that the full-timers should not betray the mission. The part-timers could complain to the larger sangha about the misconduct of any of the full-timers. Thus, the bond of alms between monastic and lay person was instrumental in the successful spread of the Dhamma.

However, this bond of alms was taken to extremes when the lay emperor Ashoka supported and interfered in the matters of sangha. The history of this disappearance of Buddhism in India is the history of the gradual weakening of this bond of alms and the disappearance of the nucleus of the Buddhist society, the monastic sangha. How could any teaching survive with the destruction of its organization and propaganda base? Buddhism eventually disappeared, because although the lay sangha strove hard, they could not give their best energies and could not organize themselves effectively.

Despite his often strong criticisms, Dr. Ambedkar did not wish to do away with the monastic sangha. On the contrary, he saw the sangha as having an important role in the awakened society. His ideal society was the Buddhist Sangha. But here is a departure from the tradition. He wanted lay persons to be part and parcel of the New Sangha. With this basic view in mind, Dr. Ambedkar expressed his views on the reconstruction of the sangha to suit modern society.

Firstly, he felt that the absence of a dhamma diksha for lay followers was a grave omission. Throughout history, the bhikkhus have been initiated and organised but the lay sangha has not. Except for a few insignificant exceptions, the Dhamma is common to both. Dr. Ambedkar wanted to correct this anomaly, and so accepted the challenge to initiate his own lay followers in the Dhamma. He also suggested the creation of lay preachers who could go about and preach the Buddha's Dhamma among the people and look after the new converts to guide their practice, rather than creating newly ordained monastics or depending on foreign monastics for this purpose. He felt these lay preachers must be paid and that they could be married. He wanted to restructure the Sangha so as to fit it in the modern society. Unfortunately, Dr. Ambedkar did not live long enough to build a movement to actualize this new understanding of the role of monastics in an awakened society.

However, the British monk Sangharakshita, who met Dr. Ambedkar thrice and helped lead the neo-Buddhist movement in India after Ambedkar's death, did develop Ambedkar's basic concept further. He has integrated Ambedkar's criticisms of the bhikkhu sangha in the creation of his new orders, the British-based Friends of the Western Buddhist Order (FWBO) and the Indian-based Trailokya Buddha Mahasangha (TBM) order nurtured by Dhammachari Lokamitra. In the spirit of Ambedkar's notion of married lay preachers who would spread the Buddha Dhamma about India, Sangharakshita has developed an intermediate form of Buddhist practitioner, called a dharmachari/charini or "dharma-farer," which dissolves the dichotomy between lay and monastic. Sangharakshita's order has sought to intensify serious training for those interested while not creating a distinction of superiority between those who choose less arduous courses. This flexibility of practice models has significantly allowed those with a high level of training to maintain a lay appearance, thereby facilitating involvement in social activities. The uniting factor of the different levels of practice is the commitment to social service within the community and the society. Sangharakshita's vision is one of a decentralized community of people sharing the same spiritual commitment without the need for ecclesiastical structure (Sponberg, 1996:90).

Dr. Ambedkar also had other concrete ideas for the creation of an awakened society based on the Buddha Dhamma. He had planned to establish a Buddhism and Religions Seminary where persons who wished to become preachers could be taught Buddhism and trained in the comparative study of other religions. He suggested the introduction of congregational worship in the Buddha Vihara every Sunday followed by a sermon. The Buddha and His Dhamma, itself, was an attempt to create a "Buddhist Bible"-a single volume work which could be a constant companion of the convert. Like the lay preacher, the Buddhist Bible represents a middle way intended to bridge the gap between the lofty ideals of monastic practice and learning and the daily needs of the larger lay sangha.

Dr. Ambedkar made many provisions to create the Dhamma as a living force in India. Besides his emphasis on the Dhamma, which he wanted to make heart of his movement, he knew the importance of social awakening and politics. After his conversion, he planned to constitute a political party, The Republican Party of India. The aim was to ensure the social, political and economic justice enshrined in the preamble of the constitution of India in order to create an ideal society. Society, according to Ambedkar, cannot do without Dhamma nor without just government.

Society has to choose one of the three alternatives. Society may choose not to have any Dhamma as an instrument of government. For Dhamma is nothing if it is not an instrument of government. This means society chooses the road to anarchy. Secondly, society may choose the police, i.e., dictatorship as an instrument of government. Thirdly, society may choose Dhamma plus the magistrate wherever people fail to observe the Dhamma. In anarchy and dictatorship liberty is lost. Only in the third liberty survives.

According to Ambedkar, the norm or the criterion for judging right and wrong in modern society is justice. Justice is ensured when the society is based on the principles of liberty, equality, and fraternity. The system of grading people as in the caste system will always lead to injustice. Ambedkar saw no solution in communism or capitalism, the two political currents dominant during his day. He found a solution in Buddhism. He said. "Man must grow materially as well as spiritually. Society has been aiming to lay a new foundation which was summarized by the French Revolution in three words, Fraternity, Liberty and Equality. The French Revolution was welcomed because of this slogan. It failed to produce equality. We welcome the Russian Revolution because it aims to produce equality. But it cannot be too much emphasized that in producing equality in society one cannot afford to sacrifice fraternity or liberty. Equality will be of no value without fraternity or liberty. It seems that the three (liberty, equality and fraternity) can coexist only if one follows the way of the Buddha" (BAWS III, 462, Italics and bracket added).

He saw the ideal society as one full of channels for conveying change taking place in one part to other parts. In an ideal society, he remarked, there should be many interests, consciously communicated and shared. There should be varied and free points of contact with other modes of association. In other words there must be social endosmosis. This is fraternity, which is only another name for democracy. Democracy is not merely a form of government. It is primarily a mode of associated living, of conjoint communicated experience. It is essentially an attitude of respect and reverence towards fellow beings. Finally, this reconstruction of the world is possible through Dhamma. Dhamma is essentially and fundamentally social. In this way, his ideal society is based on the universality of Dhamma, which consists of liberty, equality and fraternity. In the All India Radio broadcast of his speech on October 3,1954, Dr. Ambedkar clarified the usage of these terms:

Positively, my social philosophy may be said to be enshrined in three words: Liberty, Equality and Fraternity. Let no one, however, say that I have borrowed my philosophy from the French Revolution. I have not. My philosophy has roots in religion and not in political science. I have derived them from the teachings of my master, the Buddha.

The sad part of Dr. Ambedkar's movement, however, has been the lack of recognition in the entire movement of the role of Dhamma (the practice of liberty, equality and fraternity). As a result of this, the social organizations and political parties based on Ambedkar face the problems of caste and conflict. They fall asunder due to organizational problems. The success of Dr. Ambedkar's movement lies not just in education and agitation but in how effectively his followers organize themselves; that is to say how they use fraternity as a principle to make fraternity universal. Ambedkar wanted to establish universal fraternity which was not to be based on sectarian attitudes and caste prejudices. He wrote:

There are two forces prevalent in society: individualism and fraternity. Individualism is ever present. Every individual is ever asking "I and my neighbours, are we all brothers, are we even fiftieth cousins, am I their keeper, why should I do right by them?" and under the pressure of his own particular interests acting as though he was an end to himself, thereby developing a non-social and even an antisocial self.

There are many offshoots of the political party of which Dr. B. R. Ambedkar himself planned and wrote a constitution. Their main motivation is anti-Brahmanism and anti-caste. However, most of them are trapped in their own prisons of caste or the interests of their group, and therefore become antisocial. Dhamma is the way to break the prison of caste and prejudices. Dhamma is to extend fraternity both horizontally and vertically in the social structure and hence the Dhamma can help in overcoming caste identities. In conclusion, the most unfortunate part of Dr. B. R. Ambedkar's movement was his untimely death. He died just after the great conversion movement in 1956. Most of the ideas in his mind died with him. However, he left enough material and blueprints for his millions of followers to follow and organize themselves as an ideal society to set up a model for the world. The re-entry of Buddhism to India after a gap of hundreds of years has been very dramatic. Buddhism has come back as a mass movement among the untouchables.

The success of the Buddhist movement depends on the organization of a sangha of full-timers and part-timers. This sangha must transcend caste and should not get trapped in one caste or group. It needs to integrate with the larger Indian society by breaking isolation. This sangha should exemplify liberty, equality, and fraternity to live and act in harmony within itself. There is a necessity for trained dhammasevak (servants of the Dhamma). The dhammasevak must have at the same time a strong sense of history and should be ready to go beyond the great wall of caste. The new servants of the Dhamma must passionately fight for practising and propagating liberty, equality, and fraternity. In short, Dhamma can re-ethicize Indian society but it depends on how the followers of Dr. Ambedkar understand and situate the Dhamma in the various movements organized under his name and philosophy.

Think 'The System' before Taking Action: Unlike most untouchables Ambedkar's was fortunate to receive an excellent international education. Under the protection of a local Maharaja he completed his masters at Columbia, his PhD in economics at the London School of Economics and earned a law degree in England in the 1920's. During his days at university, while being introduced to western notions of individualism, equality and democracy he had the opportunity to reflect on the caste system structuring his own society. These theoretical notions went completely opposite to the intrinsic hierarchy of Hinduism that implied a natural notion of inequality. His time abroad gave him the possibility to look at his own society with an outsider's eye, and to question the so-called harmonious social structure of India. He realised that untouchability was not a universal but a social construct that could be challenged and that 95 untouchables as Indian nationals had the duty to ask for the same rights as their co-citizens.

To illustrate the perverse nature of the caste system to his Western colleagues, Ambedkar would compare it to the class system of the West.

For him in the class system there was a possibility for upward mobility, for horizontal cooperation and for revolution. In other words, according to Ambedkar, classes were not closed units. On the other hand, a social structure based on the caste system was like a closed class unit in which upward mobility was impossible and revolution unthinkable. To him, caste was like the colour of the skin or a physical attribute: it was there to stay, the same, until death.

Thus, this intrinsic fatalism imposed by God-a supreme being-impeded untouchables aspiring to greater goals. He came to the conclusion that because untouchables were an integral element participating to the "harmony of the whole" in Hinduism, they were doomed to be subdued. Thus making this system unique in its genre, as no other religion had ever created a permanent status of untouchability:

> "Untouchables are born impure, they are impure while they live, they die the death of the impure, and they give birth to children who are born with the stigma of untouchability affixed to them. It is a case of

permanent, hereditary stain which nothing can cleanse".

This questioning awaked the social activist soul in Ambedkar. He embarked on a life long quest to reform his society into recognizing the unique dignity of each of its citizens.

Using Democracy to Empower the Underdogs: Ambedkar fought on many fronts to empower his people. He understood, early on, the importance of political rights. For him this modern political empowerment could counter the power of conservative Hinduism. Thus, he took advantage of the debates going on in the mid-1920s on the shape of the electoral system of the future independent India. Ambedkar committed to create a system that would favour the schedule class giving it the political leverage necessary to become a political minority. For this reason he fought zealously for the creation of reserved constituencies. This electoral system was already in place for other religious minorities such as Muslims.

It was a system by which only members of a specific minority, in predefined circumscriptions, where allowed to vote for a candidate, member of their own group. Consequently, it allowed a community to be represented by a leader of their own choosing. This system was often wrongly mistaken with reserved seats by which a certain amount of seats were reserved for a group in certain circumscription, but in which, the candidates were elected by society as a whole. For Ambedkar, because untouchables were an existing minority in many circumscriptions; the system of 'reserved seats' was indirectly detrimental, even if seats were reserved for them, a coalition of higher castes could easily co-opt and elect an untouchable of their choice not necessarily representing the Dalits.

The shape of the Indian election system was a subject of great dissent between Gandhi and Ambedkar. For Gandhi untouchables were part and parcel of the Hindu society, and Hindus were, sole, responsible for the position of the Dalits. It was their moral responsibility to rehabilitate them into society. Therefore, Gandhi was against the idea of reserved constituencies, he argued that it would divide Hindus, isolate untouchables and break the 'harmonious' social structure of

India. For him, the position of untouchables could not, in anyway, be compared to that of Muslims, because they were Hindus.

Ambedkar agreed that the responsibility for the discriminator position of the Dalits lay with Hindus, but he did not share Gandhi's faith in upper class Hindus. They, he reasoned, would continue to maintain their entrenched prejudice. He wanted Dalits to benefit from a minority status, in order for them to become a political force and emancipate themselves without the help of others. He wanted them to become equal citizens through the full, modern implementation of democracy. Reserved constituencies were granted to untouchables by the British in the Communal Award (1932), but they had to give them up with the Poona Act (1932) after Gandhi embarked on a hunger strike in protest against the British decision.

Ambedkar saw this as a failure as it did not lead to the political independence for the Dalits. In his eyes, it perpetuated their subdued condition. Ambedkar legacy haunts the modern constitution. He was appointed Minister of justice in 1947 under Nehru, and was one of the main designers of the Indian constitution. He saw this as a unique occasion to imprint India with his modern vision of the Nation. Thus, he equipped his country with a centralised federal framework. He, also, was a fervent defender of affirmative action, and applied this policy to the educational and public sectors. In 1947 a reservation of 12.5% was introduced in the public sector for Dalits. In 1970, this reservation was raised to 16.66% in vacancies filled by other means than by open competition. For Ambedkar these safeguards were the keys to upward mobility, independence and he hoped they would lead to the questioning of the old conservative social structure.

Ideally, the constitution of a nation seeks to create both a legal framework for a political society and also to guarantee the fundamental human rights or civil liberties of its members. For this reason Ambedkar fought for the reform of Hindu Law by introducing a 'western' based civil code: the Hindu code bill. This reform was to tune India's social customs with Western values such as equality, liberalism and human rights, and protect minority groups. For instance, the bill was to establish equal gender rights to property and impose a need to legally justify a demand for divorce-to avoid widespread repudiation. This proposed reform, as one can imagine, was extremely controversial, it was met with suspicion by Hindus traditionalists and members of congress, as it directly challenged their "conservative" grip over the private sphere and questioned traditional ideas of inheritance, marriage and divorce.

It was also very problematic among Muslims, as it challenged Muslim Shariah law. With hindsight we can say Ambedkar had embarked on a very slippery slope, he wanted to introduce a Western concept of law in which one common law, protecting the 'individual' would regulate both private and public sphere. Yet the private sphere still remained framed by old rigid customs and laws that favoured groups rights over individual ones. Nehru saw the bill as a crucial step in modernizing India, but he took a moderate and practical position, to win the consent of Congress Nehru divided it into four parts; unfortunately the part on marriage and divorce, important to Ambedkar, was totally disfigured and finally rejected by congress in 1951.

Nehru did not question this decision, he felt that it was too early to shake all the conservative pillars of India, and that with time such reform would be accepted. Ambedkar, on the other hand, felt betrayed and resigned from his position in government. One can understand his disillusion; Congress was ready to approve the constitution, but not to accept the social changes that came with a modern nation. Ambedkar fight for untouchables' rights with in the constitution had tried to put the problem in a wider perspective and provide responses to questions of nationalism, democracy and social justice. He wanted, like all true humanists, to establish a social order offering access to justice and dignity for all.

Was Conversion the Ultimate Solution?

After spending most of his life trying to reform Hinduism, from above through legal-safeguards, and from below through the politicization of the untouchables, Ambedkar renounced these strategies. For him, Hinduism had definitely killed the public spirit in India, and in his opinion, social justice would never be attained unless the untouchables renounced their religion. Therefore, the last resort to attain his goal was, to call for a massive conversion to Buddhism, a religion that treated its followers as equals. Ambedkar's decision marked a turning point in his reasoning for which he finally openly admitted the difficulties of changing an old system of discrimination based on birth. Here again, Ambedkar, as a true born social activist, used his charisma to mobilize his followers. Thus, on October 1956, between 300,000 and 600,000 untouchables converted "en masse". This conversion was of course strongly criticized by the Hindus, as it appeared to them to be an outrage to Hinduism, and therefore to spirituality. Yet, for Ambedkar the event remained about social emancipation and had little to do with pure spirituality, than a spiritual one. Was conversion the solution? Results remain mitigated. More than 55% of untouchables in the Maharashtra province converted, and Buddhism went from registering 2500 followers in 1950 to 2.5 million in 1961. Yet, most of the converted came only from Maharashtra province and consequently this movement was limited geographically and did not create a strong sense of horizontal solidarity. Nonetheless, it did mark a turning point in the intellectual emancipation of the Dalits from the power of the Brahmins.

AMBEDKAR: A MITIGATED LEGACY?

During his life time, Ambedkar did not succeed in openly transforming Indian society. He constantly struggled against the conservatism of upper Hindu castes. He proposed a novel vision of the nation, a vision opposed to traditionalism and instead based on humanism. This explains, in part, why his ideas were ignored until recently and why he was described, at best, as a local social activist. Yet, India, as we know it today, owes a lot to Ambedkar. His experiences with both federal and unitary constitutions allowed him to design a suitable constitution for his country. As a social reformer, he lead India into a new-era of social political history, ensuring the active involvement of otherwise 'ignored' section of the society. It is only recently that Ambedkar has been recognised as being one of India's modern founders.

In the late 80's, his portrait was hung in the house of parliament along with those of other key politicians. Historians have also begun to recognise the his work, today he is discussed in conjunction with Gandhi, Jinnah and Nehru. Surprisingly enough, it appears that, decades after his death, Ambedkar has become the voice of the deprived. His return to the public arena owes a lot to politicians who have understood the political weight of "untouchables" votes. Political parties, such as the Bahujan Samaj Party (BSP), consider themselves as the bearers of Ambedkar's legacy and shape their political agenda around his ideas. More surprisingly, in Uttar Pradesh in the late 90's more than 15 000 statues were raised in his honour. These statues have often been profaned by fervent Hindu nationalists putting Ambedkar at the heart of the fight for public space today and reinforcing his image as the symbol of the conflict between lower and upper castes.

Ambedkar's return to the public scene should be put into perspective. It symbolizes probably more than a simple political move; and could be interpreted as the concrete proof that India is today slowly entering the postmodern era in which multiple visions of the nation are openly allowed to confront each other and offer viable alternatives to its citizens. More importantly, his fight and vision could be of great use to contemporary Europe that is becoming, because of the growing fluidity of borders, fatally more multicultural in terms of its population. Indeed, western countries today are struggling to find ways to incorporate the influx of minorities in their often rigid definition of democracy. Ambedkar's approaches, such as positive discrimination, have already been successfully used by multicultural democracies such as Canada or Australia. Yet, methods vary from one political context to other; it is more his political stubbornness to explore and stretch the concept of democracy to empower minorities that should inspire us. Like him, we should think of democracy as an involving political concept having for first principle universal representation.

The importance of Ambedkar has been recently attacked by certain intellectuals who seem to resent the celebration of Ambedkar on the national level. Dalit assertion is inevitably dealt with violence, both physical as well as ideological. Such times as these demand a nuanced understanding of the different roles which both Gandhi and Ambedkar played in reconstituting an independent India which would be truly free. For, it may be argued that regardless of the real differences between these two inspiring figures of India's struggle for freedom, both of them would represent a severe blow to the foundations of religious fundamentalism as we have come to experience in our midst.

Aims and Objectives

The central aim therefore is not limited to social upliftment of the Harijans, but economic emancipation of the poor by eliminating all forms of exploitation through capacity building among the target population and conscientisation of the masses with the help of basic education and self-employment. While formulating the objectives, the Sangh took note of the present international outlook towards development which overwhelmingly emphasise on improvement in quality of life than mere development of per capita income. The basic parameters of quality of life are education, health and environment and specifically in these three spheres, the poor including the Harijans are grossly deprived. Keeping in view above mentioned development paradigm of the international institutions, the Sangh framed following objectives:-

(i) To promote social, economic and cultural welfare of the underprivileged and weaker sections including Harijans, Adivasis, Dalits and help them to live a dignified life.

(ii) To secure human development irrespective of caste, creed, sex and religion.

(iii) To bring about growth and development of the children on holistic concept.

(iv) To disseminate popular education in lieu of elitist education of the present day, so as to ensure "Education for All."

(v) To promote vocational education and training leading to income generation.

(vi) To develop an integrated health care system and sanitation on community based sustainable programmes Strategies were formulated on the basis of stated Aims and objectives. The central strategy is to concentrate on child welfare and development with the belief that childhood is that segment of life when mind, bodies and personalities are formed and even the slightest deprivation during this period can lead to life-long impairment resulting in fundamental distortion in human development. Benefiting from the hindsight of Gandhiji who founded the Sangh and laid emphases on basic education, sanitation and gram Swaraj, the HSS, Bengal carefully blended western institutional framework with Indian cultural heritage and developed its own brand of institutions which are common with other NGOs but with the basic difference that all of them are innovative, community based and thus sustainable even without the guidance of the HSS, Bengal.

Outreach

During last 20 years, the HSS, Bengal has achieved a spatial outreach in 17 districts of West Bengal where it has 210 branches / associates, the maximum number of branches/ associates (37) being in the Midnapur district and the minimum (05) in the districts of north and south Dinajpur and Purulia. These 210 branches / associates have covered 1050 villages comprising of 2. 5 lakh people. The district-wise break-up of branches / associates and targeted population is as under:-

Only district left out is Calcutta where the need for the programme is comparatively less. HSS however is contemplating child development activities in selected slum areas of Calcutta metropolis provided funds are forthcoming. Attempts are also being made to increase the outreach in Purulia and districts of North Bengal where concentration of poor and backward scheduled caste and tribe population is highest. As funds would permit there would be progressive escalation of activities and outreach in those districts over the next reporting year.

Harijan

In the Indian caste system, a Dalit, often called an untouchable, is a person who does not have any varnas. Varna refers to the Hindu belief that most humans were created from different parts of the body of the divinity Purusha and according to which part they were created from it defines their social standing for issues such as who they can marry and what jobs they can do. . Dalits fall outside varnas system and have historically been prevented from doing any but the most menial jobs. They are also known as outcastes. Included are leather-workers (called chamar), poor farmers and landless labourers, scavengers (called bhangi or chura), street handicrafters, folk artists, clothes washers (dhobi) etc.

Terms Associated with the Dalit Caste

Dalit is the latest and currently most politically correct of many terms used for the caste. Offensive terms used mostly in the past include chura, bhangi, neech, kanjjar, and mirasi. Whereas the terms chura and bhangi are profession-based terms for scavengers, they can serve as general terms for the low-born; others are actual names of the caste. Harijan was a term for untouchable, coined by Mahatma Gandhi, which means Children of God-Hari is another name for the god Vishnu. It is now considered patronizing. The term can also be attributed to Dalit castes of Pakistan called the Haris, who are a group of mud-hut builders. Neo-Buddhist Dalits try to make 'Harijan' appear as a disgrace to all Dalits as it comes from a Hindu name. This term had already been used, in a different form, by the medieval philosopher Ramanuja who uplifted many backward caste peoples: as Thirukulattar, or People of Holy Clan. (He was probably the first to allow the untouchables into temples, albeit for limited periods).

The word 'Dalit' comes from the Marathi root dal, and means 'held under check', 'suppressed', or 'crushed', or, in a looser sense, 'oppressed'. Maharashtrian Dalit Activist and poet Namdeo Dhasal made it a symbol of pride to fight against social injustice. He said:

"Yes, I do feel that the fight to eradicate caste has to be fought by Dalits and caste Hindus together carrying forward the tradition of Adi Shankara, which got broken somewhere in between."

It is possible that Dr. Ambedkar borrowed this term from Swami Vivekananda from his quote, "Deena-Dalita-Dukhi Devo

Bhava!" ("Service to the weak, the downtrodden and the suffering masses itself is the worship of God").

Another term used for the Dalits was Matanga named after Maharshi Matanga, a Matanga Bhil and guru of Bhakta Shabari. In fact, Dalits are often addressed as 'Matanga 'in passages like Varaha Purana 1. 139. 91.

Dr. B. R. Ambedkar, a Dalit, and one of the leaders of the Indian independence movement, is considered the chief architect of the Indian Constitution, in which Article 17 abolishes untouchability. Ever since, under the aegis of the Constitution of India, a 'Reservation System' (privilege in education and other services given only to the Dalits) has been implemented for the benefit of the 'Dalits' which is a step towards affirmative action.

The terms scheduled castes/scheduled tribes (SC/ST) and non-caste tribes are also used in the Indian legal system to refer to this social group in India.

Social Background and Origins

In the context of traditional Hindu society, Dalit status has often been historically associated with occupations regarded as ritually impure: namely, any occupation involving killing, handling of animal cadavers or night soil (human feces). Engaging in these activities was considered to be polluting to the individual who performed them, and this pollution was considered to be 'contagious'. As a result, Dalits were commonly banned and segregated from full participation in Hindu social life (they could not enter the premises of a temple), while elaborate precautions were sometimes observed to prevent incidental contact between Dalits and other Hindus.

Historically, there may not have been clear demarcation between Dalit castes and the Sudra castes. Dalits are not a single identifiable race or caste. Instead, like the rest of the Hindu society, they are divided into various sub-castes known as 'jatis. One study found some association between caste status and genetic markers seeming to indicate a more European lineage.

Dalit diversity may be due to newly outcaste individuals or communities over the years. It is noteworthy that sometimes, regional tribes that are considered Dalits are sometimes seen by Indians as racially distinct. In both northern and southern India it is different. For example, in North India, in places such as Rajasthan they are usually lighter because Rajasthan was invaded several times by white tribes. In addition they also have different colour of eyes and sometimes hair. As a result in superstition, it is said to never trust a cat-eyed person. Then, in South India, they are often regarded as more closely related to Tibetans, Burmese, Khmers, Thais, and other Southeast and East Asians.

Many Dalits who have converted to other religions in the past few centuries continue to retain their Dalit heritage. In the 1991 census, Dalits numbered just over 130 million and constituted more than 16% of India's population.

Discrimination against Dalits is not limited to the Hindu community. This situation is exacerbated by the fact that non-Hindu Dalit groups have traditionally not been recognized as Scheduled Castes under hiring quota laws. The Dalit Muslims or "Arzal" (also called Mojahir in Pakistan), as well as Dalit Christians form an integral part of the caste system in South Asia among Muslims and Christians. Many Dalit Muslims are discriminated against by the upper-caste "Ashraf" Muslims, and Dalit Christians discriminated against by upper caste Christian priests and Nuns.

Some Dalits have successfully integrated into urban Indian society, where caste origins are less obvious and less important in public life. In rural India, caste origins are more readily apparent and Dalits remain excluded from local religious life, though this exclusion in its severity is in fact fast diminishing due to changing social norms of acceptable behaviour.

Dalits and similar groups are also found in Nepal, Pakistan and Bangladesh.

Dalits and Indian Politics

Mahatma Gandhi made it part of the Indian National Congress's mission to eradicate untouchability. For this reason, untouchability has been officially abolished in India, although the social practice still exists today, particularly in rural villages.

In these villages, Dalits are still not allowed to let their shadows fall upon a non-Dalit caste member (particularly a Brahmin, for fear of ritually contaminating them), and they are still required to sweep the ground where they walk to remove the 'contamination' of their footfalls. In some of these villages, rural Dalits are forbidden to worship in temples or draw water from the same wells as caste Hindus, and they usually live in segregated neighbourhoods outside the main village.

In urban areas and most villages the old concepts of a rigid caste system and untouchability usually no longer exist, though most Indians still voluntarily hold on to their caste origins, which is intended to reflect that their ancestors belonged to their castes with a sense of pride in the duties and responsibilities as required by the caste rules. In matrimonial matters, whether the wed couple is Dalit or non-Dalit, caste identity is a practical near-must. This is, however, ignored by inter-caste couples, who marry ignoring castes but due to an attraction on the basis of education or economic status, of either or both members of the couple.

While the Indian Constitution has duly made special provisions for the social and economic uplift of the Dalits, comprising the so-called scheduled castes and tribes in order to enable them to achieve upward social mobility, these concessions are limited to only those Dalits who remain Hindu. There is a demand among the Dalits who have converted to other religions that the statutory benefits should be extended to them as well as social relief to "overcome" historical injustices.

Another major politically charged issue with the rise of Hindutva's role in Indian politics is that of religious conversion. This political movement alleges that conversions of Dalits are due not to any social or theological motivation but to allurements like education and jobs. Critics argue that the inverse is true with laws banning conversion, and the limiting of social relief for these backward sections of Indian society being revoked for those who convert. Bangaru Laxman, a Dalit politician, was a prominent member of the Hindutva movement.

Another political issue is over the affirmative action measures taken by the government towards the uplift of the

Dalits by implementation of quotas in government jobs and university admissions aimed at improving Dalit representation. About 8% of the seats in the National and State Parliaments are reserved for Scheduled Caste and Tribe candidates, a measure sought by B. R. Ambedkar and other Dalit activists in order to ensure that Dalits would obtain a proportionate political voice.

Dalits and Religion

Hindu Dalits (Harijans): Many Dalits continue to debate whether they are 'Hindu' or 'non-Hindu'. Missionaries have initiated several Dalit organizations. In some regions of India and Nepal, missionaries have been successful among the Dalits, both in Eastern India and Nepal, many Dalits have come under the combined influence of Maoists and the missionaries, even attacking and murdering Hindus. Traditionally, Hindu Dalits or Harijans have been barred from many activities that were seen as central to Vedic religion and Hindu practices of orthodox sects. Among Hindus each community has followed its own variation of Hinduism. The wide variety of practices and beliefs observed in Hinduism makes any clear assessment difficult.

Some of the movements in Hinduism have welcomed Dalits into their fold. The Satnami movement was founded by Guru Ghasidas a Dalit himself. In addition, other Hindu groups have reached out to the Dalit community in an effort to reconcile with them, with productive results. On August 2006, Dalit activist Namdeo Dhasal engaged in dialogue with the Rashtriya Swayamsevak Sangh in an attempt to "bury the hatchet".

In addition, the "Pandaram" are an order of Dalit Hindu priests (a task traditionally reserved for the Brahmins) based largely in Nepal and parts of South India. These Pandaram priests maintain the same tradition as the Brahmin priests, including using Sanskrit for the rituals (a language traditionally reserved for the Brahmins). They perform religious ceremonies from weddings to death rituals. They are not generally as well trained as the Brahmin priests, but are highly respected within their community and are addressed reverentially. Also, Hindu temples are increasingly more receptive to Dalit priests, such as Suryavanshi Das, the Dalit priest of a notable temple in Bihar.

Another popular Harijan includes Babaji Palwankar Baloo, who joined the Hindu Mahasabha and was both a politician and a cricketer. He was an independence fighter.

However, extremist far-right militia groups such as the Ranvir Sena, largely run by upper-caste landlords in backward areas of the Indian state of Bihar, oppose equal treatment of Dalits and have resorted to violent means to suppress them. The Ranvir Sena is considered a terrorist organization. On the other side, extremist groups run by small minority of Dalits such as the "Dalit Panthers Movement" have committed violent acts against Brahmins and middle-caste people.

In Pakistan, a predominantly Muslim nation, more than 60% of the 1. 4 million Hindu minority are Dalits.

Muslim Dalits (Arzal): Muslim society in India can also be separated into several caste-like groups. Descendants of indigenous lower-caste converts are discriminated against by "noble", or "ashraf", Muslims who can trace their descent to Arab, Iranian, or Central-Asian ancestors. There are several groups in India working to emancipate them from upper-caste Muslim discrimination. The Dalit Muslims are referred to by the Ashraf and Ajlaf Muslims as Arzal or "ritually degraded". They were first recorded in the 1901 census as those "with whom no other Muhammadan would associate, and who are forbidden to enter the mosque or to use the public burial ground". They are relegated to "menial" professions such as scavenging and carrying night soil. Babasaheb Ambedkar, a renowned Dalit activist and the framer of the Constitution of India, wrote about the Dalit Muslims and was extremely critical of their mistreatment by upper-caste Muslims quoting that "Within these groups there are castes with social precedence of exactly the same nature as one finds among the Hindus".

In Pakistan, there are estimated to be 6.8 million Mayazurs (bonded labourers) in Punjab and another 7.5 million in Sindh. Although the Pakistani Supreme Court has ruled bonded labour unconstitutional and the National Assembly has passed laws prohibiting it, these laws remain largely unenforced due to the influence of large landlords. Furthermore, the AIBMM is striving to achieve the SC status for India's Muhajirs.

Sikh Dalits: Master Tara Singh himself helped uplift the Sikh Dalits. K.P. Singh a Dalit activist in UP was himself a Sikh. Kanshi Ram himself was of Sikh background although converted because he found that Sikh society did not respect Dalits and so became a neo-Buddhist. The Mazhabi are one Dalit of the Punjabi Dalits that are treated as outcastes from mainstream Sikh society and not allowed to enter Sikh temples. Jivan Singh, a friend of Guru Gobind Singh was a Dalit.

Christian Dalits: Converts to Christianity (facilitated by the influence of missionaries) have historically retained the caste system in their communities though many Christian leaders publicly reject caste. Joseph D'Souza, President of the All India Christian Council, has publicly pushed for a complete rejection of caste through partnership with Dalits across the country. A 1992 study of Catholics in Tamil Nadu showed that Dalit Christians face segregated churches, cemeteries, services and processions. They also face economic and social hardships due to the discrimination by upper-caste priests and nuns. One famous Dalit activist with the nom-de-plume of Bama Faustina has written books that provide a first-hand account of the discrimination against them by nuns and priests in South India.

Dalits and Neo-Buddhism

In Maharashtra, Uttar Pradesh and a few other regions, Dalits have come under the influence of the neo-Buddhist movement initiated by Ambedkar. Some of them have come under the influence of the Neo-Buddhist and Christian Missionaries and have converted away from Hinduism into religions such as Christianity and Buddhism in what they have been told is an "attempt to eliminate the prejudice they face". Activists such as Udit Raj have claimed that such conversion will solve all discrimination problems faced by Dalits. Such claims have been criticized as "fragile at best". The conversion attempts have also been criticized by Hindu advocacy groups as "unhelpful" as Casteism is a complex dynamic that extends across all religions in India. However, the Constitution of India guarantees religious freedom and their right to choose their religion, although controversies related to mass-conversions have led to laws being passed against them in some states in

India. Since then, several Christian converts have reconverted back into Hinduism as the conversions did not award them the financial rewards that the missionaries lured them with.

Resistance to the Soul: Gandhi and His Critics

Looking back at the twentieth century, as it is almost at its end, it has been marked by the bloodiest conflicts ever known to Humankind. From the death and destruction, the annals of history will forever manifest those who contributed to the barbarous events and those who attempted to resist the inhumane acts of aggressors. Belonging to the latter, one personality seems to stand out amongst the lot of humanitarians and peace loving people-Mohandas Karamchand Gandhi. Although Gandhi was a remarkable nationalist leader, he was less concerned with the ends of his actions and more with the means of achieving independence for India.

Gandhi believed in the idea of nonviolent resistance and civil disobedience. These two elements of Gandhi's plan for Indian Independence, stemmed from his philosophy of Satyagraha or soul force. When most nationalist movements of the twentieth century were being executed through the use of violence, Gandhi sought to employ a method that opposed the practice or the advocacy of violence to achieve political goals. His method was based on "Truth, Love and Self-suffering". It was through this method that any adversity could be conquered. By sacrificing one's self to your opponent's wrath without violent retaliation, your opponent would give in because of the commitment to self-sacrifice on the part of the Satyagrahis (Person practising Satyagraha).

Gandhi utilized this method of Soul Force to achieve political reform in South Africa, independence in India and to transform himself into the person that he wanted to be. Gandhi's methods gained him tremendous praise from people worldwide, including his adversaries and served as a catalyst for the mass movement towards ending the British Raj. Long after Gandhi's assassination, Gandhi and his ideas are still admired for their humanitarian and almost saintly attributes. Some revere Gandhi "...as perhaps the greatest figure of the last nineteen hundred years", while others have made serious criticisms of his ideas and methods. Rajani Palme Dutt, saw Gandhi's actions as a method of protecting the interests of the Bourgeoisie in India during a time of uncertainty.

K. Sarwar Hasan contests that Gandhi's political ideas and actions based on Hindu doctrine alienated the Muslims of India.

Hindu Nationalist V. D. Savarkar, thought that Gandhi's methods contradicted the religious outlook of Hinduism and jeopardized Hindu political interests as well. The leader of "The All Indian Depressed Class Federation" and "Untouchable", B. R. Ambedkar contends that Gandhi was a proponent of the Caste System and an antagonist towards progress that would have benefited all of India, especially the depressed classes. These men set forth a plethora of strong criticism against a man who was simply searching for the truth. It will be the goal of this work to answer these criticisms, when possible, through the use of Gandhi's ideas and historical fact.

Dutt construes a Marxist view of Gandhism and contends that Gandhi's methods were not as altruistic as they appeared to be. These methods were a means of protecting the privileges of Indian landlords and Bourgeoisie that were being jeopardized by the unbridled force of the common masses. "Non-violence" is seen as a design, constructed and utilized to restrain this force that struck fear into the hearts of the landed class and to harness the force of the masses to compel the British to make concessions. When the Rowlette act was passed in 1919 it added to the atmosphere of dissatisfaction among the Indian people. At the end of World War I many Indian people expected civil liberties to be restored.

The Rowlatt act was in favour of continuing the "war time vigours". This act caused widespread unrest and strikes in India. Dutt claims that it was Gandhi's primary intention to utilize civil disobedience and nonviolence to stop the civil unrest and strikes. The Rowlatt act and its reforms had at first been accepted by Gandhi and the Congress. Once the violence erupted, Gandhi and congress shifted their positions and assumed the leadership role of the mass movement. This was done because the members of Congress, the Bourgeoisie, were worried about the violent masses turning against them. So, Gandhi planned a program of "Non-violent non-cooperation" to cope with this matter. It would be the middle-class that would spearhead the movement while the masses were supposed to resort hand spinning, weaving and non-payment of taxes. This plan is perceived by Dutt as a scheme to eliminate the possibility of the masses posing a threat to the landed class.

The change in the position of Congress in reference to the Rowlatt, was accompanied by another phenomenon. Congress ceased to be just an organization of self-government with in the British empire but it transformed itself into a modern political party that was leading the masses into a struggle against the British. Like any other political party, Congress was bent on protecting their interests. Non-violent rhetoric "was an attempt to conciliate the interests of the masses with the big bourgeoisie and landlord interests which were opposed to any decisive mass struggle. "Dutt believes this became more obvious after the Chauri Chaura incident in which peasant rioters killed a group of policemen and Gandhi subsequently withdrew his support for the movement.

The fact that Gandhi withdraws his commitment to the movement by calling off the entire campaign and then substitute his original strategy with the "Constructive Program" indicates to Dutt that the Bourgeoisie was losing control of the movement and would attempt to regain it by calming the masses. Dutt is critical of Gandhi's actions that resulted in the suspension of the mass movement. Gandhi claims that he suspended the movement to end the violent outbreaks associated with it. Dutt believes that the Bardoli decision/resolution had an economic motive. Since the movement was cancelled at "the height of public enthusiasm" it is an indication to the Marxist that the interests of the Bourgeoisie were being jeopardized.

The enthusiasm and force of the masses at this time was potent enough to sweep away imperialism and might have done the same to landlordism in the process. This opinion is supported by the fact that the Ryots (peasants) had been instructed to resume the payment of taxes and rent once the mass civil disobedience movement was suspended. Dutt thinks that the resolution instituted by the Working Committee at Bardoli has little relation to the outbreak of violence. Three of its seven clauses specifically refer to the payment of rents by the peasants to the landlords. His conclusion is that this was a question of class interest and not a matter of suppressing the violence for its own sake. Non-violence is held to be disguise for class interest and to serve as a leash for the masses' activities that might have been counter productive to the interests of the propertied class. The keystone to this argument is that the payment or non-payment of taxes and rents is totally unrelated to the presence of mass hysteria, yet it was a major issue in the aftermath of this movement.

Dutt sees Gandhi as "an ascetic defender of property..." because he uses "...the most religious principles of humanity and love to disguise his support of the property class. "Gandhi is reduced to a" tool or mascot of the Bourgeoisie in every wave of the Indian struggle" It was Gandhi who was able to attracted and guide the masses when the Bourgeoisie leadership failed to do so. He was able to harness the enthusiasm of the people in order to gain concessions from the British and also keep the masses in check by preventing a class revolution in India through the use of his nonviolent philosophy. Further evidence to support Dutt's opinion that nonviolence was not a means of achieving independence but a method of maintaining leadership and bourgeois position is the salt march of March 1930. Gandhi limited this campaign to himself and his chosen disciples. It was by his instruction that the masses, including industrial workers were asked to be patient and continue the work of the "Constructive Program". In short, Dutt believes that Gandhi manipulated the masses by calling them to action when favourable to the bourgeoisie and then withdrawing his support if things got out of hand. Dutt claims this was the case in 1932, when Gandhi abandoned the movement once more to tend to the cause of the Harijans.

It is easy to discern why a Marxist would oppose Gandhian philosophy. A Marxist such as Dutt, advocates the violent over turning of society by the masses and the establishment of a state based on Marxist doctrine. Gandhi was opposed to violence in general, especially as a means of bringing about political change. To Gandhi, the only acceptable method of attaining freedom was through nonviolence and civil disobedience. Through this method true Swaraj could be achieved. This did not mean the mere ousting of the British imperialists from India but that Indians, through Gandhi's methods, would first learn how to master themselves.

This was the purpose of the "Constructive Program" as proposed by Gandhi in the 1920's, to help the Indian people achieve independence by first creating "an atmosphere of perfect calm", unity among all Indians and to give up foreign cloth by producing their own. It was through this program that Gandhi thought people could learn how to rule themselves as individuals. To sum it up-Inward freedom must come before outward freedom. To Gandhi Swaraj was more than just political, economic and social freedom, it was a continuous movement of spiritual liberation and self-purification. This explains why Gandhi called for peaceful protest even though many others utilized violence. "If India was to achieve independence without violence and coercion that is how India would govern herself...once the British are gone."

It is no lie that Gandhi suspended the mass movement, as Dutt claimed. In light of the occurrences at Chauri Chaura, Gandhi felt that the people were not ready for mass disobedience, since a prerequisite of a movement of mass disobedience is a law abiding citizenry. This was not the case at Chauri Chaura. The murder of the constables, who were defenceless at the hands of the crowd, was a blow to Gandhi who believed that "no provocation could have justified such an act. "He believed that" India was not ready for self-government until Indians were able to restrain themselves and have succeeded in getting control over the hooligans of India."

The notion that Gandhi was a spokesman or spin doctor for the Bourgeoisie seems absurd. Gandhi was simply a spokesman for all of humanity. He sought to help the "Untouchables" as well as the wealthy Hindus. Dutt claimed that Gandhi was guilty of manipulating the Ryots but Gandhi's actions show differently-they show that he had a genuine concern for them. Farmers in the village of Champaran were required, by law to plant three out of twenty parts of land with Indigo for their landlords. One peasant asked Gandhi to travel to Champaran and to inquire into the conditions of the Ryots there. Gandhi's inquiry led to an official investigation that found in favour of the Ryots. They were refunded a portion of the money, but the greater benefit was that this tithe was abolished. Another example of Gandhi's concern for the common folk was his actions in Ahmedabad. Mill hands were discontented with the low wages they were receiving from the mill owners. Gandhi first suggested arbitration between the two groups but that did not resolve the problem. Gandhi advises the labourers to strike and provides them with further advice on how to make the strike a success. In the end, a mutual agreement was reached and the strikers returned to work.

If Gandhi did remove his support from any civil disobedience movement it was only because it became marred with acts of violence perpetrated by his fellow countrymen. Gandhi best explains his own actions by stating "if I can have nothing to do with the organized violence of the government, I can have even less to do with the unorganized violence of the people. "Nonviolent noncooperation was not just a method of achieving Swaraj but a method of resisting evil. Gandhi did not distinguish between violent acts committed by Indians or Englishmen, to him they are equally evil.

It is obvious that a Marxist would be an opponent of Gandhism, and it come as no surprise that K. Sarwar Hasan, a Pakistani Muslim would also portray Gandhi's ideas and actions in a negative light. Gandhi's failure to attract a large Muslim following was his downfall according to Hasan. This deficiency was due to Gandhi's inability to understand and gratify the needs of the Muslim population in India.

This became evident in 1919 when the terms of the Treaty of Sevres became known to India's Muslims. This treaty proposed a dismemberment of the Ottoman Empire and caused general unrest amongst Muslims in India. Hasan's contention is that Gandhi only took action on this matter because he felt forced to do so and it was an opportunity to address issues that concerned Hindus as well. "Gandhi consolidated joint grievances and proposed that congress should launch a campaign of mass noncooperation. "Gandhi's proposal received opposition from Muslims, like Jinnah who saw Gandhi's "soul force" as a tree that would bear no fruit. The slow going pace of Gandhi's methods would only increase the divide between Muslims and

Hindus since his method possessed an ideological foundation based on Hinduism. Muslims like Jinnah believed if mass support was to be gathered for the cause of independence, it had to be done quickly.

Hasan's most stalwart criticism is that Gandhi utilized the Hindu religion and traditions to guide the quest for India's independence. Gandhi's inspiration and language, that was associated with the movement, were products of Hindu scriptures like the Gita. India's independence was referred to as Ram Raj (Rule of God-Hindu god Rama) and the struggle itself was referred to as Dharma Yudh (Hindu religious war). These associations with Hinduism coupled with the fact that Gandhi was a Hindu repelled Muslims. According to Hasan it was Gandhi's desire to establish an independent India that was free of western models. This ruled out the possibility of independent India becoming a secular state. The Muslims wanted a secular state established to ensure that their religious rights would not be trampled on. Hasan believes that Gandhi could have done more to solidify Hindu-Muslim relations. He sees Gandhi's actions as futile attempts to appease Muslims and contends that nothing concrete was ever offered to Muslims.

The fact that Gandhi was unable to rally enough Muslim support is not his downfall alone. Culpability can be found with the Muslims themselves. The fact that the Muslim community disapproved of Jinnah's joining of the Indian National Congress is proof enough that the divisions were not caused by Gandhi's actions alone, not to mention the historical rivalry. Gandhi's intentions and actions illustrate that he did not just placate the Muslims but truly desired to form a united India.

Gandhi treated Muslims as his equals. This was evident in South Africa as well as India. A main provision of his Triple Program was his commitment to strengthen Hindu-Muslim unity. He was a firm believer in the philosophy of the majority having respect for the minority. He considered Hindus and Muslims "natural brothers of India" and thought that it was more surprising to see them feud than if they should unite. His entire equation of a free India was based upon the notion of a "brotherhood of man". No distinctions were made between Hindus or Muslims or any other religion or race for that matter.

On the eve of partition, Gandhi still advocated brotherhood between the two groups even though the splitting of India was the cause of severe disappointment for him. Hasan's claim that Gandhi saw the independence movement as a Hindu Holy war is a near-sighted judgement. Gandhi was simply expressing his feeling and ideas in a medium that he was most familiar with-Hinduism. If Gandhi did disagree with Muslim opinions at times it was only because they contradicted his creed of Ahimsa and Satyagraha and his vision of an independent India. Not to mention that it was not only Muslims that Gandhi disagreed with. Hindu nationalists as well as Muslim nationalists set forth staunch opposition to Gandhi's plans and ideas.

Gandhi's actions seemed extremely unorthodox to many Hindus. V. D. Savarkar, a Hindu nationalist, saw Gandhi as a threat to the existence of Hindus in India. Savarkar believed that Gandhi's influence over Congress hurt the Hindu cause, because Gandhi gave in to Muslim demands. Gandhi supposedly jeopardized Swaraj by taking up the Khilafat issue. Muslim leaders in India tried to coerce Amir Nuillakhan of Afghanistan to invade India. Gandhi was aware of this vision to establish an Afghanistanian kingdom in India, yet did not distance himself from those that supported this invasion. In short, Gandhi's continual appeasement of the Muslims endangered the interests of Hindus according to Savarkar.

This criticism serves to calcify the previous argument that Gandhi was in favour of a united India and had no ill will towards the Muslims or their interests. Gandhi probably would not have minded if a Muslim was head of the government as long as he shared the same views on brotherhood and equality among all people as Gandhi did. Gandhi did say that "Muslims in India were once Hindus, they just accepted Islam. "Savarkar's criticisms stems from the criticisms that Gandhi made about Hindus that suggested that they were too closed minded to accept Muslims as their brothers and fellow countrymen.

Criticism directed at Gandhi seems expected from the three previous sources, criticism from an Untouchable seems surprising. B. R. Ambedkar is under the impression that Gandhi was an advocate of the caste system. Gandhi saw the caste system as the backbone of Hindu society and did nothing to put an end to this evil practice even though it was the cause of misery for the Untouchables that Gandhi was supposedly trying to help. Ambedkar attempted to support his claims by stating that Gandhi believes that "intermarriages were not necessarily for national unity, that dining together does not create peace and that the abandonment of the caste system in favour of a social system based on western ideals was a detriment to all. Ambedkar assumes that Gandhi is undemocratic in thought because he opposes a social system similar to that of western nations that made discrimination illegal.

Ambedkar interprets Gandhi's views as conservative, reactionary, downright archaic and unrealistic. Gandhi's opposition to machinery and his commitment to Charka (the spinning wheel) is rejected by Ambedkar who believes that such modern devices will end economic and social ills in so far as progress will liberate the depressed classes of India not Gandhi's idealism. Gandhi's views will never be able to help the common man, so states Ambedkar. The only thing that will elevate him is culture. Culture advances and liberates humanity. It is the only thing that divorces humans from animals. But culture cannot be transmitted if people do not possess leisure time. Leisure time will only become available if the toils of life are lessened. In Ambedkar's opinion machines would produce leisure time by reducing the labour of the common person and this leisure time could be used for a "life of culture".

Gandhi saw the caste system as a blemish to Hinduism. If he ever said that the caste system possessed positive attributes it was only because he was in search of the truth. Which means he thought it was to this end that the both the positive and negatives of the caste system should be examined. Gandhi was a friend to the Untouchables and despised their plight. He fought against the system of Untouchability by admitting Untouchables into the Ashram. Even though he was criticized for doing this and lost monetary support from many Hindus, he stuck to his guns. Gandhi believed that "it was a sin to believe anyone else is inferior to ourselves... Sin pollutes us not another human's touch. Caste is a blot to Hinduism that must be ended". Gandhi criticizes his fellow Hindus for treating the Untouchables the same way the British treated Indians. His assumption was that, if the British were incorrect in their conduct then Hindus must be as well. Untouchables should be "treated as blood brothers as they are in fact. We (Indians) must free ourselves from this miserable condition then true Swaraj can be achieved".

Gandhi was correct in his assumption that peace and brotherhood would not be a product of intermarriages, dining together and the adoption of a social system based on a western model. In Gandhi's view all these things were useless if there was not a change in the conscience of Hindus. No law can force someone not to discriminate, only one's own convictions could do that. Ambedkar's assumption that a social system based on western ideals would bring about "civilization" in India was held in contempt by Gandhi. To Gandhi, civilization was equated with good conduct.

Western culture was plagued by various maladies such as materialism, competition and overindulgence. An assimilation in that direction would only hurt India and the depressed classes. Industrialization as advocated by Ambedkar would only cause the further exploitation of the Untouchables. Labour saving machines would result in more unemployment, further starvation, poverty and homelessness. It would provide benefits for the few and suffering for the many. Gandhi believed progress would not be thwarted by the refusal of labour saving machines because the only progress that mattered was that considered all people. To Gandhi, progress is only progress if all Indians progressed together. The only device that considered the needs of all Indians was the spinning wheel. With it people could become self sufficient and labour for their benefit.

Gandhi was an ordinary man who had great ideas. These critics misunderstood many of Gandhi's ideas. Their lack of comprehension is the cause of their criticisms. Their lack of vision is the cause of these criticisms. Gandhi was a dreamer and these men did not share the same dreams as Gandhi.

It is no secret that Gandhi's ultimate dream did not come true-an independent united India. Does this mean that "the method" failed? Gandhi believed "the method" could never fail since it was a method of truth and love. If anything failed, he admitted "...I did." In his life long search for the truth he like any other human being made mistakes and attracted criticisms. Even if these criticisms were all true, does that negate what Gandhi did for India and humanity?

Ambedkar View on Salvation

Ladies and Gentlemen

You must have come to know by now that this Conference has been purposefully called upon to brood over the declaration of Conversion which I made recently. The subject of conversion is very dear to me. According to me, the whole of your future depends upon this subject. I have no hesitation in saying that you have clearly understood the gravity of this problem. Had it not been so, you would not have assembled here in such large numbers. I am very happy to see this (gathering).

Since the time of the declaration of Conversion, our men have conducted several meetings at various places and expressed their views and opinions, which I hope must have reached you. But we have had no opportunity so far to gather, and to discuss and decide the problem of conversion at one place. I was much more concerned for such an opportunity. You will all agree that planning is very necessary for making the movement of Conversion a success. Conversion is not a children's game. It is not a subject of entertainment. It deals with how to make man's life successful. Just as a boatman has to make all necessary preparation before he starts on a voyage, so also we have to make such preparation. Without preparation, it will be impossible to reach the other shore.

But just as the boatman does not collect luggage unless he gets an idea of the number of passengers boarding the boat, so also is the case with me. Unless I get an idea as to how many persons are willing to leave the Hindu fold, I cannot start preparation for conversion. When I expressed to some workers of Bombay that I would not be able to judge the public opinion unless we meet at a conference, they shouldered the responsibility of this conference voluntarily, without putting up any excuse about expenses and labour. What pains they had to take, has already been described by our revered leader and the President of the Reception Committee, Shri Rawji Dagduji Dolas, in his speech. I am extremely indebted to the Reception

Committee of the Conference for arranging the meeting, after making such strenuous efforts.

Some people may raise an objection as to why the conference is called (with the participation) only of the Mahars. If the declaration of Conversion is meant for all the Untouchables, why has a meeting of all the Untouchables not been convened? Before starting the discussion on the issues before the conference, I feel it obligatory to reply to these questions. There are various reasons for convening a conference of the Mahars alone.

Firstly, neither any safeguards nor any social rights are to be demanded from the Hindus through this conference. The only question before this conference is, what should be done for the betterment of our life? How to carve out the path for our future life? This question can be solved, and needs to be solved, by the respective castes separately, discussing it through their respective conferences. This is one of the reasons why I have not called a conference of all the Untouchables.

There is another reason for convening a conference of Mahars only. About ten months have passed since the declaration of Conversion was made. During this period, sufficient efforts have been made to awaken the public conscience. I felt that this was the proper time to judge the public opinion. In my opinion, the holding of meetings of each caste separately is the simplest way to judge the opinion. In order to materialize (give substance to) the problem of conversion, it is very necessary to judge the public opinion. And I believe the public opinion judged through the meetings of each caste separately will be more representative and reliable than the opinion arrived at through a common meeting of all the Untouchable castes. In order to avert this situation, and to ensure the (knowledge of) public opinion, this meeting of Mahars alone has been called.

Although the other communities are not included, they will not be at a loss. If they do not intend to convert, they have no reason to regret their not being included in this conference. If at all they wish to leave their religion, nothing can come in their way simply because they have not participated in this conference. The other communities, like the Mahars, are free to hold meetings and express their public opinion. I would advise them to hold such meetings, and whatever help is needed from me shall be extended to them to the best of my capacity.

This much is enough as introduction. Now I turn to the main subject. For a common man, this subject of conversion is important as well as difficult to understand. It is equally difficult to grasp the subject. It is not an easy task to satisfy the common man on the subject of conversion. I realise that unless you are all satisfied, it is difficult to bring the idea of conversion into reality. I shall therefore try my level best to explain the subject as simply as possible.

The Material Aspect of Conversion

There are two aspects of conversion: social as well as religious, material as well as spiritual. Whatever may be the aspect or line of thinking, it is necessary to understand at the beginning the nature of Untouchability and how it is practised. Without this understanding, you will not be able to realise the real meaning underlying my declaration of Conversion. In order to have a clear understanding of the problem of Untouchability and its practice in real life, I would want you to recall the stories of atrocities perpetrated against you.

The instances of beating by the caste Hindus for the simple reason that you have claimed the right to enrol your children in the Government school, or the right to draw water from the public well, or the right to take out a marriage procession with the groom on horseback, are very common. You all know such instances, as they happen right before your eyes. But there are several other causes for which atrocities are committed on the Untouchables by the caste Hindus—causes which, if they are revealed, the foreigners will be surprised to hear.

The Untouchables are beaten for putting on clothes of superior quality. They are whipped because they used utensils made of metal like copper, etc. Their houses are burnt for having purchased land for cultivation. They are beaten for putting on the sacred thread on their body. They are beaten for refusing to carry away dead animals and eat the carrion, or for walking through the village road with socks and shoes on, or for not bowing down before a caste Hindu, or for taking water in a copper pot while going out in the field to ease (defecate). Recently, an instance has been noticed where the Untouchables were beaten for serving chapatis at a dinner party. You must have heard of, and some of you must also have experienced, such types of atrocities. Where beating is not possible, you must be aware as to how the weapon of boycott is used against you.

You all know how the caste Hindus have made your daily life unbearable by prohibiting you from labour, by disallowing your cattle from grazing through the jungle (uncultivated land), and by prohibiting your men from entering into the village. But perhaps very few of you have realised as to why all this happens! What is at the root of their tyranny? To me, it is very necessary for us to understand it.

Spiritual Aspect of Conversion

Uptil now, we have discussed why conversion is necessary for material gains. Now, I propose to put forth my thoughts as to why conversion is as much necessary for spiritual wellbeing. What is Religion? Why is it necessary?... 'That which govern people is religion'. That is the true definition of Religion. There is no place for an individual in Hindu society. The Hindu religion is constituted on a class-concept. Hindu religion does not teach how an individual should behave with another individual. A religion, which does not recognize the individual, is not personally acceptable to me. Three factors are required for the uplift of an individual. They are: Sympathy, Equality and Liberty. Can you say by experience that any of these factors exist for you in Hinduism?

No Equality in Hinduism

Such a living example of inequality is not to be found anywhere in the world. Not at anytime in the history of mankind can we find such inequality, which is more intense than untouchability... I think, you have been thrust into this condition because you have continued to be Hindus. Those of you who have become Muslims, are treated by the Hindus neither as Untouchables nor as unequals. The same can be said of those who have become Christians. That God is all pervading is a principle of science and not of religion, because religion has a direct relation with the behaviour of man. Hindus can be ranked among those cruel people whose utterances and acts are two poles apart. They have this Ram on their tongues and a knife under their armpits. They speak like saints but act like butchers.

Thus we are not low in the eyes of the Hindus alone, but we are the lowest in the whole of India, because of the treatment given to us by the Hindus. If you have to get rid of this same shameful condition, if you have to cleanse this filth and make use of this precious life; there is only one way and that is to throw off the shackles of Hindu religion and the Hindu society in which you are bound.

The taste of a thing can be changed. But the poison cannot be made amrit. To talk of annihilating castes is like talking of changing the poison into amrit. In short, so long as we remain in a religion, which teaches a man to treat another man like a leper, the sense of discrimination on account of caste, which is deeply rooted in our minds, can not go. For annihilating caste and untouchables, change of religion is the only antidote.

Untouchables are not Hindus

What is there in conversion, which can be called novel? Really speaking what sort of social relations have you with the caste Hindus at present? You are as separate from the Hindus as Muslims and Christians are. So is their relation with you. Your society and that of the Hindus are two distinct groups. By conversion, nobody can say or feel that one society has been split up. You will remain as separate from the Hindus as you are today. Nothing new will happen on account of this conversion. If this is true, then why should people be afraid of conversion? At least, I do not find any reason for such a fear.

Revolution-Not Reform

Changing a religion is like changing a name. Change of religion followed by the change of name will be more beneficial to you. To call oneself a Muslim, a Christian, a Buddhist or a Sikh is not merely a change of religion but also a change of name. . Since the beginning of this movement of conversion, various people have raised various objections to it. Let us now examine the truth, if any, in such objections.

A congenital idiot alone will say that one has to adhere to one's religion because it is that of our ancestors. No sane man will accept such a proposition. Those who advocate such an argument, seem not to have read the history at all. The ancient Aryan religion was called Vedic religion. It has three distinct characteristic (features). Beef-eating, drinking and merrymaking was part of the religion of the day. Thousands of people followed it in India and even now some people dream of going back to it. If the ancient religion alone is to be adhered to why did the people of India leave Hinduism and accept Buddhism? Why did they divorce themselves from the Vedic religion?... Thus this Hindu religion is not the religion of our ancestors, but it was a slavery forced upon them.

To reform the Hindu society is neither our aim nor our field of action. Our aim is to gain freedom. We have nothing to do with anything else.

If we can gain freedom by conversion, why should we shoulder the responsibility of reforming the Hindu religion? And why should we sacrifice our strength and property for that? None should misunderstand the object of our movement as being Hindu social reform. The object of our movement is to achieve social freedom for the untouchables. It is equally true that this freedom cannot be secured without conversion.

Caste can't be Destroyed

I do accept that the untouchables need equality as well. And to secure equality is also one of our objectives. But nobody can say that this equality can be achieved only by remaining as Hindu and not otherwise. There are two ways of achieving equality. One, by remaining in the Hindu fold and another by leaving it by conversion. If equality is to be achieved by remaining in the Hindu fold, mere removal of the sense of being a touchable or an untouchable will not serve the purpose. Equality can be achieved only when inter-caste dinners and marriages take place. This means that the Chaturvarnya must be abolished and the Brahminic religion must be uprooted. Is it possible? And if not, will it be wise to expect equality of treatment by remaining in the Hindu religion? And can you be successful in your efforts to bring equality?

Of course not. The path of conversion is far simpler than this. The Hindu society does not give equality of treatment, but the same is easily achieved by conversion. If this is true, then why should you not adopt this simple path of conversion?

The Caste Notion and the Nation

Ambedkar counterpoised the concept of nation as against the concept of caste, which was the pre-eminent mode of social organisation in India. For him, the idea of a nation was not just political sovereignty. A nation was a people who were socially bound as one. India however was divided by caste groups and people were unable to think in any other terms except as caste groups or caste sub-groups.

"The Hindus often complain of the isolation and exclusiveness of a gang or a clique and blame them for antisocial spirit. But they conveniently forget that this antisocial spirit is the worst feature of their own Caste System.

One caste enjoys singing a hymn of hate against another caste as much as the Germans did in singing their hymn of hate against the English during the last war. The literature of the Hindus is full of caste genealogies in which an attempt is made to give a noble origin to one caste and an ignoble origin to other castes. The Sahyadrikhand is a notorious instance of this class of literature. This antisocial spirit is not confined to caste alone.

It has gone deeper and has poisoned the mutual relations of the sub-castes as well. In my province the Golak Brahmins, Deorukha Brahmins, Karada Brahmins, Palshe Brahmins and Chitpavan Brahmins, all claim to be subdivisions of the Brahmin Caste. But the antisocial spirit that prevails between them is quite as marked and quite as virulent as the antisocial spirit that prevails between them and other non-Brahmin castes. There is nothing strange in this.

An antisocial spirit is found wherever one group has 'interests of its own' who shut it out from full interaction with other groups, so that its prevailing purpose is protection of what it has got. This antisocial spirit, this spirit of protecting its own interests is as much a marked feature of the different castes in their isolation from one another as it is of nations in their isolation.

The Brahmin's primary concern is to protect 'his interest' against those of the non-Brahmins and the non-Brahmin's primary concern is to protect their interests against those of the Brahmins. The Hindus, therefore, are not merely an assortment of castes but they are so many warring groups each living for itself and for its selfish ideal. There is another feature of caste, which is deplorable. The ancestors of the present-day English fought on one side or the other in the war of the Roses and the Cromwellian War. But the descendants of those who fought on the one side do not bear any animosity—-any grudge against the descendants of those who fought on the other side.

The feud is forgotten. But the present-day non-Brahmins cannot forgive the present-day Brahmins for the insult their ancestors gave to Shivaji. The present-day Kayasthas will not forgive the present-day Brahmins for the infamy cast upon their forefathers by the forefathers of the latter. To what is this difference due? Obviously to the Caste System. The existence of Caste and Caste Consciousness has served to keep the memory of past feuds between castes green and has prevented solidarity."

Ambedkar devoted much effort to illustrate this in great detail. This is no surprise. Ambedkar was the chairman of the Drafting Committee of Constituent Assembly that drafted the Indian Constitution, which has lasted up to date with several amendments. He, like other leaders of the independence movement, was aware of the deep division within the Indian society. Nehru, the first Prime Minister of India was very much saddened by this historic reality. In the famous book-The Discovery of India-which he wrote from prison, where he was confined to by the British Raj, there are several references to this tragic historic reality. Mahatma Gandhi was deeply aware of the problem and knew that future of India would very much depend on this issue.

In fact all the great thinkers, poets and writers of India have said something or other strongly on the issue. However, it fell on Ambedkar, the beloved leader of the Untouchables, who also belonged to this group, to analyse this problem in its full details and suggest a path to its solution. Ambedkar's writings have now been brought out in fourteen thick volumes. All his writings directly or indirectly refer to the issue of caste and the nation. Ambedkar demonstrated how the absence of solidarity led to the weakening of a people, making them indifferent and fear-ridden; as a result cooperation becomes impossible.

"Indifferentism is the worst kind of disease that can infect a people. Why is the Hindu so indifferent? In my opinion this indifferentism is the result of Caste System which has made Sanghatan and cooperation even for a good cause impossible"

The notional foundation of Sanghatan and cooperation is at the heart of Ambedkar's views on the concept of the nation. He, as an eminent jurist, realised that this foundation cannot merely be a juridical one.

The juridical conception of the nation are based on the theory of sovereignty which based on the classical legal theory of contract. However, Sanghatan and cooperation are social realities, not merely legal or political ones. Their existence or not is a ground reality.

Thus the notions of Sanghatan and cooperation have to be derived from the ground reality of a given society at a given time. India as a legal entity, a colony under British Raj for most his lifetime and later an independent sovereignty with a constitutional framework, in the formulation of which he participated, was one thing.

The ground reality of India as a society was quite another. A democratic constitution however liberal, could not create this ground reality. The ground reality was primarily a social issue and not a political or a juridical issue. Here, the notions must be derived from the ground reality and if different sets of notions were to be introduced it had to be done by a change in the ground reality, which would involves everyone in society. What then was at issue was not the contract, but consensus. The consensus is not an abstraction; it is a social reality.

In fact Ambedkar's thought can be divided into two parts. Why he thought there was a fundamental impediment-caste-which prevented Indian people from reaching a consensus regarding any important aspect of their social life, and the solutions he proposed to get rid of this great impediment.

The Concept of Power Involved in this Discourse

The concept of power that Ambedkar had to discuss in dealing with the above mentioned two issues were not juridical notions of sovereignty and of the sovereign individual who passed his power to the state, but the issue of social power as actually found in the existing Indian society. He clearly saw the illusion of political power, when divorced from the social bases of power, when such great leaders such as Gandhi and Nehru were unable to achieve any of the fundamental ambitions they had set out to achieve, on the use of Indian independence for altering the nature of Indian society.

Ambedkar engaged in many debates with both the Socialists and people who held right wing views, as well as those who held the view that economic development was the solution to the social division of castes.

"One may contend that economic motive is not the only motive by which man is actuated. That economic power is the only kind of power no student of human society can accept. That the social status of an individual by itself often becomes a source of power and authority is made clear by the sway, which the Mahatmas have held over the common man.

Why do a millionaire in India obey penniless Sadhus and Fakirs? Why do millions of paupers in India sell their trifling thickets, which constitute their only wealth and go to Benares and Mecca? That, religion is the source of power is illustrated by the history of India where the priest holds a sway over the common man often greater than the magistrate and where everything, even such things as strikes and elections, so easily take a religious turn and can so easily be given a religious twist. Take the case of the Plebeian of Rome as a further illustration of the power of religion over man. It throws great light on this point. The Plebs had fought for a share in the supreme executive under the Roman Republic and had secured the appointment of a Plebeian Consul elected by a separate electorate constituted by the Commitia Centuriata, which was an assembly of Plebeian. They wanted a Consul of their own because they felt that the Patrician Consuls used to discriminate against the Plebeian in carrying on the administration. They had apparently obtained a great gain because under the Republican Constitution of Rome one Consul had the power of vetoing an act of the other Consul. But did they in fact gain anything? The answer to this question must be in the negative. The Plebeian never could get a Plebeian Consul who could be said to be a strong man and who could act independently of the Patrician Consul. In the ordinary course of things the Plebeian should have got a strong Plebeian Consul in view of the fact that his election was to be by a separate electorate of Plebeian.

The question is why did they fail in getting a strong Plebeian to officiate as their Consul? The answer to this question reveals the dominion which religion exercises over the minds of men. It was an accepted creed of the whole Roman populous that no official could enter upon the duties of big office unless the Oracle of Delphi declared that he was acceptable to the Goddess. The priests who were in-charge of the temple of the Goddess of Delphi were all Patricians. Whenever therefore the Plebeian elected a Consul who was known to be a strong party man opposed to the Patricians or 'communal' to use the term that is current in India, the Oracle invariably declared that he was not acceptable to the Goddess. This is how the Plebeian were cheated out of their rights. But what is worthy of note is that the Plebeian permitted themselves to be thus cheated because they too like the Patricians, held firmly the belief that the approval of the Goddess was a condition precedent to the taking charge by an official of his duties and that election by the people was not enough. If the Plebeian had contended that election was enough and that the approval by the Goddess was not necessary they would have derived the fullest benefit from the political right which they had obtained. But they did not. They agreed to elect another, less suitable to themselves but more suitable to the Goddess which in fact meant more amenable to the Patricians. Rather than give up religion, the Plebeian give up material gain for which they had fought so hard. Does this not show that religion can be a source of power as great as money if not greater?" He goes on to say.

"Religion, social status and property are all sources of power and authority, which one man has, to control the liberty of another. One is predominant at one stage, the other is predominant at another stage. That is the only difference. If liberty is the ideal, if liberty means the destruction of the dominion which one man holds over another then obviously it cannot be insisted upon that economic reform must be the one kind of reform worthy of pursuit. If the source of power and dominion is at any given time or in any given society social and religious, then social reform and religious reform must be accepted as the necessary sort of reform.

One can thus attack the doctrine of Economic Interpretation of History adopted by the Socialists of India. But I recognise that economic interpretation of history is not necessary for the validity of the Socialist contention that equalisation of property is the only real reform and that it must precede everything else. However, what I like to ask the Socialists is this: Can you have economic reform without first bringing about a reform of the social order?"

In this aspect of economic interpretation of power, Ambedkar's views expressed in the text published in 1937 and many other texts, which are a very integral to his analysis of caste, bear similar perspectives as the views of Foucault expressed in his lectures in 1971, on Truth and Power.

"What is at stake in all these genealogies is the nature of this power which has surged into view in all its violence, aggression and absurdity in the course of the last forty years, contemporaneously, that is, with the collapse of Fascism and the decline of Stalinism. What, we must ask, is this power-or rather, since that is to give a formulation to the question that invites the kind of theoretical coronation of the whole which I am so keen to avoid-what are these various contrivances of power, whose operations extend to such differing levels and sectors of society and are possessed of such manifold ramifications? What are their mechanisms, their effects and their relations? The issue here can, I believe, be crystallized essentially in the following question: is the analysis of power or of powers to be deduced in one way or another from the economy? Let me make this question and my reasons for posing it somewhat clearer. It is not at all my intention to abstract from what are innumerable and enormous differences; yet despite, and even because of these differences, I consider there to be a certain point in common between the juridical, and let us call it, liberal, conception of political power (found in the philosopher of the eighteenth century) and the Marxist conception, or at any rate a certain conception currently held to be Marxist. I would call this common point economism in the theory of power. By that I mean that in the case of the classic, juridical theory, power is taken to be a right, which one is able to possess like a commodity, and which one can in consequence transfer or alienate, either wholly or partially, through a legal act or through some act that establishes a right, such as takes place through cession or contract. Power is that concrete power which every individual holds, and whose partial or total cession enables political power or sovereignty to be established. This theoretical construction is essentially based on the idea that the constitution of political power obeys the model of a legal transaction involving a contractual type of exchange (hence the clear analogy that runs through all these theories between power and commodities, power and wealth). In the other case-I am thinking here of the general Marxist conception of power-one finds none of all that. Nonetheless, there is something else inherent in this latter conception, something which one might term an economic functionality of power. This economic functionality is present to the extent that power is conceived primarily in terms of the role it plays in the maintenance simultaneously of the relations of production and of class domination which the development and specific forms of the forces of production have rendered possible. On this view, then, the historical raison d'etre of political power is to be found in the economy. Broadly speaking, in the first case we have a political power whose formal model is discoverable in the process of exchange, the economic circulation of commodities; in the second case, the historical raison d'etre of political power and the principle of its concrete forms and actual functioning, is located in the economy. Well then, the problem involved in the researches to which I refer can, I believe, be broken down in the following manner: in the first place, is power always in a subordinate position relative to the economy? Is it always in the service of, and ultimately answerable to, the economy? Is its essential end and purpose to serve the economy? Is it destined to realize, consolidate, maintain and reproduce the relations appropriate to the economy and essential to its functioning? In the second place, is power modelled upon the commodity? Is it something that one possesses, acquires, cedes through force or contract, that one alienates or recovers, that circulates, that voids this or that region? Or, on the contrary, do we need to employ varying tools in its analysis-even, that is, when we allow that it effectively remains the case that the relations of power do indeed remain profoundly enmeshed in and with economic relations and participate with them in a common circuit? If that is the case, it is not the models of functional subordination or formal isomorphism that will characterize the interconnection between politics and the economy. Their indissolubility will be of a different order, one that it will be our task to determine."

In fact the whole study of caste by Ambedkar, which takes many volumes to fully study, falls under what Foucault describes as genealogy. Forced by the need to explain the theory and practice of caste, which could not be explained in terms of the usual economic and social theories, Ambedkar was forced to explain them in other ways. The learned jurist who had obtained many degrees from several western universities, was not able to rely on any of the theories he learned to explain the Indian caste system. What he wrote might fall under what Foucault later called subjugated knowledge.

"On the other hand, I believe that by subjugated knowledge one should understand something else, something which in a sense is altogether different, namely, a whole set of knowledge that have been as inadequate to their task or insufficiently elaborated: naive knowledge, located low down on the hierarchy, beneath the required level of cognition or scientificity. I also believe that it is through the re-emergence of these low-ranking knowledge, these unqualified, even directly disqualified knowledge (such as that of the psychiatric patient, of the ill person, of the nurse, of the doctor-parallel and marginal as they are to the knowledge of medicine-that of the delinquent etc.), and which involve what I would call a popular knowledge (le saviour des gens) though it is far from being a general commonsense knowledge, but is on the contrary a particular, local, regional knowledge, a differential knowledge incapable of unanimity and which owes its force only to the harshness with which it is opposed by everything-surrounding it-that it is through the reappearance of this knowledge, of these local popular knowledge, these disqualified knowledge, that criticism performs its work."

He further goes on to say, "What emerges out of this is something one might call a genealogy, or rather a multiplicity of genealogical researches, a painstaking rediscovery of struggles together with the rude memory of their conflicts. And these genealogies, that are the combined product of an erudite knowledge and a popular knowledge, were not possible and could not even have been attempted except on one condition, namely that the tyranny of globalising discourses with their hierarchy and all their privileges of a theoretical avant-garde was eliminated.

Let us give the term genealogy to the union of erudite knowledge and local memories, which allows us to establish a historical knowledge of struggles and to make use of this knowledge tactically today. This then will be a provisional definition of the genealogies which I have attempted to compile with you over the last few years."

In fact, the work of both Ambedkar and Grundtvig, are works that of genealogies, though they did not think of their work in that way. It is important to note this aspect when considering the contributions made to education within the context of discourse on power. Grundtvig beautifully combines erudite knowledge with folk memories. Folk School was a meeting place where erudite knowledge and folk thinking were to mix and merge, where academic and popular forms of thinking were to be fused. That was the living dialogue, and the genuine enlightenment.

7

DR. AMBEDKAR AND THE CONSTITUTION

INTRODUCITON

"Without going into the merit of constitution, however good and faultless a constitution may be, but if those who implement it are incompetent and useless, that constitution results in an evil. Similarly however defective a constitution may be, but if its executors are good the same constitution results in the good of the people", such was the view expressed by Dr. Baba Saheb Ambedkar while replying to the discussion on the Constitution on November 26, 1949. How prophetic were his statement! The, Congress rulers during the last 40 years have made a travesty of the Constitution. They needlessly amended the original charter several times to perpetuate their single-party rule. Actually the Congress rulers have no moral right to speak on the sanctity of the Constitution.

Hindutva Challenge and Congress: In recent years the Congress has been facing a formidable challenge from the protagonists of Hindutva. It must be noted that the Hindutva challenge is to the Congress, and not to the Constitution, the judiciary or the democratic system. But a systematic Goebellsian propaganda blitzkrieg is conducted by the Congress and those whose vested interests lie in perpetuating the Congress rule and the Congress culture to present Hindutva as the worst challenge to the Constitution. The vilification campaign is joined by all those who have an eye on the main chance, and the Congress party is the highest bidder.

The Congress hangers-on have formed a Constitution Preservation committee as a part of this anti-Hindu propaganda campaign. Anything is grist for their propaganda mill. No falsehood or abuse is too base or too mean for them. They have no compunction to use shady methods. They argue: (1) The Sangh Parivar is out to scrap the Indian Constitution. (2) Its aim is to establish the system propounded by Manu. (3) If elected to power, Bharatiya Janata Party will rescind all legal provisions giving certain social rights to the dalits. (4) The dalits will again be dumped in the traditional ditch of untouchability and all the disabilities associated with it. The source of this offensive of falsehoods is far from any love for the Constitution. The whole business springs from the single-point programme of perpetuation of the Congress rule, the sole host of these parasites. Political propaganda should be matched on a political plane.

Yet there is enough occasion to have a hard look at the issue in dispute, "Dr. Baba Saheb Ambedkar, Constitution and Hindutva". Let us first consider Hindutva.

Hindutva is, these days, being discussed from various angles. The dominant being the accusation that Hindutva is none else than the abuse of Hindutva for political mileage by Sangh Parivar. Even the courts of law have taken the stand that Hindutva is a religious concept. And following this, elections of several Members of Parliament and State Legislative Assemblies have been declared void. But Hindutva is not a mere religious concept. At least the Sangh Parivar does not subscribe to this view. Hindutva is a concept that is related to nationhood. The part "Hindu" in the word "Hindutva" is not used to denote a group of people following any particular way of worship. The late V.D. Savarkar has defined the word "Hindu" as "the one whose country, India, spreads between the two seas and who regards it as his fatherland and sacred land".

RSS has not defined Hindu, and Hindutva. But what the Sangh understands by these words has been amply clarified. Sangh believes Hindu to be a way of life. Guruji has stated regarding this way of life: "We have perceived the entire society as a body. It is the great social person (virat samajapurush). All men are indeed limbs and organs of the great social corpus spiritualis. Society as a mammoth humanoid body and the eternal undying spirit that dwells in that body and this realization is the specific and unique aspect of the Indian spiritual thinking. All existent objects, including all human beings are parts of that eternal existence. And that is the fount of the basic unity. Since the eternal spirit inform everyone in equal measure, the social system should be so organised as to make everyone happy. A social order where all will have equal self-interest."

Shri Guruji calls these "the principles of Hindu way of life". He further says: "The ever present principle of Hindu life, that one truth pervades in all, is the ultimate truth. That alone is the link that joins all. The selfsame truth appears in diverse forms. Therefore it is our natural duty to create all manner of scope for all to lead their life according their diverse tastes".

It should be, noted that Shri Guruji does not define Hindu-Hindutva in religious terms. He does not link Hindutva with any specific method of worship. It should be appreciated that he sheds light on the fact that the substance of Hindutva relates to the wellbeing of mankind. The Sarsanghchalak Shri Balasaheb Deoras while addressing the Maharashtra State-level camp at Tuljai declared: "The Sangh goal is to create an egalitarian society free from exploitation."

The concept of Hindutva does not imply total trust in a single scripture, neither does it strictly adhere to a single religious regimen. It does not reserve all its faith for one Prophet, nor does it profess to tailor society to the measurements given by a religious tone. Deoras has elaborated the thoughts on social system intended in Hindutva in his book Hindu Organisation and Social Equality where he says: "Untouchability should be eradicated from our society permanently, It must go lock, stock and barrel. The Hindutva of the Sangh does not accept the sense of high and low based on caste. So there is no question of Sangh justifying the present caste inequality."

The Hindutva of the RSS-is not based on any religious sect, so it has no room for religious hatred against any sect. Guruji says: "There is a deliberate attempt to create confusion around the word Hindu. Some are driven by their selfish motives to describe Hindus as opposed to Muslims, Christians, Sikhs,

Jains and dalits."

They do not do this after any serious study of the issue. The Hindu thinking and the Hindu way of life have been in the world even before Islam and Christianity were yet to emerge. How could Hindus be against a religion that was not in existence, either Islam or Christianity, Sikhs, Jains, etc. are indeed under the general conceptual umbrella of Hinduism. To oppose them is a indulge in suicidal attempt to cut one's limbs. The term Hindu is never used to oppose or discriminate against any sect. The term is a positive one and could never be construed to mean anything negative.

Constitutional Idealism: While discussing the Constitution, one has to bear in mind this wider meaning of the term Hindutva. Our Constitution has three types of idealism. The political idealism, social idealism and economic idealism. The blend of these three ideals becomes the national idealism. The Constitution explains to us the objectives to be kept always before our eyes in the context of individual-society relationship.

The freedom struggle was not at all limited to political freedom only. India aimed at three kinds of freedom. The political freedom was to be followed by social and economic freedoms. The great leaders at the helm of the freedom struggle had mainly the Hindu society before, their vision. The Muslim community did not fully participate in the freedom struggle. Muslim leaders were without any big following. There was hardly any Muslim League representative in the Constituent Assembly. The kind of political freedom the leaders in the freedom struggle had envisaged is reflected in the Constitution in the form of the fundamental rights. This freedom was not demanded by the Muslims. Because their overwhelming majority had demanded a separate land for Muslims. And the factor of social freedom in the struggle for the freedom of the country was a hundred-per-cent Hindu social reform movement. Untouchability, social inequality, traditional superstition, injustice to women, child-marriage, widow remarriage an so on and so forth were all issues of social reforms in Hindu society.

The incursion of social justice in the Constitution is the outcome of these agitations for social reforms. The demand for the country's liberation from the foreign economic yoke and all-out efforts for gaining that were the activities of Hindus. Though the Parsis like Jamshedji Tata and Dadabhoy Naoroji were at the forefront of the country's economic liberation they were different only in their manner of worship. They were in fact a factor in the all-round movement for economic emancipation carried out by Lokmanya Tilak, Mahatma Gandhi, Lalchand Hirachand in their own way. The economic ideal enshrined in the Constitution is the fruit of their efforts.

Because the ideals of political, social and economic liberaties are enshrined in the Constitution the responsibility for their fulfilment devolves on the government machinery and the citizens are granted some of these liberties in the form of the fundamental rights. All these are intended to achieve the goal of highest interests and welfare of the people, and therefore Hindutva cannot have any quarrel with these.

The noble ideals included in the Constitution, if viewed uninhibited by political considerations and those of Hindutva, would appear to have no contradictions. Hindutva does not deny individual liberty, equality and fraternity. It also does not deprive anyone of his freedom of worship. The founding fathers of our Constitution felt that such ideals must be enshrined in our Constitution, because they were deeply impressed by Indian traditions in social thought. In this context Dr. Ambedkar's interpretation is very significant.

He says: "I have not borrowed liberty, equality and fraternity from the French Revolution. I have learnt them from the teachings of Lord Buddha. To allow every person to adopt a way of worship dictated by his conscience is in the best of Hindu tradition. It is not in the Hindu tradition to oppress anyone only because he happens to worship his lord in a different manner. This has been beautifully expressed in the Mahimnastotra which says: "O Lord, you are the destination of all people reaching you by various ways, straight or crooked according to their taste as waters of various rivers flowing whichever way reach the sea." The Constitution also merely paraphrases the contents of this stotra (praise to Lord).

Social Justice : The social ideals of our Constitution are as important as the political ones. There was dual slavery in our country. One political and the other social. Under the social slavery it was mainly the scheduled castes which were trampled under the injustices by higher castes. They had no political or social rights. Their lowest state in society was determined by their birth. Great savants raised a relentless revolt against this social slavery prevalent in the Hindu society. Sages like Maharshi Dayanand, social reformers like Mahatma Phule, political leaders like Mahatma Gandhi and Swatantrya Veer Savarkar ceaselessly agitated against this social slavery. Ambedkar fought the final battle against the Hindu society. The strugglers reflected in our Constitution.

"I entered the Constituent Assembly to safeguard the interests of the dalits", said Dr. Ambedkar while explaining his purpose in joining the Constituent Assembly. He further stated: "I did not go there to draft the Constitution. But that responsibility crane upon me for certain reasons.

It is a matter of pride for me to have been associated with the architects of the Constitution." Dr. Ambedkar's is the lion's share in clearly defining the social and economic ideals in our Constitution. Article 17 of the Constitution eradicates untouchability. Article 15 guarantees that no discrimination would be allowed on the basis of religion race, caste, gender or domicile. Article 16 guarantees that the State will grant equal opportunities to all citizens. And the same Article 16 makes provision for reservations for the backward people.

Political Democracy: This is a special feature of our Constitution. All adults enjoy the right to vote. All votes are of equal weightage. This right of the citizens is very important and this has invested the common man with full control on the State power. With the ballot-power the Constitution itself grants to the majority of the citizens the power to rule. To extend the right to select their rulers to the common people is politically a revolutionary measure. Politicians playing caste-card organise their parties on various caste-lines and try to acquire majority. The Ahirs, the Jats, the Rajputs, the Yadavs, the dalits and the Muslims are yoked together to present what is named as Bahujan Samaj. But this is an election strategy. Some others try to garner castes other than the Brahmins, the Kshatriyas and the Kayasthas, and try to present them as Bahujan Samaj.

But Hindutva is opposed to such fissiporous business of strengthening divisive caste sentiments through politician means because a very narrow sentiment is detrimental to national unity. The political organisation of the Indian society should be undertaken on the basis of the wide and comprehensive content of Hindutva. If caste is conceived as the basis of political activity the hallowed social ideals in the Constitution would be gathering dust in the statute. The protagonists of Hindutva in the widest ken of the term-aspire to bring a Hindu-again in the wide connotation-rule in the country. The adult franchise granted in the Constitution is bound to result in the majority rule, i.e., Hindu rule. No one can change this foregone conclusion. The limited demand of the Hindutva protagonists is that those politicians who play caste politics, who foster communal division for their politician ends and who deny the just share of the national life to the dalits and the backward sections of society should not be allowed to usurp power by formenting fissiparous, communal and caste passions. Hindutvists are not opposed to the principle of political democracy consecrated in the Constitution. Their objection and opposition is to the policies of implementing the democracy promoted by political parties with their eye on the main chance without any compunction regarding national interests.

Economic Justice: Our Constitution has vowed to render economic justice to all citizens. The directive principles laid down in the Constitution have recorded the economic goals to be achieved by the States. Article 36 to 51 comprise such directive principles, Two of them are relevant here. Article 38 enjoins on the State to establish a social system which will ensure social, political and economic justice to its citizens.

Article 39 directs the State to formulate policies of distribution of physical means which will result in the greatest good of all and will provide adequate means of livelihood to all its citizens, men and women. The principle of equal remuneration for equal work should be implemented. The States should not allow centralisation of wealth and the means of-production which harm the society.

A part from these, there are other directives which have extensively discussed the responsibilities of the States regarding adult education, unemployment, children, women, etc., and how the States should execute these responsibilities. The administrators and the government are guided by these directive principles to achieve, the goals included in the preamble of the Constitution. Dr. Ambedkar in commenting on this says: "These directive principles are not mere decorative pieces showing noble sentiments. The executive and the judiciary should keep those principles in their minds while taking any decisions in future." The economic ideals in the Constitution guide the States in their actions in the relevant field. In the present age the government field of action is not limited to maintaining peace and order. It will be seen that these ideals are but the concrete form of the Hindu directive principle:

> Sarve Santu Sukhinah, Sarve Santu Niramayah,
>
> Sarve Bhadrani Pashyantu ma Kashchit Duhkhabhag Bhavet.
>
> (Let all be happy and healthy. Let all see the vision of universal wellbeing. Let no one suffer miseries.)

If liberty and equality are to materialise in the practical life of the people then economic justice should be granted to all without exception. All the rights enumerated in the Constitution are swallowed by the enormous dragon of poverty and destitution. Dr. Ambedkar says: "On 26 January 1950, India will awake in political freedom, but in the social and economic field the darkness of inequality will persist. We must strive to remove this contradiction between political freedom and economic and social bondage, as soon as possible. If we do not succeed in removing this contradiction, then those masses who are the victims of this contradiction will certainly raze to ground the lofty edifice of political democracy, the Constituent Assembly has so painstakingly and assiduously erected."

Hindutvists have never suggested that the State may deny economic equality-economic justice. On the contrary they have for so long been opposing those very policies that have impaired economic justice. Because the political policies so far carried out have denied this very economic justice to the masses, the rich have snowballed into affluent giants, the poor have been lowered into utter destitution. The directive principles have evaporated in their implementation. The State apparatus has installed and operated an economic machinery that diligently preserves the vested interests of a particular tiny but powerful group. The country is groaning under the unbearable load of foreign debt. Indigenous industries are facing insurmountable difficulties created by multinationals riding on the backs of the ruling coterie. The economic policies that help these multinationals to ascend the ruling backs are wrong. And so these policies should be opposed. Opposition to these policies cannot be construed to mean opposition to economic ideals enshrined in the Constitution.

Framework of Constitution: The Hindutva ideology is not in conflict with the framework of the Constitution that lays down the political, economic and social ideals and the ideals regarding freedom of worship. The foregoing discussion would have brought to light two reasons for this. One, the framework of Constitution upholds certain guiding principles and these principles are but a reflection of the noblest ideals held dear for centuries by Indian thinkers. And two, the Hindutva philosophy has already assimilated the ideals our Constitution so explicitly proclaims. Therefore the Hindutva protagonists have no warrant to wage a war against the lofty values they have cherished all their life.

Congress and Constitution: The malicious, mendacious and mean campaign to malign the Hindutva camp springs from causes that are far from the high plane of the directive principles. These are: One for the last several decades the Congress has been operating the Constitution for its narrow political ends. There is nowhere any proof of Congress efforts to bring into practice the noble values enshrined in our Constitution. Whenever their was imminent threat to the Congress hold on political power, the Congress has never flinched from abusing and wrongfully amending the Sections of the Constitution to save its rule from being overthrown. In 1969 the threat to Indira Gandhi's premiership was staring in the face. So she abused the economic ideal of the Constitution to nationalize the banks and abolish the privy purses of the native princes and shouted from the housetops the slogan of "Garibi Hatao".

In 1975 she was again threatened with loss of her seat in the Lok Sabha; she took recourse to the Emergency, abrogated fundamental rights granted by the Constitution, amended the very preamble by interpolating the words "secular" and "socialist". The Constitution cannot slap any specific restricting ideology on the society. The State cannot be bound by such partisan ideology. Dr. Ambedkar astutely skirted these two words but equally sagely incorporated the ideas of freedom of worship and economic justice. He intended to ensconce the soul of these ideas, whereas the late prime minister, Indira Gandhi wanted to use these words as catchwords to attract and abuse popular sentiments without granting anything of substance.

For, the Congress programme for the last four decades had nothing really secular or really socialistic. This travesty of the directive principles is a breach of the sanctity of the Constitution. The Hindutvists' present struggle is against the Congress. But how can the fight against the Congress be considered as a fight against Constitution? The, propaganda that the Hindutvists are opposed to the Constitution is politically motivated to save the Congress rule.

> For some years now all the political parties have been celebrating 14 April,
>
> Dr. Ambedkar's birthday in a big way; for most of them it is a ritual.

Some of the major parties indulge in unalloyed hypocrisy in that they do two things simultaneously. One, their think tanks attack Dr. Ambedkar mercilessly; they are very angry that there are more statues of Dr. Ambedkar than that of Gandhiji, and that, too, of a larger size; angry because Dr. Ambedkar is called the father/architect of the Indian Constitution. They are dismissive of the perpetual suffering and unequal status of the depressed section of our population and Dr. Ambedkar's fight for their right to be human. Two, on 14 April the leaders garland Dr. Ambedkar's "oversized" statues, hail him as the architect of the Constitution and as one who sowed the seeds of social democracy and social equality. The think tank-the 'ideologues' of 'patriotic' political formations-shed crocodile tears over Ambedkar's disagreement with

Gandhiji on a number of issues. They, however, conveniently forget what Gandhiji thought of Ambedkar: "If Ambedkar does not break our heads, it is an act of self-restraint on his part. Dr. Ambedkar has had to suffer humiliations and insults which should make any one of us bitter and resentful. Had I been in his place, I would have been as angry. We shall be unfit to gain Swaraj so long as we keep in bondage a fifth of the population. In the history of world religions there is perhaps nothing like our treatment of the suppressed classes. Caste Hindu well-wishers of untouchables have no right to speak for them."

Dr. Ambedkar was a revolutionary, rationalist-humanist, human rights intellectual-activist, a man who looked ahead of his time. He wondered "why the Hindus having traditions of charity and humanity-their regard for animal life-should behave so heartlessly towards their fellow human beings and in such unreasonable ways. The Hindu community is set in the steel frame of the caste system, in which one caste is lower than another in social gradation involving particular privileges, rights, inhibition and disabilities with regard to each caste. This system has created vested interests which depend upon maintaining the inequalities resulting from the system".

He, therefore, "unfurled the banner of equality". He was not satisfied with the abolition of untouchability only, leaving the caste system along with "the inequalities inherent in the system". Dr. Ambedkar embraced Buddhism because the Buddhist dharma is based on scientific reasoning, it seeks to achieve human freedom, equality, liberty and fraternity. According to him Buddhism is the only religion which does not sanctify poverty and inequality: nirvana is the way "to remove injustice and inhumanity that man does to man." Buddha taught "social freedom, intellectual freedom, and political freedom. He taught equality, equality not between man and man only but between man and woman. His concern was to give salvation to man in his life on earth, and not to promise it to him in heaven after he is dead".

Many progressives whisper that Dr. Ambedkar accepted a cabinet post in Pandit Nehru's government because he wanted, political, power. Like all political leaders he too wanted power, but unlike most of them he accepted a cabinet post to empower those who have remained depressed and deprived for centuries. But for him the progressive provisions in the Constitution might not have been incorporated. He devoted his whole life to the cause of human rights of the depressed; his mission in life was to restore human dignity to those who have been victims of an ugly and unjust hierarchical social order which gave rise to injustice and, inequality. "My hear breaks", he said, "to see the pitiable sight of your faces and hear your sad voices".

To the Hindus he said. "If you say that Hindu religion is our religion, then your right and ours must be equal. But is this the case?" Dr. Ambedkar fought a relentless battle against this social order and was one of the very few Indian leaders who was forthright, and called a spade a spade: "I hate all injustice, tyranny, pompousness and humbug". Dr. Ambedkar believed that if he succeeded in his struggle-struggle for a just social order-it will prove a blessing for all Indians, not merely any group or community. He wanted the dominating section of our people to adopt a strong position against the hierarchical social order.

Dr. Ambedkar will be remembered for all time to come as the architect of the Indian Constitution, specially for the Fundamental Rights and Directive Principles Chapters which, aim at eradicating "all injustice and tyranny" and ushering in social democracy and social equality. He was however, disappointed that the dominating section of our society did not rise to the occasion and did not water the plants that he had planted. Our political rulers have failed Ambedkar and his vision. It is now for human rights groups and grassroots activists to make social democracy and equality a way of life in the absence of which political democracy will always stand on a shaky foundation.

Dr. Ambedkar's signal contribution was the enactment of the article in the Constitution (Article 32) which guarantees a citizen the fundamental right to move the Supreme Court directly for enforcement of his or her fundamental rights instead of first approaching the High Court before a single judge and thereafter in appeal before a division bench. The rationale was to secure speedy and inexpensive justice. Dr. Ambedkar regarded this provision as "the very soul of the Constitution and the very heart of it". The tendency of some judges of the Supreme Court to relegate citizens to the High Court even in cases where there is a clear violation of their fundamental rights is certainly not in keeping with the heart and soul of the Constitution. Hero worship is endemic in our country and the personality cult flourishes. In the process, the tendency is to entrust heroes and heroines with vast powers and uncritically accept their authority without insisting on accountability. Dr. Ambedkar was aware of these lurking dangers. In the Constituent Assembly, he emphasised John Stuart Mill's caution, namely, not "to lay liberties at the feet of even a great man, or to trust him with powers which enable him to subvert their institutions".

Baba Saheb was aware that hero worship in our country plays a part in politics unequalled in magnitude to the part it plays in any other country. He warned: "Bhakti in religion may be a road to the salvation of the soul. But in politics, Bhakti or hero-worship is a sure road to degradation and to eventual dictatorship." We did not heed this prophetic warning and had to suffer the spurious June 1975 Emergency.

The slogan "India is Indira and Indira is India" was repeatedly chanted in the sycophantic hero worship of the charismatic leader. Recently, we witnessed nauseating sycophancy when Congress leaders and politicians vied with one another in their heartrending attempts to persuade Sonia Gandhi to revoke her sensible decision to decline the Prime Ministerial office. Dr. Ambedkar attached great importance to constitutional morality in the working of the Constitution. He endorsed the view of the Greek historian Grote, that constitutional morality required "a paramount reverence for the forms of the Constitution, enforcing obedience to authority acting under and within these forms". He stressed that diffusion of constitutional morality should be "not merely among the majority of any community but throughout the whole-since even any powerful and obstinate minority may render the working of a free institution impracticable without being strong enough to conquer ascendancy".

Dr. Ambedkar then posed the question: "Can we presume such a diffusion of constitutional morality?" His frank answer was, "Constitutional morality is not a natural sentiment. It has to be cultivated. We must realise that our people have yet to learn it." Surveying the present scene it is apparent that we have not yet learnt it. Indeed constitutional morality seems to be alien to our legislators and people at the centre of power.

Political Career: In the course of the next few years Ambedkar founded the Independent Labour Party, took part in the provincial elections that were held under the Government of India Act, 1935, was elected to the Bombay Legislative Assembly, pressed for the abolition of agricultural serfdom, defended the right of industrial workers to strike, advocated the promotion of birth control, and addressed meetings and conferences throughout the Bombay Presidency. With the outbreak of World War II in 1939, Ambedkar regarded Nazi ideology as a direct threat to the liberties of the Indian people.

Ambedkar exhorted the public to support the British government in prosecuting the war and encouraged Untouchables to join the Indian Army. In 1941, Ambedkar was appointed to the Defence Advisory Committee and in the following year joined the Viceroy's Executive Council as Labour Member, a post he occupied for the next four years. During the same period he transformed the Independent Labour Party into the All-India Scheduled Caste Federation, founded the People's Education Society, and published a number of highly controversial books and pamphlets. Among the latter were Thoughts on Pakistan, What Congress and Gandhi have Done to the Untouchables, and Who Were the Sudras?

Participation in Drafting the Constitution: In 1947, India achieved independence and Ambedkar, who had already been elected a member of the Constituent Assembly, was invited by J. Nehru, the first prime minister of the country, to join the Cabinet as Minister for Law. A few weeks later the Assembly entrusted the task of framing the Constitution to a Draft Committee, and this committee elected Ambedkar as its chairman. For the next two years, he worked on the Draft Constitution, writing it almost single-handed. Despite ill health, Ambedkar completed the Draft Constitution by the beginning of 1948 and later that year introduced it in the Constituent Assembly. Thereafter he steered it through the legislative process and in November of 1949 it was adopted by the Assembly with very few amendments. Ambedkar's resignation from the Cabinet in 1951 marked the virtual end of his political career. In the general elections of January 1952 he failed to win a seat in the Lok Sabha or House of Representatives, and was equally unsuccessful when he contested a by-election the following year. In March 1952 he was, however, elected to the Rajya Sabha, the less influential upper house of parliament, as one of the seventeen representatives of the State of Bombay. He was soon vigorously attacking the government from his new position.

Architect of Indian Constitution: Dr. Ambedkar was the main architect of the Indian Constitution. He was born in a very poor low caste family of Madhya Pradesh. In U.S.A., he did his M.A. in 1915 and Ph.D. in 1916. From 1918 to 1920, he worked as a Professor of Law. Dr. Ambedkar set up his legal practice at the Mumbai High Court. Ambedkar was the main inspiration behind the inclusion of special provision in the Constitution of India for the development of Schedule Caste people. Dr. Ambedkar was the Law Minister of India from 1947 to 1951. He took part in the Satyagraha of untouchables at Nasik in 1930 for opening the Hindu temples to them. Dr. Ambedkar was emancipator of the 'untouchables' and crusader for social justice. This liberator of the down trodden was affectionately called "Baba Saheb". He was posthumously awarded 'Bharat Ratna' in the year 1990.

Ambedkar's Movement: While coming back to India in 1923, Ambedkar again experienced humiliation. The upper caste lawyers would not even have tea at his desk. But his greatest consolation was his clients, whom he treated with liberal mind. His reputation and fame among the Depressed Classes began to grow. He visualised and struggled for a casteless and equal India.

By the time he returned to India, Bhimrao had equipped himself fully to wage war against the practice of untouchability. In 1924 he started the organisation 'Bahiskrit Hitakarini Sabha' (Outcastes Welfare Association), for the upliftment of the untouchables. Ambedkar adopted a two-pronged strategy. First, the eradication of illiteracy and economic uplift of the downtrodden and second, initiating nonviolent struggle against visible symbols of casteism, like denial of entry into temples and drawing water from public wells and tanks.

The problems of the downtrodden were centuries old and difficult to overcome. Their entry into temples was forbidden. They could not draw water from public wells and ponds. Their admission in schools was prohibited. Ambedkar won two major victories when the High Court of Bombay gave a verdict in favour of the untouchables.

On 25th December 1927, he led the Mahad March at the Chowdar Tank at Colaba, near Bombay, to ensure the untouchables right to draw water from the public tank. The marchers were met with the brutality of caste Hindus. He then burnt copies of the 'Manusmriti' publicly terming it a document of discrimination with a number of his supporters. It was an act of great courage to do so in the den of violent Chitpawan Brahmins in Maharashtra. The two struggles shook the religious foundation on which the caste system is built. This marked the beginning of the anti-caste and ant-priest movement in Maharashtra. The temple entry movement launched by Dr. Ambedkar in 1930 at Kalaram temple, Nasik is another landmark in the struggle for human rights and social justice.

He was fully convinced that nothing could emancipate the Dalits except through a complete destruction of the caste system. He continued his movement to attack the base of caste system in every possible way.

In the meantime, the Simon Commission visited India and Dr. Ambedkar met the commission in Pune in which Ambedkar presented his position on depressed classes. He then followed it up during the round table conference after which Ramsay McDonald announced 'Communal Award' as a result of which several communities including the 'depressed classes' were given the right to have separate electorates. Gandhiji wanted to defeat this design and went on a fast unto death to oppose it. On 24th September 1932, Ambedkar and Gandhiji reached an understanding, which became the famous Poona Pact. According to this Pact, in addition to the agreement on electoral constituencies, reservations were provided for untouchables in Government jobs and legislative assemblies. The Pact carved out a clear and definite position for the downtrodden on the political scene of the country. For the first time in Indian history it opened up opportunities of education and government service for them and also gave them a right to vote.

Dr. Ambedkar attended all the three Round Table Conferences in London and each time, forcefully projected his views in the interest of the 'untouchable'. He exhorted the downtrodden sections to raise their living standards and to acquire as much political power as possible. He was of the view that there was no future for untouchables in the Hindu religion and they should change their religion if need be. In 1935, he publicly proclaimed," I was born a Hindu because I had no control over this but I shall not die a Hindu".

Ambedkar - The Socialist: It is also interesting to note and which not many Ambedarkites have ventured, that Dr. Ambedkar was a socialist to the core of his heart. The disappointing relation with the communist movement stands as the single most unfortunate paradox of contemporary Indian history. It didn't come out of much of ideological differences, which certainly existed in the form of certain unclear theoretical constructs in the mind of Ambedkar-as from the attitudes of the communist leaders towards the Dalit movement. These leaders in the Trade Unions of Bombay dogmatically regarded the caste question as an unimportant super-structural issue, which would automatically disappear when the revolution takes place. Their orthodox outlook regarding untouchability, caste disparity, discrimination was the basics on which Ambedkar's entire thesis on Communism was formed. For historical reasons the leadership of this communist movement however came from the middle class educated youth who had to come from upper castes communities, the majority being the Brahmin itself.

Ambedkar's writing on Marxism is heavily reflects his frustration with the Bombay-Communists. This legacy to identify Marxism with its self-appointed practitioners still appears to be followed by Dalits. They cite examples of the parliamentary communist parties to show the lacuna or inapplicability of Marxism. It is necessary for them to understand that Marxism intrinsically solicits criticism but it presupposes its careful study.

As Anand Teltumde puts it, although Ambedkar could not discuss the philosophy of communism in the manner it deserved, he was never antagonistically disposed towards it. Rather, he acknowledged the beauty of communist philosophy and said that it was closer to his own. Preoccupied with the mission of liberating the Dalits, he insisted, quite like Marx, that the test of the philosophy was in practice, and opined that if communists worked from that perspective, to win success in India would be far easier than in Russia (Janata, 15 January, 1938). He always regarded communism as the ultimate benchmark to assess his highest ideal-Buddhism. With unpleasant experience with communist dogma and vulgarity of his times, he did sound polemically against Communism and appeared at times even professing its doom but it all underscored his wrath against the dogma that occupied the communist practice.

Despite all these aspects of Ambedkar's disagreements with Communism it is cannot be ruled out that Ambedkar was not a Socialist. He was a socialist of a different kind. One of his prime conflicts with Marx was 'dictatorship of the proletariats', which he condemned saying that dictatorship of any kind is unethical. His stood for greater democracy of, by, for and among the oppressed ones in every field. At one stage he was clearly of the opinion that the historical conflict is between the exploited and exploiters and that all.

It is with this idea that Dr. Ambedkar, formed the Independent Labour Party, participated in the provincial elections and was elected to the Bombay Legislative Assembly. During these days he stressed the need for abolition of the 'Jagirdari' system, pleaded for workers' Fight to strike and addressed a large number of meetings and conferences in Bombay Presidency. In 1939, during the Second World War, he called upon Indians to join the Army in large numbers to defeat Nazism, which he said, was another name for Fascism.

He stood for the nationalisation of property like land, banks etc. Ambedkar was also an advocate of women's rights. He struggled for women's liberation from the caste-entrenched patriarchal system. At the conference of the Depressed Classes Women in Nagpur in 1942, he stated: 'let every girl who marries stand by her husband, claim to be her husband's friend and equal, and refuse to be his slave'. He resigned from the Nehru's cabinet as Law Minister only when the cabinet refused to pass the Women's Rights Bill. This strongly proves that his idea of Socialism was embedded in his core agenda of freedom for all from all forms of bondage.

Ambedkar and After: The post Ambedkar Dalit movement had witnessed several ups and downs. On one side a categorical awakening among the Dalits had grown beyond all levels of history and on the other it has somewhere stagnant after Ambedkar mainly due to ideological disposition of stagnation. It would be opportune to look at the post Ambedkar Dalit movement and do a stock taking of the changes within the Dalit politics to understand the phenomenon. Subash Gatade says that the ups and downs through which the Dalit politics passed through after the death of Dr. Baba Saheb Ambedkar can be broadly divided into three phases-Rise and Fall of the Republican Party, emergence of the Dalit Panthers and thirdly the growing assertion of Dalits for political power and their consequent refusal to remain satisfied merely with education and job opportunities arising out of the policy of reservation.

At this stage there is another factor that developed among Dalit castes too. These are organising themselves under the banners of their respective caste and sub-caste for achieving their rights. Consequently their guns are trained besides the Varna system also on the so-called rich Dalit castes or the creamy layer in them, which they feel, have monopolised a large part of the reserved posts. The Mahar/neo-Buddhists vs. Matang and Charmakar debate in Maharashtra, Mala vs. Madiga in Andhra Pradesh are symptomatic of this rising trend. This propensity is similar in most states where the marginalized Dalits are organising themselves into a movement for castewise categorisation of reserved seats in educational institutions and jobs etc., which could not avail of the quota for historical reasons, could avail of it.

It is indeed ironical that at a time when the issue of Dalit assertion has got acceptance even in the mainstream polity in the 90s a counter tendency has emerged which seem to fracture the new found identity. One could also perceive the whole process as an explosion of identities hitherto suppressed by the hegemonic caste and class structure. In the beginning of the 70s the term Dalit denoted a broad, homogenous fraternity. This is no more the case. If you just say Dalit you are making an incomplete statement. It would be necessary to also specify whether he is a Mala or a Madiga or a Matang or a Charmakar. This process has thrown up new 'icons' from among the different castes and the sub-castes as well. This clearly gives a broader picture of the fact that how much the individual caste identity had become more important than the collective one of the 70s.

Another aspect that the Dalit movement in the post-Ambedkar era failed to address is that of the direct challenges of communal fascism. Communal-fascism is exploring its way to elaborate its base, activities and action. It appears that building of philanthropic and religious institutions like Saraswati Sishu Mandir, Vanvasi Kalyan Ashram, Sanghs, Deen Dayal Shodh Sansthan, Sanskriti Bihar, Vikas Bharit, Gayatri Pariwar, Brahmakumari Samaj, etc. are some of the strategies adopted to create inroads among the Dalits & Adivasis. Another strategy applied is the steady and systematic capturing of the community panchayats and organisations. The best example of this is Gujarat where the communal fascists have got their stranglehold and successfully executed the carnage against the Muslims by communalising Dalits and Adivasis. Resultant is the perpetual assurance of control over these communities plus a bonus of sustaining casteism. Expansion of caste fascism has so far and is disintegrating the Dalit ideology, theology, and identity and intimidated their very existence. Apparently this ruptures the community, deteriorates the noble notions of sharing, caring and cooperation, expansion of patriarchy and battered the inkling of community ownership over resources. Let us not forget Ambedkar was the greatest fighter against religious fascism and historical caste fascism.

Thirdly Dalit movement neither understand the politics of imperialist globalisation not address it in any form. Rather than entering the debate in a critical way from the subaltern perspective, it remained passive to the process of globalisation, and many times joined the sustaining party. Globalisation in India marked through Economic Reforms launched in July 1991 in India were in nature of a crisis management response to the economic and political crises that erupted in early 90s. The blue print for the Reforms was provided by the combination of macroeconomic stabilisation and structural adjustment programme of International Monetary Fund (IMF) and World Bank respectively, which had been adopted by many countries before in similar situations.

This had quantitative and qualitative adversities on food security, employment, inflation, poverty alleviation schemes as well as social security. For example reservation in the educational institutions and the financial assistance in the form of scholarships and freeships had gone out of context, with the advent of education as an industry. Without education, all constitutional safeguards including the reservation in services would be futile. The Reforms have already resulted in freezing the grants to many institutions and in stagnating, if not lowering, the expenditure on education. The free market ethos has entered the educational sphere in a big way. Commercialisation of education is no more a mere rhetoric; it is now the established fact. Commercial institutions offering specialised education signifying the essential input from utilitarian viewpoint have come up in a big way from cities to small towns.

It is the same way that the employment sector had its impact due to the thus called 'economic reforms'. Howsoever, unsatisfactory the results of the implementation of reservation in employment may be, its importance from the Dalit viewpoint cannot be under emphasised. As could be evidenced by the organised private sector, where it would be difficult to find a Dalit employee (save of course in scavenging and lowliest jobs), without reservations Dalits would have been totally doomed. The importance of reservations thus could only be assessed in relation to situations where they do not exist. Whatever be their defects and deficiencies, they have given certain economic means of livelihood and some social prestige to the sons and daughters of over 1.5 million landless labourers. Whether they get real power or not, over 50,000 Dalits could enter the sphere of bureaucratic authority with the help of reservations. Besides these tangible benefits promised by the policy, it has instilled a hope in Dalit community. This hope predominantly manifests in the form of spread of education among them. Their emotional bond with the nation and its Constitution despite heaps of injustice and ignominy they bear every moment of their life may also be significantly attributable to the Reservation Policy.

The selling out the PSU, the disinvestments of PSUs, promotion of privatisation, the letting off of land to the corporates, etc. had crafted formulae of neo-colonisation. This is high time that Dalit leadership across the country enters this debate in a big way, which it had until now failed to do.

Coming back to Ambedkar, he was not dogmatic but pragmatic. He had rightly confronted the forces of fascism, communalism and capitalism. He believed that any system that promotes unequal human relationships should not thrive. Unfortunately, his socio-economical writings were kept aside while his writings on religion and caste system of 30s were used more by the representatives of the movement, thus clearly alienating a vast masses of the unorganised labour away from the mainstream Ambedkarite movement. That is why today, despite globalisation resulting in wars and multiple conflicts, yet Dalits simply remain as silent spectators, just waiting for their turn of reservation. Dalits are confined to use the Dalit card for just reservation in education and employment, nothing else.

The forth barrier of the post Ambedkar Dalit movement is the emergence of a new sect of Dalit elite. This Dalit elite whom Baba Saheb had opposed tooth and nail in his lifetime had become the Sarkari Babu Sahab clan, who not only take the benefits of reservations but also conveniently forget the community once they get there. It is also observed that while this sect functions throughout with the brand 'Dalit', also engage in all the corrupt practices that was once the cornerstone of Brahministic culture and ethics. It is interesting that Ambedkar fought for the rights of Dalits and had a broader vision, which couldn't be inculcated by post-Ambedkar Ambedkarites. He wanted to give his people an identity so that they get out of Varna System, but here what we see is the stimulation of the culture of varna and caste within the Dalit communities.

Despite the leaps and bounds, the Dalit movement made in Indian context, the failure of Ambedkarite movement to address the questions of fascism, communalism, globalisation, imperialism and the most importantly patriarchy in relation with casteism has altogether dragged the Dalit movement to the crossroad in the present context.

Any pragmatic and progressive movement cannot stand on the selective criticism of a few religious texts or political ideologies and conveniently keeping quiet on other questions. A movement cannot be built on superfluous philosophy of negativism. It has to provide its own alternative to the people. To quote V.B. Rawat, Dalits have their own distinct identity and culture and those claiming to provide them an alternative God really misquote Ambedkar and kill their revolutionary spirit as suggested by many Dalit activists.

Ambedkar's popularity among the Dalits is not due to the corrupt Dalits who use all tactics to grab money and power but the poor Dalits who consider him as the liberator. There are many reasons for the same. Ambedkar is a uniting factor for Dalits. No doubt that he has become an icon of Dalits from North to South from Hindi heartland to the southern Tamil Nadu.

However he himself was against 'hero worship' of any time. He believed in the exploration of knowledge on historical and scientific basis. This has to be a regular, rather ongoing, process which is only possible by addressing the problems of the oppressed and exploited masses. The undeniable fact is the Ambedkar is mainly known among the working class Dalits. The only way to salute Bhimrao is by truly standing against oppressive structure, for equality and justice.

8

CONFERENCES OF AMBEDKAR'S

INTRODUCTION

Dr. Ambedkar: I should like to raise the point, which my friend Mr. Joshi made before we adjourned. The Lord Chancellor, as the Chairman of this Sub-Committee, invited some of the delegates to submit any views they might have on these particular matters, and a few delegates including myself submitted a letter to the Chairman of the Sub-Committee, and expressed our wish that letter should be submitted to the Sub-Committee for consideration. I do not find in the Report any reference to that letter, and I was informed by Lord Sankey that letter was not placed before the Sub-Committee, but was sent to you, Sir, as Prime Minister. I do not think that was quite a proper way of dealing with it.

The letter was submitted to the Chairman of the Sub-Committee, for the Sub-Committee's use and it expressed certain definite views we held on the question of Federation. I am bound to make this comment because, speaking for myself, the Report as drawn up is so much at variance with the principles expressed in the letter that I find we shall have at some stage to raise a debate on this question, and I should like to know what steps the Lord Chancellor proposes to take.

Lord Sankey: I am very much obliged to Dr. Ambedkar for raising the point he has done, because I should have liked to have raised it myself, and it gives me the opportunity of saying a few words which I should have said at the beginning........ This is not a complete picture........ soon you are going to be presented with the complete picture, and Dr. Ambedkar, I shall want your assistance,.........Now with regard to the letter. Dr. Ambedkar, that you were good enough to send to me, I have considered it very carefully, and it will be vital to discuss it when we come to No. 6.

Dr. Ambedkar: All I should like to know, if I may say so, is whether you will place that letter before the Committee. At what stage you may do so is a matter which I must leave to you.

Lord Sankey: One moment, Dr. Ambedkar. I am going to do a good deal more than that; I am not only going to place your letter before the Committee. I am going to draw the Committee's attention to it myself.

First Sitting-4th December 1930

Dr. Ambedkar: I propose to divide my remarks under three heads : (1) provincial autonomy, (2) responsibility in the provinces, (3) provincial services. I make a distinction between provincial autonomy and provincial services. It seems to me that the question of provincial autonomy raises the definition of the relations of the provincial Executive and Legislature vis-a-vis the Central Government and the Central Legislature. The first remark I would offer with the attitude of those who hold that the time has arrived when the provincial Governments ought to be left with as complete an autonomy as is possible under the circumstances, and they should be free from such control as the Central Government now exercises.

But, Sir, I cannot help making this further observation, that viewing the problem of provincial autonomy from the standpoint of the particular class I represent in this Conference and of the interests of India as a whole and the working classes in particular, I think that in any future constitution that we propose to devise for endowing the Provinces with provincial autonomy we must take into consideration certain facts which are bound to limit the character of that autonomy.

The first limiting factor in the provincial autonomy is that it must be made subject to such questions of a provincial character which are, although provincial in nature, also of an All-India character. The Provinces may have their say with regard to these subjects, and yet the Central Government should not be excluded from its jurisdiction with regard to them. For instances, I would like to draw an illustration from labour legislation, legislation affecting tenants and affecting agriculture. These, no doubt, in a country like India, must become provincial subjects yet I do not think they can be viewed entirely from such a small compass. They cannot be regarded as entirely provincial and without an All-India character. The Central Government must have some jurisdiction over subjects of this character, notwithstanding that it cuts across provincial autonomy.

Secondly, I should state that in dividing the powers of Government between the Central and the Provincial Governments in the future constitution of India with a view to giving the Provinces as complete an autonomy as possible, it will also be necessary that such powers as remain undefined must be left with the Central Government. Well, I do not think that there is no other view on that point. But I say that in the present situation in India, where the separatist tendency exists to such an extent as we all know it, where provincial and local parochialism is more dominant than national feeling, while we are building up a Federated India with complete autonomy of the units, we still have the problem of making India as a whole a strong and united country. I would make this further observation, namely, that I do not think that the reservation of powers in the Central Government is likely to affect the autonomy of the Provinces. The reservation of powers as interpreted by the Judicial Committee of the Privy Council in the case of Canada has not had this overriding effect. It means a power that comes into existence in an emergency in a field not specifically allotted to the Provinces. I do not think that the Provincial autonomy should be really affected.

The second thing I should like to observe in connection with this question of Provincial autonomy is that autonomy must be limited by the affording of protection for the interests of the minorities and of the Depressed Classes. As I visualise the situation in India as it will result from the new constitution, I find there will be certain Provinces in which some communities will be in a majority, but in all the Provinces the Depressed

Classes, whom I represent, will be in a minority. They will be in a minority in every Province. I cannot understand how we can at this state permit the Provincial majorities to have a complete uninterrupted and undiluted sway over the destinies of these poor people, without any right of appeal being given to the latter in regard to mal-administration or neglect of their interests. There must be some authority somewhere, over and above the Provincial Government, which will be in a position to intervene and rescue them from any adverse position in which they may be placed by the Provincial majorities.

These are the three things, which, in my opinion at any rate must limit the autonomy of the future Provincial Governments of India.

Coming to the question of the character of responsibility in the Provincial Governments, my first observation is that the whole question of responsibility in the Provincial Legislature is entirely dependent upon the kind of Legislature that you are going to get in the Provinces. If the Legislature that you are going to get in the Provinces is a Legislature which is going to be a mirror of the whole population of the Province, if it is going to be thoroughly representative and not merely representative as a museum is, where there are a few specimens of every species for the observation of the general onlooker; if every minority and every class which fears its existence will be jeopardised is placed on a position to make its influence felt, then I think in a Legislature of that sort there will be no harm in conceding the principle that Provincial responsibility may be introduced to the fullest extent. That is my first observation.

Making that a condition that the Legislatures shall be fully and adequately representative of all the classes, I see no objection to the subjects, which are now, reserved being transferred to popular control.

Coming to the question of whether the responsibility in the Provinces should be joint or should be individual I have not the slightest hesitation in saying that the responsibility not only should be joint but must be joint. I have been a member of Legislative Council, and I have seen how Ministries in the Provinces have worked. It has been a most painful experience for me, as it has been the experience, I believe, of many of those who have had the misfortune or the good fortune to be members of a Legislative Council, to find that Ministries have been working as a kind of loose confederation, without having any complete or unanimous view on a particular policy which they adopted. There have been divided counsels, and cases of Ministers not being very willing to support each other.

What has been the result? The result is this, that in no instance have we had any considered policy put forward by the Cabinet as a whole, worked out in detail and placed before the Legislative Council. Things have been done by fits and starts, and I do not think we want our responsibility in future to be bungled in that fashion.

Turning now to the question of communal representation in the Cabinets, I must confess that I am not very much drawn to the suggestion, which is often made that there should be communal representation in the Cabinet. I am not, of course, oblivious of the fact; in fact, I am very conscious of it that if the minority communities are not represented in the Cabinet it is very possible, and even very likely, that in matters of administration which affect their daily lives their interests may be affected very prejudicially by the policy of Ministers whose dominant interest is communalism. I do not forget that for a moment, but my submission is that there is a better way of dealing with that sort of evil, and it seems to me that if the minorities could get constitutional and statutory guarantees laid down in the Constitutional Act itself against anything likely to injure their interests being done or left undone by the Cabinet, the danger which most of us apprehend from the fact that the Cabinets may be communally dominated, will vanish, and we shall not have much cause to insist on communal representation in the Cabinet. Although I am very desirous that the Chief Minister, whoever he is, should recognise or should be made to recognise the interest of having most of the important minorities represented in the Cabinet, we cannot for the moment forget that, after all, a Cabinet office is a very responsible office.

A Cabinet Minister has not merely to look after the interests of the minorities; he has to see to the safety and interest of the Province as a whole. That demands ability and competence; it does not merely demand a communal outlook, and it is from that point of view that I look at the matter. I should like to have the interests of the minorities and the Depressed Classes safeguarded in such a manner that constitutionally it would be impossible for Ministers drawn from the majority communities to do anything prejudicial to the minorities or to neglect their interests.

Coming to the question of the relations between the Governor and his Ministry, I think one thing is obvious, namely that no constitution, if it is really to embody full responsible Government and collective responsibility, can permit the Governor the power to interfere in the day-to-day administration of the country. That would run quite across the system of responsible Government and collective responsibility. The Ministry must be allowed to carry on the day-to-day administration on the basis of joint responsibility.

When we come to the question of the emergency powers which it is suggested should be left with the Governor. I find myself in a somewhat difficult position, because I do not understand exactly what is meant. Is it meant that when an emergency arises the Governor should simply dismiss the Ministry and have nothing to do with it, and should promulgate whatever laws, ordinances or measures he thinks are necessary to meet the situation, notwithstanding the fact that they are opposed by the Ministry? I do not know what is wanted. I can quite understand the Governor should have the absolute, undoubted and unrestricted power of dismissing a Ministry which he thinks is not acting in the best interests of the country, but I cannot understand how there can be responsible Government in a Province in which the Governor is allowed to do a thing without a Ministry. It is one thing to say that the Governor should have a Ministry with which he agrees in a particular emergency, but it is quite a different thing to say that when an emergency arises the Governor should simply disregard the Ministry altogether. I think this point will have to be worked out in some deal, for, as I say, I do not quite understand it.

Coming to the question of the Services, there is one observation I am bound to make. I quite agree in principle that with provincial autonomy the power of regulating the Services in a Province should belong to that Province, and that the Provinces should have full liberty to Indianise the Services as they desire and according to their means and circumstances. The observation which I feel bound to make, however, is this: I cannot forget that Indians are communal minded. We do hope it is only a hope that a time will come when all Indians will cease to look at problems from a communal point of view in administrating matters which are left to their charge, but that is only a hope; it is not a fact. The fact is that Indians do discriminate between class and class, community and community, in administering such discretion as is left to them in their administration of the law. That is a fact I cannot get over; it is a fact from which I have suffered immensely. My fear with regard to the future constitution of India is that having regard to the present position of the depressed classes, having regard to the fact that education is not widely spread amongst them, and having regard to the fact that there is hardly a single individual holding a gazetted post in the Bombay Presidency for instance:

A Member: There is one.

Dr. Ambedkar: Yes, there is one, and that is the exception, which proves the rule. You know how much trouble I had to get him in. I very much fear that this Indianisation may work out as a tyranny, and therefore, from my particular point of view, I should like to emphasise that at any rate for some time it will be necessary to maintain a British element in the Services. I do not say there should be no Indianisation, but I do say that, having regard to our interests, it should be rather slower than some people desire it to be. These are the general remarks that I wish to offer from our point of view.

Third Sitting-8th December 1930

Dr. Ambedkar: May I make a suggestion? It seems to me this question of Second Chambers is so important that it cannot be discussed properly and adequately by being tacked on to the series of heads we are now discussing. In my opinion a special day ought to be allotted to this subject. I see very little connection between the subject of Second Chambers and that of the protection of minorities, or any of the other matters enumerated in items I and 2. It seems to me this is a very important question. I find nothing in this list of heads dealing with the composition of the Legislature; if you were to add a head "Composition of the Legislature" we should have a proper opportunity of discussing the whole subject.

Chairman: I cannot see how you can separate this whole subject and split it up.

Dr. Ambedkar: The question of Second Chambers can certainly be separated from that of minorities.

Chairman: Not entirely. Whether there is to be a Second Chamber or not affects almost every other subject that comes up, the powers of the Governor vis-a-vis the Executive and the Legislature, the powers of the Legislature and so on. I think you had better let us go on, and if at the end we find the discussion has not been adequate, we will try to arrange for a further discussion on this subject by itself.

Fourth Sitting-9th December 1930

Dr. Ambedkar: It may be. But I am taking these two communities for the moment because they are important. It seems to me that any argument, which is based upon that fact is an argument, which leads to a conclusion which, will never enable us to transfer law and order. Therefore it seems to me that is an argument which ought not to be adopted or accepted. It seems to me also that the noble Marquess assumes that although a Mohammedan or a Hindu will be in charge of the department of law and order, he will be entirely subject to the whims of the particular community to which he belongs. My submission, Sir, is this, that assumes that the future of political parties in India will be so constituted that they will be divided on religious lines and not on the lines of political or economic differences. As I view the situation it seems to me that in the future constitution of India the Executive will be so divided that we shall see less of the religious and racial distinctions coming to the surface and we shall find a Hindu Minister having a party and a following containing a large element of Mohammedans, and a Mohammedan Minister with a following of Hindus in his group, if that happens, and I take it is almost a certainty that it will happen, I do not understand how, for instance, a Hindu Minister who is in charge of law and order could administer law and order in such a manner as to offend the susceptibilities of a part of the group which supports him in office. It seems to me therefore that the fears so far as this particular aspect of the matter is concerned are rather unfounded.

The second thing which seems to be agreed upon more or less is this, that not only should the Executive be a unified Executive but that the responsibility of this unified Executive should be joint and not several. With these conclusions, Sir, I agree, but the points of difference that have arisen in the course of the debate to which we have listened largely relate to the composition of the Executive and it seems to me that there arise three different questions for our consideration in connection with the composition of the Executive. The first question is: should the Executive be confined to members of the Legislature or should it be open to individuals who are officials or non-officials and who are outside the Legislature? The second question is: should it consist of members of the minority communities? The third question is: whether the Governor should have the responsibility of appointing the Ministers himself or whether he should appoint the Chief Minister and leave the matter of the selection of his colleagues to that Chief Minister.

Now, Sir, on all these three questions my answer is in the affirmative. Personally, I do not see why the membership of the Cabinet should be rigorously restricted and confined to the members of the Legislature. I also do not see why there should not exist some provisions whereby the Executive should not be made as representative as possible of all the communities that are represented in the Legislature.

Thirdly, regarding the power of the Governor to compose his Ministry, it seems to me that we must admit that it is his prerogative right to constitute the Ministry and that you must have discretion left to him in the matter of selecting his men. But, Sir, when I say that I answer these three questions in the affirmative, namely, that the Executive need not be confined to the members of the Legislature, that some provision should exist whereby different communities may be represented in the Cabinet, and that the Governor should have left with him abundant discretion in order to form his Cabinet, I say when I make these admissions I make them subject to one supreme condition. That supreme condition is that however the Executive is composed, it shall abide by one principle, namely that it shall accept joint responsibility. If, for instance, this principle of joint responsibility is made obligatory upon the Executive, it seems to me that the importation of a foreign element into the Cabinet will not be a disturbing factor as it is supposed to be. If, for instance, the newcomer who does not belong to the Legislative Council comes into the Cabinet and accepts joint responsibility along with the Cabinet, I do not see any reason why such a procedure should not be permitted. It was pointed out that it may so happen that when a Ministry is censured and it goes out, the official or the one who does not belong to the Legislature will remain while the other members of the Cabinet will go out; that when a new Ministry is formed, he will be again tacked on to the Ministry and that he will be perpetually in the Council. It seems to me with all respects that is a somewhat fallacious view, because, unless the members who are drawn from the Legislature to form the Ministry are prepared to take him along with them and are prepared to bear the responsibility of his actions, they will not consent to work with when he accepts their advice and they accept his advice. If, for instance, a Prime Minister were so situated that he could safely take an outsider into his Cabinet and at the same time maintain the confidence of the House, I do not see why the Chief Minister should be prevented from having that privilege accorded to him.

In the same way, Sir, if, for instance, it was found possible that the Governor should have powers to see that the different minority communities are represented in his Cabinet, and if at the same time it is made perfectly clear that whoever is appointed to the Cabinet must accept joint responsibility with the others, then I submit there is no harm in allowing this sort of thing. It seems to me therefore that the point which it is necessary to emphasise is that the Governor may have the power which as I say belongs to him as of right to compose the

Ministry in any way he likes provided that the Ministry does not violate in its operation the principle of its being, namely, that it is to work on the principle of joint responsibility.

Now the next question to which I will address myself, Sir, is how best to achieve this result, how best to bring out a responsible and unified Executive. It seems to me there are two ways open to us. One way is to define in the constitution itself the character of the Executive by law; the other is to leave to convention the constitution of the Executive. Both these ways are adopted, as you all know. We all know that in the Dominions of Canada, South Africa and Australia, responsible Government of a unified character is entirely a matter of convention. Everyone of us knows that in the Canadian Act or in the Acts of South Africa or Australia the words "responsible Government "do not arise. It is not even mentioned in the Canadian Act, as I found to my great surprise, that the Ministers who are to advise the Governor are to be members of the Legislature, although as a matter of fact they are. On the other hand, as we know, in the constitutions of Ireland, Malta and Rhodesia this is a subject which is not left to convention, it is something which is incorporated in law. In Ireland we know that the Prime Minister is a creature of statute, the joint responsibility is also defined by law.

I therefore think that we shall have to make our choice between the two, and in making the choice I for one would be guided by two considerations. I fully realise that when a matter is left to convention it is possible that the convention may be wrongly worked, that it may be abused, and may be abused with impunity. The danger of matters being left to convention in a country like India seems to me to be greater because there are no parties in India which have a keen eye on the way in which the constitution works and we may have Ministers less interested in working the constitution in the right spirit than in maintaining their seats in the Cabinet. On the other hand it seems to me that where matters are defined by law it must necessarily take away all the discretion that must necessarily be left to a Governor.

In a country like India where the political field with all its communal and racial difficulties is an absolutely uncharted sea, it seems to me that we must so contrive that sufficient discretion will be left with the Governor. My concrete suggestion therefore is this, that joint responsibility of the Executive should be prescribed by law and that everything else should be left to the discretion of the Governor, so that we shall have satisfied both the conditions : we shall have provided that whatever responsibility there is, is joint responsibility and that the composition of the Executive is at the same time not hampered in such a manner that the communities which do require to be represented in the Cabinet may be represented or that the necessity which Prime Minister may feel of having a non-official, I mean an outsider, in his Cabinet is provided for.

If we do that, if we insist by law, not leaving it to the discretion of the Governor, that the Executive shall be a joint Executive with joint responsibility, I think all other matters may be left without any fear of abuse to the choice of the Governor.

Now Sir, the next topic which I will take for consideration is that of the powers of the Governor vis-a-vis his Executive. The present relations between the Governor and the Minister, as well we all know, are defined in section 52, sub-clause 3. That clause says that in all transferred matters-and all matters will now be transferred, none being reserved-the Governor shall be guided by the advice of his Ministers; and it adds a further proviso that if he sees sufficient cause to dissent from the advice of his Ministers he may cause action to be taken otherwise than in accordance with that advice. With all due respect to those who framed that clause, and they did it with the best intention of providing responsible Government, I cannot help saying that this clause as it now stands is a perversion of responsible Government; it makes responsible Government a matter of convenience, a matter which may be accepted and followed when it suits the Governor, whereas as a matter of fact what we want is that responsible Government should be a matter of obligation. If responsible Government means anything it means this, that in whatever action the Governor takes in any field he has the support of a Ministry which has the confidence of the House. That is a fundamental proposition which we cannot ignore.

It does not of course mean that a Governor must always accept the advice of his Ministry; it leaves it open to the Governor to throw out the Ministry, to say he will not abide by their advice; but then if the Governor chooses to differ from his Ministry his obligation is not to act on his own initiative but to find some other Ministers who will support his action. So that the proposition is that at all times when the Governor takes action he takes action which is in conformity with the views of Ministers who have the confidence of the House. My submission therefore is that this clause, namely section 52, must be so altered as to make it plain that unless specific provision is made to the contrary by statute there may be cases which, I will come to a little later, the Governor shall always act upon the advice of the Ministers.

Now, Sir, I do readily agree that there may be cases in which it is necessary to provide the Governor with overriding powers, powers in respect to which he will not be obliged to follow the advice of his Ministers but will have the right of independent action. Those cases are mentioned in paragraph 50, page 36 of Volume 2 of the Report of the Simon Commission. The first is that he should have overriding powers in order to preserve the safety and tranquillity of the Province; secondly, he should have overriding powers in order to prevent serious prejudice to one or more sections of the community as compared with other sections; and then lastly it mentions certain cases where the Governor may have fixed upon him specific responsibility as apart from the responsibility of the whole of the Executive, in which case it says that he should also have overriding powers.

With regard to these items my first submission is this, that if you are going to give the Governor to over-ride his Ministers to preserve the peace, safety and tranquillity of the Province, it seems to me you are taking away a very large part of responsible Government in the Provinces.

After all, what we are striving for is that the Provinces shall be governed in all matters, including even the peace, safety and tranquillity of the Province, by a Governor on the advice of his Ministers; and, if you reserve powers to the Governor to act contrary to their advice, it seems to me you are to a very large extent nullifying the powers of responsible Government. I should not, therefore, give the Governor overriding powers in a matter of this sort, unless some way could be found whereby this large formula, which seems to me to eat-up the whole situation, might be very narrowly defined.

Coming to the other question, namely prejudice to one section of the community as compared with the others, my own view is that although this is a very salutary thing my preference is that such matters as are likely prejudicial to affect the interests of any particular community should be governed by statute; it should not be left to the sweet will of the Governor. I say that for this very good reason. After all, a Governor has to keep in touch with a Cabinet which is supported by a majority in the Legislature. He can never work at cross purposes with the Cabinet; the greatest amity must prevail between them, and I am not sure the Governor would always be so minded as to quarrel with a Cabinet which represented a majority in the House merely in order to protect a minority which, in his eyes, might not be very important. Although, therefore, I agree with the underlying suggestion there. I rather prefer that the interests of the minorities should be protected in a firmer manner than is suggested, and for myself I should be prepared to delete this clause.

Regarding the other items 3, 4 and 5, I agree that in cases of this sort the Governor must have overriding powers, because they are cases where he personally is made responsible for the administration of those subjects.

Coming to the next subject, the powers of the Governor vis-a-vis the Legislature, I will divide my remarks under three heads. There is first of all budgetary legislation; secondly, ordinary legislation and thirdly, emergency legislation. The Governor has today powers of certification with regard to the provision for reserved subjects, and that will necessarily go with the abolition of anarchy. Secondly, the Governor has authority to authorise expenditure for the safety and tranquillity of the Province.

It seems to me that if you are going to leave questions of peace and tranquillity to be settled by a responsible ministry, the Governor should not possess this power of authorising expenditure for the safety and tranquillity of the Province. In the next place, he has the power of certifying Bills, which are of two sorts. He may certify that a particular Bill which is being discussed in the Legislature shall not be discussed because it affects the safety and tranquillity of the Province, and he has also the power to certify a Bill which is in the interests of the safety and tranquillity of the Province even though the Legislature may not desire to pass it in the ordinary course. It seems to me both these powers should go; they will not be necessary in the future constitution of India. He has also powers of previous sanction; certain subjects have to be previously sanctioned by him before they can be discussed, and in my opinion this power should go.

Sir Ahmad Sayed Khan: Discriminatory legislation?

Dr. Ambedkar: That should be dealt with by Statute; I should not leave it to the Governor. The Governor must have the power of veto, and in view of the fact that there will be no Second Chamber in those Provinces which do not want it, it is very necessary that the Governor should have the power of veto. The Governor today has also the power of returning a Bill to the House for reconsideration. This is a very useful power which exists in the constitutions of the various Dominions, and I think it should be retained. The Governor has also power to reserve a Bill for the consideration of the Governor-General and the cases in which he should do so are defined by Statute.

That is a matter, I think which might be more conveniently considered when we consider the relations of the Provincial Governments to the Central Government, but I should like to make one observation on this subject. We should so endeavour to contrive our Provincial constitution that it will function independently, as far as possible of the interference of the Central Government in those domains which have been transferred to its control. We must make a constitution under which there will be no occasion for constant intervention by the Central Government, either administratively or legislatively by the reservation of Bills.

With regard to the question of safeguards for Law and Order and for minorities, I have already stated that Law and Order should be transferred, but I am prepared to make one suggestion, for what it is worth. In cases of emergency, when Law and Order are being jeopardised, I suggest the Governor should have power to pass orders finally, without respect to the advice of the Ministry, regarding the posting and transfer of Police officers. I think that is very necessary; it is essential.

Sir Cowasji Jehangir: In case of emergency only?

Dr. Ambedkar: Yes, but not in other cases.

Dr. Paul: Not in normal times?

Dr. Ambedkar: Not in normal times, no, but in cases of emergency when a riot has taken place or a disturbance has occurred, it is very necessary that an impartial officer like the Governor, who is not swayed by what is happening in the Cabinet, should have the ultimate power to see that people are not transferred from one place to another to suit one community or the other community when a riot is actually proceeding. It seems to me that it gives him sufficient power for the purpose of safeguarding the administration of Law and Order.

With regard to the question of minorities, it was suggested by some speakers that a Second Chamber would afford protection to minorities, and my friend Mr. Wood threw out the suggestion that I had not carefully considered the position of the Depressed Classes in relation to a Second Chamber. I should like to assure my friend that I have given the matter most careful consideration, and I thoroughly agree with my friend Mr. Paul that these Second Chambers, far from being a protection to minorities, will be really milestones round their necks.

There is one subject I did not touch on before, but which I should like briefly to mention now, namely, the relation of the Governor to his Cabinet. Should he preside over the Cabinet as a matter of right or should he not? Should there be the system which prevails in this country where the Cabinet holds its meetings without the King being there, and if so what should be the means of communicating the results and decisions arrived at by the Cabinet to the Governor? I do not know if that arises on this item; if it does not, I will not waste time in discussing it.

Chairman: We have generally discussed the whole question, so that if you desire to continue I shall not object.

Dr. Ambedkar: In that connection I want to say one thing. The Simon Commission has suggested that a Cabinet Secretary should be appointed who would be of the same status as an I.C.S. Officer, and who would act as the liaison officer of the Cabinet to the Governor. In throwing out that suggestion the Commission says it has drawn on the practice that has now become prevalent in this country, namely, that the Cabinet now always has a Secretary, which formerly it did not have. I should like to submit, however, that it is one thing to say that the Cabinet should have a Secretary, but it is a totally different thing to say that Secretary should have access to the Governor over the heads of the Ministers.

In this country the practice does exist, probably, of appointing a Secretary, but I do not think any Cabinet or Prime Minister in this country would consent to that Cabinet Secretary having access to His Majesty over the heads of the Ministers or over the head of the Prime Minister; such a thing would be intolerable. We know that in this country the Cabinet throughout all its history has laid emphasis on the fact that the persons who will be near to His Majesty should be persons who will bear the same complexion as the Ministry, and we know that has been carried so far that even the Ladies of the Chamber who wait upon the Queen are required to be nominated by the Prime Minister and the Cabinet. The situation suggested, therefore, seems to me almost impossible. I do not think any Cabinet which is working on the principle of joint responsibility will consent to have a Secretary of this kind attached to it.

On the other hand, if the Governor is given the power to preside over the Cabinet when it is discussing its policy, I doubt very much whether that will work, because although the Ministry may, and indeed must, communicate to the Governor the decisions at which it has arrived, I do not think the Ministry will consent to disclose to the Governor the reasons which have led it to come to those decisions. The reasons may be very particular and very delicate, and you all know that the Cabinet is very jealous not to let the Governor know the reasons why it has arrived at a particular decision.

The explanation of that is that the Governor holds in his hands a tremendous power for undoing the Ministry for he may not agree to the Ministry's advice to dissolve the House, but may instead of being embodied in a Statute, the matter should be left to the Instrument of Instructions, which may provide that the Governor can attend if he desires to do so, but it should not be obligatory at all. On the other hand, it should be made obligatory for the Cabinet to communicate to the Governor all the recommendations at which it arrives at its meeting. That is all I desire to say on that point.

Dr. Ambedkar: We should like to say one thing on that point that the Second Chamber should not be constituted first, and then its abolition should be left to constitutional resolution requiring a certain majority. What we suggest is that if the situation is such that it should be left as a matter of discretion in certain Provinces, then first of all a resolution might be passed by the Provincial Legislature expressing its desire for a Second Chamber, and then, that the Second Chamber should be constituted. It should not be first imposed on the Provincial Legislature by the constitution.

Fifth Sitting-15th December 1930

Dr. Ambedkar: Sir, I should like to make one or two observations on the amendment which the noble Marquess has moved. I should like to state at once that the position which he has taken up seems to me to be absolutely logical. In this report we are going to provide that certain interests and minority groups may be represented by nomination in the Legislative Council. At the same time we are also making provision in this report that the Governor shall be given an obligation to endeavour to secure that his Cabinet shall be representative of all interests and of all minorities.

Now, Sir, unless you provide that in the making up of this Cabinet, the Governor shall also have the right to include members who represent certain important interests by nomination, it seems to me that you are creating an absolutely illogical position. Either you must provide that there shall be no nomination to the Legislative Council at all, that all interests, no matter how minute, shall be secured by election to the Legislative Council, or, if there is to be nomination then you must provide that a nominated member shall have the right to be in the Cabinet if his colleagues are prepared to work with him on the principle of joint responsibility. There is no escape from one or other of those positions.

Now. Sir, it is stated by friends who are sitting on this side that if we accept this principle, that a nominated member shall be a member of the Cabinet, or at least that there shall be no ban upon him, it will run counter to the principle of responsibility. I really cannot understand that position. These gentlemen who are saying it will run counter to the principle of responsibility are prepared to take the votes of nominated members. I am taking the report as it stands. I do not know what future amendments there will be. Supposing the report as it stands is carried, that there shall be certain members in the Legislative Council who shall be nominated.

Is it the position of these gentlemen that their votes are illegal? If those who form the Cabinet who are drawn from the elected portion of the House can validly use the votes of members who are nominated to the Legislative Council, if those votes can logically become the basis of the policy of a Government, I cannot see how a member who is one of that nominated group should not become a member of that Cabinet. I fail altogether to understand it. If, as I say, they can take these votes of nominated members and utilise them for their own purposes. I cannot understand what objection there can be to the inclusion of a member from the nominated group in the Cabinet. I therefore say the position of the noble Marquess is perfectly logical. It seems to me we have to make a choice whether we shall make a provision of the sort suggested by the noble Marquess in his amendment, or whether we shall agree to the other proposal which my friends say they will move at a later stage, that there shall be no nominative element in the Legislative Councils at all. Personally I would much rather have the whole Legislative Council elected with no trace of nomination at all. From that point of view I am not very much in favour of the amendment suggested by the noble Marquess; but if in this Committee or at any later stage nomination remains, then I think I shall have to agree with the noble Marquess and accept the amendment he has proposed. Diwan Bahadur Ramachandra Rao: I must express my surprise at the speech to which I have just listened.

Dr. Ambedkar: You may, but you cannot have it both ways.

Diwan Bahadur Ramachandra Rao: He knows very well that even under the existing system nominated members are not eligible for appointment as ministers. Section 52 clearly lays it down that no minister shall hold office for a longer period than six months unless he is an elected member of the local Legislature.

Dr. Ambedkar: That is in the melting pot.

Opposition to Co-option in Legislature

Dr. Ambedkar: I am afraid I shall have to oppose this amendment. First of all, such experience of co-option as we have had in Bombay is not very encouraging. It has developed into the worst sort of scandal; the amount of corruption and bribery that take place are such that I for one should not like to introduce this principle in the constitution of the Legislature of Bombay.

A further objection is this. If the various communities that do not find themselves elected at the polls are to get representation of a real sort, representation which is independent of the influence of any other community, I think co-option is a principle which is certainly not going to help them, for it may very well happen that when representatives of the various communities stand for co-option only those will be in fact co-opted as may happen to be subservient to and willing to play into the hands of the majority. It seems to me this would be worse than no representation at all, and I am afraid on that ground I must oppose the amendment. But I submit, Sir, that this Sub-Committee ought to make a recommendation that the future constitution of the Provincial Legislatures should be such that there should be no nominated members at all.

Diwan Bahadur Ramachandra Rao: That is far better, of course.

Dr. Ambedkar: That is my own view of the matter. I am certainly opposed to co-option.

Diwan Bahadur Ramachandra Rao: I agree that some statement that the Legislature should be wholly elected ought to be inserted in this report, and unless some such indication is given of the views of this Subcommittee the nominated element will continue, though I believe it is the desire of most of our members that it should disappear. A statement to that effect ought to find a place in the report. I have no doubt whatsoever that everyone of us is quite alive to the evils of nomination, and we are anxious it should disappear as early as possible. Under these circumstances I am not prepared to support the amendment, and I would favour the proposal made by my friend, Dr. Ambedkar.

Chairman: What was the proposal? I have no words here.

Dr. Ambedkar: We should say it is the view of the Sub-Committee that hereafter the Legislative Councils in the Provinces should be wholly elected.

Chairman: That is another amendment altogether, you will have to send it in writing if you want to move that.

Chairman: I will take your decision on this point.

Raja Narendra Nath: I support Sir A. P. Patro. I think the power of nomination should be strictly confined to the representation of interests, which cannot be given by election.

Dr. Shafa'at Ahmad Khan: Yes.

Raja Narendra Nath: There may be in certain Provinces some communities, such as the one to which Dr. Ambedkar belongs, for which it would be impossible to arrange election.

Dr. Ambedkar: I should not have anything to do with a constitution which did not provide the franchise for my community.

Raja Narendra Nath: The franchise will have to be arranged on a very different basis if it is to be provided for the community to which Dr. Ambedkar belongs, and therefore a limited power of nomination should be provided.

Chairman: It seems to me the majority of the Sub-Committee is in favour of clause (c) as it stands in the Report.

In Subcommittee No. III (minorities)

Second Sitting-31st December 1930

Dr. Ambedkar: Mr. Chairman, I am sure you will readily agree that the task which has fallen upon me to represent the case of the Depressed Classes is a heavy one. I think it is for the first time that the case of the Depressed Classes from the political point of view has come to be considered. The disabilities of the Depressed Classes were mentioned in almost every despatch that was recorded by the Government of India in connection with the political advancement of the country; but the despatches only mentioned the difficulties and never attempted to give any solution oı those difficulties.

The problem was just allowed to rest there. In view of that, and in view of other matters, namely, that in a Committee consisting of so many members we are only two to voice the grievances of 43 millions of people, and grievances which the Committee will agree are unparalleled by the case of any other community that exists in India, I submit that the task is really an enormous one, and I should have expected more latitude in the matter of time allowed to me for presenting this case.

But I anticipated that probably such would be the fate that would befall me, as it did, of course, at the Plenary Session; and, in anticipation of that, I and my colleague, Rao Bahadur Srinivasan, thought it advisable to submit to this Conference a written memorandum giving in clear-cut language what the Depressed Classes desire by way of political safeguards in the future constitution of India.

That memorandum has already been submitted and circulated among the members of this Committee, and I hope everyone of them has received it. In view of this fact, that the case of the Depressed Classes is in the possession of the members of this Committee, I do not wish to ask indulgence from the Chairman for a larger period to present the case. I will therefore summarise, only to emphasize, what I have stated in the memorandum which is already in the hands of the members of the Committee.

Sir, the first observation that I will make is this, that although there are various minority communities in India which require political recognition, it has to be understood that the minorities are not on the same plane, that they differ from each other. They differ in the social standing which each minority occupies vis-a-vis the majority community. We have, for instance, the Parsee community, which is the smallest community in India, and yet, vis-a-vis its social standing with the majority community, it is probably the highest in order of precedence.

On the other hand, if you take the Depressed Classes, they are a minority which comes next to the great Muslim minority in India, and yet their social standard is lower than the social standard of ordinary human beings.

Again, if you take the minorities and classify them on the basis of social and political rights, you will find that there are certain minorities which are in enjoyment of social and political rights, and the fact that they are in a minority does not necessarily stand in the way of their full and free enjoyment of those civic rights. But if you take the case of the Depressed Classes, the position is totally different. They have in certain matters no rights, and, where they have any, the majority community will not permit them to enjoy them.

My first submission to this Committee, then, is that it should realise that although, to use an illustration, the minorities are all in the same boat, yet the most important fact to remember is that they are not all in the same class in the same boat; some are travelling in "A" Class, some in "B" Class and some in "C", and so on. I have not the slightest doubt in my mind that the Depressed Classes, though they are a minority and are to that extent in the same boat as other minorities, are not even in "C" or "D" Class but are actually in the hold.

Starting from that point of view, I agree that, in some respects, the position of the Depressed Classes is similar to that of the other minorities in India. The Depressed Classes, along with the other minorities; fear that under any future Constitution of India by which majority rule will be established and there can be no shadow of doubt that majority rule will be the rule of the orthodox Hindus-there is great danger of that majority with its orthodox Hindu beliefs and prejudices contravening the dictates of justice, equality and good conscience, there is a great danger that the minorities may be discriminated against either in legislation or administration or in the other public rights of citizenship, and therefore it is necessary to safeguard the position of the minorities in such a manner that the discrimination which is feared shall not take place.

From that point of view, however, what is asked is that the minorities shall have representation in the Legislature and the Executive, that they shall have representation in the public services of the country, and that the constitution shall provide that these shall be imposed on the future legislatures of India, both Central and Provincial, certain limitations on their legislative power which will prevent the majorities from abusing their legislative power in such a manner as to enact laws which would create discrimination between one citizen and another. I say, this circumstance-this danger of discrimination is common to all minorities, and I, as a representative of the Depressed Classes, join with the demand which the other minorities have made in this regard. Now, Sir, I will come to those circumstances which mark off the Depressed Classes and the other minority communities in India. I will at once say that the way in which the position of the Depressed Classes differs from the position of the other minority communities in India is this, that in the first place the Depressed Classes are not entitled, under present circumstances, to certain civic rights which the other minorities by law enjoy. In other words, in the existing situation the Depressed Classes suffer from what are called civic disabilities. I will give you just one or two illustrations, because I know I have not much time at my disposal.

Take the case of employment in the Police or in the Army. In the Government of India Act it is provided that no subject of His Majesty shall be deprived of the right of being employed in any public service by reason of his caste, creed or colour. Having regard to that, it is obvious that every member of the Depressed Class community who is capable, who is in a position to satisfy the test laid down for employment in any public department, should have the right to enter that public department.

But what do we find? We find this. If a Depressed Class man applies for service in the Police Department today, he is told point blank by the executive officers of the Government that no member of the Depressed Classes can be employed in the Police Service, because he is an untouchable person. In the case of the Military the same situation obtains. Up to 1892 practically the whole of the Madras Army and the whole of the Bombay Army consisted of members drawn from the Depressed Classes.

All the great wars in the history of India have been fought with the help of sepoys drawn from the Depressed Classes, both in the Bombay Presidency and in Madras. Yet in 1892 a rule or regulation was made which debarred the Depressed Classes from entry into the Military Service, and even today, if you ask a question in the Legislative Council as to why this is done, the answer is that the bar of untouchability does create insuperable difficulties in the recruitment of these classes.

I am quite sure that this disability is as effective as it was imposed by law, and the section in the Government of India Act, which says that all His Majesty's subjects shall have free entry into employment provided they are otherwise fit, is altogether set at naught. I can cite many other cases. For instance, there is the difficulty the Depressed Classes find in getting themselves accommodated in public inn when they are travelling, the difficulty they find in being taken in an omnibus when travelling from one place to another, the difficulty they find in securing entry to public schools to which they have themselves contributed, the difficulty they find in drawing water from a well for the building of which they have paid taxes, and so on. But I need not go into all these cases. The one circumstance which distinguishes the position of the Depressed Classes from that of the other minorities is that they suffer from civic disabilities which are as effective as though they were imposed by law.

The second and, in my opinion, the most hideous distinction which marks the Depressed Classes is that the Depressed Classes are subject to social persecution unknown in any other part of the world. In that connection I want to read to the Sub-Committee a small extract from the Report of a Committee appointed by the Government of Bombay in the year 1928 to investigate into the position of the Depressed Classes.

That Committee tried to find out whether there were any impediments in the way of the Depressed Classes enjoying such rights as the law gave them in common with other citizens of the State: Although we have recommended various remedies to secure to the Depressed Classes their rights to all public utilities we fear that there will be difficulties in the way of their exercising them for a long time to come. The first difficulty is the fear of open violence against them by the orthodox classes. It must be noted that the Depressed Classes form a small minority in every village, opposed to which is a great majority of the orthodox who are bent on protecting their interests and dignity from any supposed invasion by the Depressed Classes at any cost. The danger of prosecution by the Police has put a limitation upon the use of violence by the orthodox classes and consequently such cases are rare.

The second difficulty arises from the economic position in which the Depressed Classes are found today. The Depressed Classes have no economic independence in most parts of the Presidency. Some cultivate the lands of the orthodox classes as their tenants at will. Others live on their earnings as farm labourers employed by the orthodox classes and the rest subsist on the food or grain given to them by the orthodox classes in lieu of service rendered to them as village servants. We have heard of numerous instances where the orthodox classes have used their economic power as a weapon against those Depressed Classes in their villages, when the latter have dared to exercise their rights, and have evicted them from their lands, and stopped their employment and discontinued their remuneration as village servants. This boycott is often planned on such an extensive scale as to include the prevention of the Depressed Classes from using the commonly used paths and the stoppage of the necessaries of life by the village Bania. According to the evidence sometimes small causes suffice for the proclamation of a social boycott against the Depressed Classes. Frequently it follows on the exercise by the Depressed Classes of their right to the use of the common well, but cases have been by no means rare where a stringent boycott has been proclaimed simply because a Depressed Class man has put on the sacred thread, has bought a piece of land, has put on good clothes or ornaments, or has carried a marriage procession with the bridegroom on the horse through the public street.

We do not know of any weapon more effective than this social boycott which could have been invented for the suppression of the Depressed Classes. The method of open violence pales away before it, for it has the most far-reaching and deadening effects. It is more dangerous because it passes as a lawful method consistent with the theory of freedom of contact. We agree that this tyranny of the majority must be put down with a firm hand if we are to guarantee the Depressed Classes the freedom of speech and action necessary for their uplift." A third thing which the Depressed Classes fear more than any other community is that whatever representation they may be granted in the new legislature, they will always be in a very small minority, and consequently, having regard to the apathetic attitude of the orthodox classes towards the Depressed Classes, there is always the danger of the interests of the Depressed Classes, being neglected altogether, or some action taken which may ultimately prove to be prejudicial to their interests.

As against these special circumstances which affect the Depressed Classes, we propose the following safeguards. First of all, we want a fundamental right enacted in the constitution which will declare "untouchability" to be illegal for all public purposes. We must be emancipated, so to say, from this social curse before we can at all consent to the constitution; and secondly, this fundamental right must also invalidate and nullify all such disabilities and all such discriminations as may have been made hitherto. Next, we want legislation against the social persecution to which I have drawn your attention just now, and for this we have provided in the document which we have submitted by certain clauses which are based upon an Act, which now prevails in Burma. I need not go into that detail just for the moment. Then what we want is this, that liability of the executive officers of the Crown for acts of tyranny or oppression shall be made effective. Today under sections 110 and 111 of the Government of India Act that liability is not real. And lastly, what we want is a right to appeal against acts of neglect of prejudice to the Central Government and failing that, to the Secretary of State and a Special Department in the Government of India to take charge of our welfare.

This is, in general, the cases for the Depressed Classes, and the safeguards that they want. Let me just say a word or two as regards the most important of them-namely, their right to adequate representation in the legislature. Now, on the question of the granting of representation of the Depressed Classes, we are absolutely unanimous that representation shall be by election and not by nomination. The system of nomination has produced in the case of the Depressed Classes, results which we all say are abdominable. The system has been abused in a manner in which it was never expected that it would be abused, and it has never given the Depressed Classes the real and independent representation which they must have as their safeguard. Under no circumstances, therefore, will the Depressed Classes accept representation by nomination.

As to the question of joint or separate electorates, our position is this-that if you give us adult universal suffrage the Depressed Classes, barring a short transitional period which they want for their organisation, will be prepared to accept joint electorates and reserved seats; but if you do not give us adult suffrage, then we must claim representation through separate electorates. That is our position.

Now regarding the question of the number of seats, it is not possible, of course, for us to state definitely what that number should be, except to state that we will not tolerate any invidious discrimination. We insist upon equality of treatment. But the whole question, in my opinion, is entirely a relative question: it is a question that can be determined only in connection with, and by taking into account, the seats that will be allotted to the other minority communities; but I will make two observations in this connection.

The first observation that I will make is this-that we, the Depressed Classes, demand a complete partition between ourselves and the Hindus. That is the first thing. We have been called Hindus for political purposes, but we have never been acknowledged socially by the Hindus as their brethren.

They have taken to themselves all the political advantage with our numbers, with our voting strength, have given to them, but in return we have received nothing. All that we have received is a treatment which is worse than the treatment that they themselves have accorded to other communities whom they do not call Hindus. That must be the first thing, therefore, that we want to be done.

The second thing that I will say concerns the question of weightage. Now, this system-I will be plain, to my mind has been abused. I am not against the principle of weightage. I do not accept the principle that in all circumstances every minority must be confined to its population ratio. A minority may be so small that its population ratio may give a representation which may be wholly inadequate for the purpose of its protection. It may be a representation which may be of no consequence at all.

If, therefore, you want to protect a minority adequately and really, then in certain circumstances the principle of weightage will have to be conceded. But the distribution of weightage must be subject to some uniform and intelligible principle. In our opinion weightage is to be conceded because a minority is weak, either in numbers, or because its social standing is low, or its educational standing is backward as compared with others, or because its economic strength is not sufficient to place it on a fighting par with other communities.

Member: Quite right.

Dr. Ambedkar: But I cannot understand, for instance, how weightage can be allowed on the ground of political importance, or loyalty, or services rendered either to the Empire or to the British Government. I think if we adopt that principle, we shall land ourselves in very difficult circumstances from which it will be difficult to extricate ourselves.

Regarding the question of the representation of the Depressed Classes in the Central Legislature. If you have again adult suffrage for the election of members of the Central Legislature, then, of course, the Depressed Classes will claim separate representation in the Legislature, such number of seats being allotted to them in conjunction with the seats allotted to other minorities.

But if your representation is to be by a suffrage which is higher or much higher, based on property, and so much higher that the Depressed Classes will probably be entirely left out, then I am afraid the Depressed Classes will have to claim indirect election to the Central Legislature, carried on by electoral colleges composed of members of the Depressed Classes, in the Provincial Legislature, in Municipalities, and in district local boards. That is all that I have to say so far as the Depressed Classes are concerned.

Having said all that I need say let me add one thing in conclusion that this whole question of minority representation is really the crux of the whole situation, and if the majority community desire that all minorities should associate with them in having or in claiming, a constitution which will give India what they call Dominion Status, or what we prefer to call Government by the people, for the people and in the name of the people, then I am afraid that the majority community must see to it that all fears of the minorities are set at rest.

Otherwise it may not be possible for us to take what I do not conceal from myself is the risk that most of us are taking in claiming Dominion Status.

Fifth Sitting-14th January 1931

Chairman: The proposal that has just been made makes it impossible for us to go on and adopt the Draft Report that is in front of us, because, of course, it changes the whole circumstances. If you would be agreeable, I should propose to adjourn this Sub-Committee now, and I will also, you being agreeable, propose to remain in the Chair and to ask that those of you who are specially interested should meet and we must include Dr. Ambedkar.

Dr. Ambedkar: I am obliged to you, Sir.

Chairman: Oh, yes, we must include him and see whether by an exchange of opinions across the table we could not come to an agreement.

Sir P. C. Mitter: I should like to join, Sir, in those discussions.

Dr. Ambedkar: We have heard just now these proposals and percentages being disposed of, but really it strikes me that if you add up all these they not only go over 100 per cent but they practically take no notice of many other communities that are existing in the Punjab and Bengal and in other places.

If these communities, the Sikhs, the Mohammedans, the Hindus are going to appropriate 49 and 20 and so on, what is left for the other people? Are they to be taken into account or not? That is a very serious question, Mr. Prime Minister.

Lt. Col. Gidney: May I just raise my humble voice-it is a very small voice. I know-in this conflict? I support what Dr. Ambedkar has just said. Surely you are not going to take the political rupee and give 15 annas and 9 pies to the major communities, leaving 3 pies to be scrambled for by the other minorities. On behalf of the smaller communities I maintain we should have some say in this distribution.

Chairman: That is just the point. I think that we had better discuss this matter with a smaller body and a little but more informally.

Mr. Foot: And no notes taken?

Chairman: And I shall remain in the Chair, you being agreeable, and see what can be done to straighten out the situation that has been opened up by the very hopeful suggestion made by Sir Muhammad Shafi.

Chairman: But you see, in so far as these suggestions can be made workable, they will come in the details that will have to be worked out.

Dr. Ambedkar: I quite see that.

Chairman: Partly legislative and partly administrative.

Dr. Ambedkar: But what I would like to say is this, that in view of the fact that the paragraph tries to summarise what was put before this Committee by the different communities, what was put by the Depressed Classes, as something specifically for themselves, apart from what other communities needed, ought to come in by way of completion.

Chairman: But it says "without discrimination" and so on.

Dr. Ambedkar: Mr. Prime Minister, you will excuse me; it is one thing for the constitution to say that no man shall be discriminated against, and that every man shall be guaranteed the free enjoyment, and so on; but I know as a matter of fact that we are hard up against facts, and that people will not allow us to enjoy the rights which are given to us by the constitution. I am as certain of that as I am certain of my existence. I do not want merely a paper guarantee. The whole community will be against us, and we shall certainly never enjoy one-tenth of what is given to us. I therefore desire that the constitution should not only declare that we shall have specific rights that every community will have, but that the constitution should also provide ways and means by which we shall be protected in the exercise of those rights.

Chairman: The point is, supposing a legislature does not pass a law which will suit you, then the constitution has been broken.

Dr. Ambedkar: No. What I suggest is this : That in the memorandum which I have circulated I have suggested certain ways and means by which we think our rights could be protected in the matter of their exercise. The Committee here, for instance, may not agree that is an appropriate way of doing it; the Committee may suggest that there are some other means of doing it. I am quite prepared and open for consideration of these other ways and means; but what I want to submit is this, that this draft ought to report that the Depressed Classes did suggest that they were not satisfied with the mere declaration that they were placed on an equal footing with other communities; but they pressed in that rights be given to them by the constitution. I am not asking for anything more than that. That is by way of completion of the report. In the memorandum which I submitted, you will see I do recommend a certain procedure for that.

BIBLIOGRAPHY

Ambedkar, B. R.: *Annihilation of Caste: An Undelivered Speech*, Arnold Publishers, New Delhi, 1990.

Bailey, F. G.: *Caste and the Economic Frontier: A Village in Highland Orissa*, University of Manchester, Manchester, 1957.

Benjamin, Joseph: *Scheduled Castes in Indian Politics and Society*, Ess Ess Publications, New Delhi, 1989.

Beteille, A.: *The Backward Classes and the New Social Order*, OUP, New Delhi, 1981.

Bondurant, Joan V.: *Conquest of Violence; The Gandhian Philosophy of Conflict*, University of California Press, Berkeley, 1965.

Chatterjee, Partha: *Caste and Subaltern Consciousness*, Oxford University Press, Delhi, 1994.

Desai, I. P.: *Anti-reservation Agitation and Struggle of Gujarat Society*, Adjanta Publications, Delhi, 1985.

Dubois, Abbe: *Hindu Manners, Customs and Ceremonies*, AES, New Delhi, 1983.

Engineer, Asghar Ali.: *Mandal Commission Controversy*, Ajanta Publications, Delhi, 1991.

Fiske, A.: *The Untouchables in Contemporary India*, University of Arizona Press, Tucson, 1972.

Ganesan, L.: *Relevance of Reservation*, Valentina Publications, Madras, 1991.

Ghurye, G. S.: *Caste and Class in India*, Popular Books, Bombay, 1950.

Glen, M. and Johnson, S. B.: *Social Mobility Among Untouchables*, Vikas, New Delhi, 1979.

Gorhe, Neelam: *Social Development and Dalit Women*, Gyan Pub. House, New Delhi, 1995.

Hardgrave, Robert L. Jr.: *The Dravidian Movement*, Popular Book Depot, Bombay, 1965.

Hocart, A. M.: *Caste*, Mathew and Co., London, 1950.

Ishwaran, K.: *Shivpur: A South Indian Village*, Routledge, London, 1968.

Jatav, D.R.: *Dr. Ambedkar's Role in National Movement*, Boudha Sahitya Samelan, New Delhi, 1979.

Kadam, K.N.: *Dr. B.R. Ambedkar: The Emancipator of the Oppressed*, BR Publishing, Delhi, 1994.

Kamble, J. R.: *Rise and Awakening of Depressed Classes in India*, National Publishers, New Delhi, 1979.

Karve, Irawati: *Hindu Society: An Interpretation*, Sangam Press, Poona, 1961.

Keer, D.: *Dr. Ambedkar. Life and Mission*, Popular Prakashan, Bombay, 1954.

Kosambi, D. D.: *Introduction to the Study of Indian History*, Popular Prakashan, Bombay, 1975.

Krishnaiah Chetty, V.B.: *Scheduled Castes and Development Programmes in India*, Vohra, Allahabad, 1991.

Kuber, W.N.: *Dr. Ambedkar: A Critical Study*, People's Publishing House, New Delhi, 1973.

Lakshmanna, C.: *Caste Dynamics in Village India*, Nachiketa Publications, Bombay, 1973.

Lal, Shyam: *Caste and Political Mobilisation: The Bhangis*, Panchsheel Prakashan, Jaipur, 1981.

Lokhande, G.S.: *Bhimrao Ramji Ambedkar: a Study in Social Democracy*, Intellectual Publishing House, New Delhi, 1977.

Mahar, Michael J.: *The Untouchables in Contemporary India*, University of Arizona Press, Arizona, 1972.

Majumdar, D. N.: *Caste and Communication in an Indian Village*, Asia Publishing House, Bombay, 1958.

Mallik, Suneila: *Social Integration of the Scheduled Castes*. Abhinav, New Delhi, 1979.

Maw, Martin: *Visions of India*, Vertag Perer Lang, London, 1990.

Nagaraj, D. R.: *The Flaming Feet: A Study of the Dalit Movement*, South Forum Press, Bangalore, 1993.

Naidu, A. Nagaraja: *Caste and Land in Colonial South India*, Rawat Publications, New Delhi, 1994.

Narwade, S.S.: *Dr. Babasaheb Ambedkar Ani Hyderabad Sanathan*, Sugava Prakashan, Pune, 1988.

Nath, Trilok: *Politics of the Depressed Classes*, Deputy Publications, Delhi, 1987.

O'Malley, L. S. S.: *Indian Caste Customs*, Vikas Publishing House, Delhi, 1974.

Pantavane, G.: *Patrikar Dr. Babasaheb Ambedkar*, Abhijit, Nagpur, 1987.

Paranjpe, A. C.: *Caste, Prejudice and the Individual*, Lalvani Publishing House, New Delhi, 1970.

Patwardhan, Sunanda: *Change Among India's Harijans: Maharashtra a Case Study*, Orient Longmans, New Delhi, 1973.

Prabhavathi, M.: *Dalit Women in Contemporary Indian Situation*, Gyan Publishing House, New Delhi, 1995.

Punekar, S.M.: *Harijan Contribution to Medieval Thought*, Prasaranga, Bangalore University, Bangalore, 1991.

Rajasekharaiah, A.M.: *B.R. Ambedkar: the Politics of Emancipation*, Sindhu Publications, Bombay, 1971.

Ram, Nandu: *Beyond Ambedkar: Essays on Daits in India*, Har-Anand Publications, New Delhi, 1995.

Rege, Sharmila: *Sati: A Critical Analysis*, University of Poona, Poona, 1989.

Robbin, J.: *Dr. Ambedkar and His Movement*, Dr. Ambedkar Publishing Society, Hyderabad, 1964.

Rodage, S.: *Subhedar Ramji Ambedkar*. Ramaji Prakashan, Wakvali Dapoli, 1989.

Sampla, B.R.: *Yug Purush Ambedkar*, Bheen Patrika, Jullundur, 1978.

Sarkar, J.: *Caste, Occupation and Change*, B. R. Publishing Co., Delhi, 1984.

Shabbir, M.: *B.R. Ambedkar. Study in Law & Society*, Rawat, Jaipur, 1997.

Shah, Ghanshyam: *Caste Association and Political Processes in Gujarat*, Popular Prakashan, Bombay, 1975.

Sharma, G. S.: *Legislation and Cases of Untouchability and Scheduled Castes in India*, Allied Publishers, Bombay, 1975.

Silverberg, James: *Social Mobility in the Caste System in India*, Mouton Publishers, The Hague, 1968.

Singh, K. K.: *Patterns of Caste Tensions*, Asia Publishing House, Bombay, 1967.

Singh, Mohinder: *The Depressed Classes*, Hind Kitab Ltd., Bombay, 1947.

Singh, S. N.: *Reservation: Problems and Prospects*, Uppal Publishing House, New Delhi, 1987.

Srinivas, M. N.: *Caste in Modern India and Other Essays*, Asia Publishing House, Bombay, 1962.

Stevenson, Margaret S.: *Without the Pale: The Life Story of An Outcaste*, Association Press (Y.M.C.A.), Calcutta, 1930.

Suman, R.D.: *Dr. Ambedkar: Pioneer of Human Rights*, Bodhisattva Publications, New Delhi, 1977.

Tope, T.K.: *Dr. B.R. Ambedkar, A Symbol of Social Revolt*, Maharashtra Information Centre, New Delhi, 1964.

Tripathy, R. B.: *Dalits: A Sub-Human Society*, Ashish Publishing House, New Delhi, 1994.

Varale, B.H.: *Dr. Babasaheb Ambedkarrancha Sangaki*, Shrividya Prakashan, Pune, 1988.

Venkateshwarlu, D.: *Harijan-Upper Class Conflicts*, Discovery, New Delhi, 1990.

Webster, John: *The Christian Dalits: A History*, Indian Society for Promoting Christian Knowledge (ISPCK), Delhi, 1994.

Wolf, G.: *Re-inventing Tradition*, Indian Institute of Advanced Studies, Shimla, 1992.

INDEX

J

K

L

M

P

R

S

T

♦♦♦